W.S. GRAH
SPEAKING TOWA

CW00816325

LIVERPOOL ENGLISH TEXTS AND STUDIES, 43

W.S. GRAHAM
SPEAKING TOWARDS YOU

EDITED BY RALPH PITE
AND HESTER JONES

LIVERPOOL UNIVERSITY PRESS

First published 2004 by
Liverpool University Press
4 Cambridge Street
Liverpool L69 7ZU

Copyright © 2004 Liverpool University Press

The right of Ralph Pite and Hester Jones to be identified as
the editors of this work has been asserted by them in
accordance with the Copyright, Designs and Patents Act,
1988

British Library Cataloguing-in-Publication data
A British Library CIP record is available

ISBN 0-85323-569-4 hardback
ISBN 0-85323-579-1 paperback

Typeset in Garamond by
Koinonia, Bury, Lancashire
Printed and bound in the European Union by
Bell and Bain Limited, Glasgow

Contents

Notes on Contributors

Matthew Francis is a poet and novelist, and lecturer in creative writing at the University of Wales, Aberystwyth. He is editor of the *New Collected Poems of W. S. Graham* (Faber and Faber, 2004), and author of a forthcoming monograph on Graham, *Where the People Are* (Salt, 2004).

Fiona Green is a lecturer in the Faculty of English, University of Cambridge and a Fellow of Jesus College. She writes on twentieth-century British and American poetry.

Hester Jones is a lecturer in English at the University of Liverpool. She has written on eighteenth-century literature and women's writing. She is preparing a study of the relation between gender and spirituality in twentieth-century fiction and poetry.

Tony Lopez is Professor of Poetry at the University of Plymouth and the author of twenty books of poetry, most recently *False Memory* (Salt, 2003), *Data Shadow* (Reality Street, 2000) and *Devolution* (The Figures, 2000).

Edwin Morgan taught at the University of Glasgow until 1980 when he retired as professor. His *Collected Poems* was published by Carcanet in 1990. In 2000, he was awarded the Queen's Gold Medal for poetry.

Adam Piette is Reader in English at the University of Glasgow. He has published monographs on European modernism and on World War II writing. Currently, he is on three-year research leave sponsored by the Leverhulme Trust and is working on a study of Cold War American culture that focuses on Nabokov.

Ralph Pite is Reader in English at the University of Liverpool. He has recently completed a study of Thomas Hardy, *Hardy's Geography; Wessex and the Regional Novel* (Palgrave, 2002) and is working on a biography. He has also published on Romanticism, ecocriticism and modern poetry.

His collection of poetry, *Paths and Ladders* was published by The Brodie Press in 2003.

Peter Robinson is a Visiting Professor of English Literature at Tohoku University, Sendai, Japan. He is the author of five collections of poetry, the most recent of which is *About Time Too* (Carcanet, 2001). A selection of his translations appeared in *The Great Friend and Other Translated Poems* (Worple Press, 2002). Two volumes of literary criticism are published by Oxford University Press: *In the Circumstances: About Poems and Poets* (1992) and *Poetry, Poets, Readers: Making Things Happen* (2002). His *Selected Poems* appeared from Carcanet in 2003.

Ian Sansom has recently published *The Truth About Babies* (Granta, 2002) and is about to publish *Ring Road* (Fourth Estate, 2004).

Acknowledgements

Anthony Astbury particularly deserves our thanks for his generosity and enthusiasm in support of this volume. Adrian Poole's and Peter Swaab's insightful comments on the essays were very valuable. The kind and name-less person at Edinburgh University Press who sent us the publisher's very last copy of *Edinburgh Review* 75 has made it infinitely easier to complete the book. Sally West compiled the index with impressive thoroughness and skill despite the short notice we gave her. Helen Tookey and Andrew Kirk have made the production process a pleasure for us.

We are also grateful to Jonathan Bate, Bernard Beatty, Robin Bloxsidge, Geoffrey Godbert, Michael Snow and Austin Wormleighton for the different kinds of help they have given the volume.

We wish to thank Michael and Margaret Snow for permission to reproduce extracts from W. S. Graham's poetry, and the estate of David Wright for permission to reproduce 'Incident in Soho' by David Wright. Edwin Morgan's essay is reprinted from *Cencrastus* (1981) with the author's permission.

Abbreviations

AN	W.S. Graham, *Aimed at Nobody: Poems from Notebooks*, ed. Margaret Blackwood and Robin Skelton (London: Faber and Faber, 1993)
CP	W.S. Graham, *Collected Poems: 1942–1977* (London: Faber and Faber, 1979)
ER75	'The Life and Work of W.S. Graham', *Edinburgh Review*, 75 (1987), pp. 6–109
IP	W.S. Graham, *Implements in their Places* (London: Faber and Faber, 1977)
Lopez, *PWSG*	Tony Lopez, *The Poetry of W.S. Graham* (Edinburgh: Edinburgh University Press, 1989)
N	W.S. Graham, *The Nightfishing* (London: Faber and Faber, 1955)
Nightfisherman	W.S. Graham, *The Nightfisherman: Selected Letters*, ed. Michael and Margaret Snow (Manchester: Carcanet, 1999)
UP	W.S. Graham, *Uncollected Poems* (Warwick: Greville Press, 1990)
WT	W.S. Graham, *The White Threshold* (London: Faber and Faber, 1949)

Introduction: Contacting Graham

RALPH PITE AND HESTER JONES

W.S. Graham lived nearly all his working life in the far west of Cornwall and had little to do with literary circles, either in London or elsewhere. In the 1940s, he published three collections with small presses before T.S. Eliot took him on at Faber and Faber. He published two collections with them – *The White Threshold* (1949) and *The Nightfishing* (1955). After that, despite the good reception that *The Nightfishing* received, he seems to have been forgotten by his publishers. Another volume did not appear until 1970 even though Graham had been writing and publishing quite frequently in the intervening years. Nevertheless, that 1970 volume, *Malcolm Mooney's Land*, and its successor, *Implements in their Places* (1977), were notable successes and led to Graham's *Collected Poems: 1942–1977*, published in 1979. On his death in 1986, he was widely mourned as 'a poet of international stature' and 'the most important writer writing in England' (*ER75*, pp. 100, 102).

Sixteen years later, these claims do not sound ridiculous or painfully dated. Graham's work has remained current. It has, if anything, gained in stature and extended its readership, particularly during the 1990s. *Uncollected Poems* was published in 1990 (by the Greville Press, Warwick); *Aimed at Nobody*, a selection of unpublished work from notebooks, appeared in 1993, and a *Selected Poems* appeared in 1996 (both from Faber). In the same year, *Conductors of Chaos*, an anthology of contemporary, experimental poetry edited by Iain Sinclair, included a selection from Graham, citing him as one of the major influences on and inspirations for these contemporary writers.[1] And not only is Graham profoundly respected and admired, he is fondly remembered. The number of the *Edinburgh Review* devoted to him in 1987 contains vivid recollections of Graham the man – the performer, the friend, the drinker, the writer. These memories still survive undimmed.

Michael Snow has written a vivid memoir of W.S. Graham, published in *Aquarius* 25/26 (2002). This volume of the magazine is devoted to

Graham himself and his contemporary George Barker. The Graham half includes other reminiscences (by Harold Pinter, Michael Hamburger and Matthew Sweeney), plus valuable critical essays by Peter Riley, Robert Calder and others. Added to this are manuscript letters, a journal by Ronnie Duncan covering his holiday in Crete with Graham in 1977, accounts of Graham reading in public and an interview with Benjamin Creme, one of the artists Graham knew in Glasgow.

A further sign of Graham's growing reputation is the new *Collected Poems*, edited by Matthew Francis, one of the contributors to this volume. The new *Collected* will include the poems Graham himself excluded in 1979 as well as previously uncollected work. Still, despite all this interest among readers and writers of very different kinds, an article recently written about him is entitled 'The Strange Disappearance of W.S. Graham'.[2] He's gone and not forgotten, yet how much he is remembered, and for what, both seem uncertain.

It has been suggested quite frequently that Graham was the victim of literary fashion and, more specifically, of the Movement. His early writing, influenced by the Apocalyptic school and by Dylan Thomas in particular, contradicted all the tenets of the Movement. It wasn't lucid, down-to-earth and prosaic. It didn't seek the conversational, Augustan-suburban of Davie or Larkin. On the contrary, Graham's poems from the 1940s are almost always hard to make out at first reading. They are grandiose in their pretensions and aim at the Romantic sublime. *The Nightfishing* was, moreover, unlucky to appear in the same year as Larkin's *The Less Deceived*, a volume that helped to crystallize the Movement style. Soon after, Angry Young Men took over the British theatre and an anti-Romantic spirit – sulky in London, sour in Oxbridge – began to dominate English letters. The obscure and experimental were driven to the margins and Graham went with them. Only after his fifteen years in the wilderness did he start to gain some of the recognition he deserved. By then, according to this account of his career, he was too old to make the most of it and was accepted only on rather condescending terms, as an eccentric writer, left over from High Modernism. His poetry published in the 1970s was also more straightforward than anything he had written before. Though verbally inventive, it could be accommodated by an aesthetic that preferred immediacy and by an audience used to clarity.

There is some truth to this version of Graham's life and career. Neglect made him a poor man and, especially in the late 1950s and early 1960s, into an almost despairing one. It is a shame that 'The Dark Dialogues', for instance, written around 1958, was scarcely read in Britain until 1970. It is one of his very best poems and would have offered in the 1960s an alternative method to Larkin's, Hughes's or Plath's. Imagine Alvarez's *The New Poetry* with Graham included.

Nonetheless, seeing Graham as a victim of the Movement oversimplifies him and his place in post-war poetry. The fight between experimentalists and traditionalists also seems a quarrel no longer worth pursuing. Graham has been hailed by experimental poets but the personal directness of his later poems makes part of his output attractive to a wider audience. Does that mean that he falls uncomfortably between the two schools? Or does it suggest that post-war poetry does not divide up so easily into these two models?

This collection of essays suggests that both may be true. Graham was uncomfortable with poetic labels and schools. His writing arises out of a sense of non-affiliation, partly chosen and partly imposed on him. He felt an outsider amidst a privileged, English literary world because of his working-class origins and Scottish background. He could never quite join the clique. Secondly, however, and perhaps more importantly, his writing is eclectic. It has some of its roots in Modernism, some in the Apocalyptic school and others in the tradition of Scottish poetry. He draws on Burns and Dunbar, Eliot, Beckett and Joyce, and on other writers too: Browning, Malory, Tennyson. He read his contemporaries intently. There are, for example, echoes of Plath. In this he reflects an overlap between the experimentalist and traditionalist schools that can be found in Larkin too, supposedly Graham's absolute opposite.

In the second of the essays collected here, Tony Lopez brings out the overlap, showing the common interest Graham and Larkin had in Dylan Thomas during the 1940s. Larkin confessed his youthful attachment to W.B. Yeats. He said less about his enthusiasm for Dylan Thomas. With Thomas in the background, Larkin's move into the colloquial poetry of *The Less Deceived* proves to be not very different from Graham's development in the same period, since Graham too moved on from Thomas. The poets have in common Dylan Thomas and the desire to go beyond him. And this, as Peter Riley remarks, is not so unusual: 'It is a not uncommon pattern in the careers of British poets born around 1910 to 1920 for their way of writing to move from a highly-wrought, difficult, linguistically and/or conceptually challenging textuality, to a simpler, more directly addressed and less problematic one – a process of normalisation'.[3] In following such a pattern, both Larkin and Graham are mainstream.

Subsequent essays in the collection follow on from Lopez's both in exploring connections between Graham and other writers, thinkers and artists, and in questioning the received account of his place among post-war poets. Adam Piette links 'The Nightfishing' to Heideggerian philosophy and the pre-Socratics, both of whom Graham came across either during his time as a student at Newbattle Abbey in 1938–39 or soon afterwards. Ralph Pite explores Graham's relations with the St Ives painters – Roger Hilton, Peter Lanyon and Bryan Wynter particularly. Matthew Francis discusses Graham's workbooks, seeing them as works of art in their own right, and revealing new links between Graham and Surrealist art and between Graham and Joyce. Peter Robinson reconsiders Graham's indebtedness to Dylan Thomas, arguing that it has been exaggerated at the expense of other influences. Fiona Green follows out the intricate literariness of Graham's most apparently straightforward poems, his elegies for friends and relatives. Hester Jones discovers in Graham's epistolary poems echoes of T.S. Eliot, John Donne and subtly disguised biblical allusions. Ian Sansom begins the collection by finding contacts between Graham and his contemporaries in both Scotland and America, connections that illuminate poems from early and late in Graham's career.

Taken together, these essays do justice to the breadth of Graham's reading and influences. They show him to be experimental and traditional simultaneously, modernist and also involved in his frequently anti-modernist historical moment. They contest the ways in which Graham has been pigeonholed and implicitly question the ways in which poetry from the post-war period has been categorized (and polarized).

In discovering Graham's contacts with other writers, the essays also return to his pronounced sense of how difficult contact between people always is. Ian Sansom draws attention to Graham's central and urgent desire that his reader should be made to 'listen'. Peter Robinson sees Graham as peculiarly alert to the writer's dependence upon language – language which may obstruct as much as facilitate the communication that the writer seeks. Fiona Green reads Graham's elegies as poems animated by the complex paradox of their own project: how can one make contact with someone who is dead? What is really being attempted as one makes a gesture of this kind? For Hester Jones, Graham regards communication with another person as next to impossible and as literally miraculous. His spirituality, she argues, coincides with the process of stretching out towards other people.

Making contact was one of Graham's continual preoccupations. Much of his writing, from every period and in every style, betrays what Edwin Morgan calls (in his important review of Graham's *Collected Poems*, reprinted here), 'Graham's obsessional interest [...] in trying to define the communicative act and art of poetry itself'. The same preoccupation also comes to the fore in his extraordinary letters, first published in any number in *The Nightfisherman* (1999). These letters, sensitively edited by Michael and Margaret Snow, reveal many sides of Graham that were previously unknown and illuminate the poetry in innumerable ways.

The essays fall into two groups. Following Ian Sansom's essay, which provides an introductory survey of Graham's work as well as shrewd insights into it, there are four essays that run chronologically: Tony Lopez discusses Graham's work of the 1940s, culminating in *The White Threshold* and in particular its title poem; Adam Piette reads Graham's next major work, 'The Nightfishing', written in the late 1940s, first published in book form in 1955; Ralph Pite then considers the impact on Graham of his move to live permanently in Cornwall from 1954 onwards and the influential presence in 'The Dark Dialogues' (1958) and 'Malcom Mooney's Land' (1966) of Graham's artist friends. Both these poems first appeared in book form in 1970, in *Malcolm Mooney's Land*, and Matthew Francis, in the following essay, discusses the previously unpublished material that Graham was working on in the late 1960s – the 'clusters' that generate much of the distinctive work published in his 1970s volumes and that stand as independent, idiosyncratic 'works' themselves.

Peter Robinson's essay continues this chronological study of Graham to some extent by finding Graham's finest accounts of 'dependence' in his late, personal poems addressed to his wife. His piece also, however, draws on many periods of Graham's writing, as do the two that follow. Fiona Green considers the genre of elegy from all stages of Graham's career, culminating in his elegy for his close friend, the painter Bryan Wynter. Hester Jones traces the thread of spirituality in Graham's work from his early essays and letters through 'The Nightfishing' to 'The Thermal Stair'. In the course of doing so, she discusses the previously uncollected poem, 'Letter X – My dear so many times'. Edwin Morgan's review of Graham's *Collected Poems*, first published in 1980 and reprinted here for the first time, addresses matters that underlie many of the earlier discussions: Graham's need to speak and to be heard, his doubts about the medium of poetry and his desire for a home.

Because Graham's poetry remains relatively little known, and in order to help these essays illuminate his work, some of the poems analysed here have been reprinted in between the essays. Each poem is one either directly considered in the essay that follows or is important to its concerns. Michael and Margaret Snow began a similar practice in their edition of Graham's letters and we are very glad to repeat it here, with their generous permission as Graham's literary trustees.

The first poem quoted is 'Listen. Put on Morning', in which Graham says: 'A man's imagining / Suddenly may inherit / The handclapping centuries / Of his one minute on earth'. It became one of his familiar preoccupations that through imagination and, especially, through language, people may come into contact with the deep past. In this formulation he seems to emphasize that it is a 'man' who performs this imaginative activity. Graham's poetry often arises out of and refers to male friendship – especially friendships with other writers and artists: John Minton and Roger Hilton, Dylan Thomas and Robin Skelton. Women tended to be on the periphery of Graham's culture of hard-drinking male camaraderie. On the other hand, Graham grew increasingly wary of the process whereby a writer might 'inherit' the past through language. As he put it in 'Implements in their Places', language seemed to him a 'terrible surrounder / Of everything', predetermining perception as much as expression. It created the appearance only of 'common ground', where 'sly irreconcilabilities' still lurked. Especially in his later work but not exclusively there, Graham attempts to unpick an oppressive language and this endeavour links him (perhaps unexpectedly) to contemporary women writers who find language to be a male oppressor.

The last of the poems we include in the book is the last section of Graham's sequence 'Johann Joachim Quantz's Five Lessons', a series of five dramatic monologues. These are spoken by the real-life famous flautist, Johann Joachim Quantz, to his imaginary pupil, Karl. Much in Quantz's instructions to his young student echoes in Graham's own work. It too is characterized by 'good / Nerve and decision'. He can be 'light as feathers' but is always 'definite'. He speaks with sometimes extraordinary directness and plangency but the more feelingly because he does not 'intrude too much / Into the message'. His work might be seen, in fact, as an acceptance of the impersonal note of High Modernism on the condition that the personal is able to survive within it. But, whatever one's view of this and other literary-historical questions, Graham, like Quantz's pupil, Karl, 'will be all right'. Moreover, it has been our experience, in editing this book and learning lessons from Graham's extraordinary craft and sensitivity, that (to adapt the poem once more) our hearts have lifted to his playing.

Notes

1 Iain Sinclair (ed.), *Conductors of Chaos* (London and Basingstoke: Picador, 1996).
2 Elizabeth Lowry, 'The Strange Disappearance of W.S. Graham', *Thumbscrew*, 5 (Summer 1996), pp. 15–33.
3 Peter Riley, 'W.S. Graham: First and Last', *Aquarius* 25/26 (2002), pp. 95–105 (95).

Listen. Put on Morning

Listen. Put on morning.
Waken into falling light.
A man's imagining
Suddenly may inherit
The handclapping centuries
Of his one minute on earth.
And hear the virgin juries
Talk with his own breath
To the corner boys of his street.
And hear the Black Maria
Seaching the town at night.
And hear the playropes caa
The sister Mary in.
And hear Willie and Davie
Among bracken of Narnain
Sing in a mist heavy
With myrtle and listeners.
And hear the higher town
Weep a petition of fears
At the poorhouse close upon
The public heartbeat.
And hear the children tig
And run with my own feet
Into the netting drag
Of a suiciding principle.
Listen. Put on lightbreak.
Waken into miracle.
The audience lies awake
Under the tenements
Under the sugar docks
Under the printed moments.
The centuries turn their locks
And open under the hill
Their inherited books and doors
All gathered to distil
Like happy berry pickers
One voice to talk to us.

Yes listen. It carries away
The second and the years
Till the heart's in a jacket of snow
And the head's in a helmet white
And the song sleeps to be wakened
By the morning ear bright.
Listen. Put on morning.
Waken into falling light.

2

'Listen': W.S. Graham

IAN SANSOM

W.S. Graham remains an anomaly. Praised during his lifetime by T.S. Eliot and published by Faber and Faber (Graham – jokingly – called them 'Fibber & Fibber'), he is nonetheless most admired and respected by those poets and critics who disdain mainstream poetry publishing and who style themselves as renegades. In Iain Sinclair's anthology of so-called 'elective outsiders', *Conductors of Chaos* (1996), for example, Graham is one among the five poets of 'previous generations' nominated as significant father figures. The others are David Gascoyne, Nicholas Moore, J.F. Hendry and David Jones.[1]

To a certain extent, therefore, Graham straddles the great divide in contemporary poetry, between the mass-marketed super-league on the one hand and the worthy unknowns and solipsistic self-publishers on the other. He remains in poetry's shadow cabinet. There are perhaps several reasons for this. He was not, apparently, an easy man to get on with, which might have been a boon but turned out to be a bane to his reputation. According to Julian MacLaren-Ross, in his *Memoirs of the Forties*, Graham was the sort of man who, if 'you greeted him by saying "Good After-noon", he would morosely reply, "What's good about it?"'.[2] This seems not to have gone down especially well in Fitzrovia in the 1940s.

Tony Lopez maintains that this unfavourable account reflects more on MacLaren-Ross than on Graham (see *ER75*, p. 10). Graham's friend David Wright evokes MacLaren-Ross in the Wheatsheaf in Soho, 'teddy-bear coated and malacca-caned, [holding] court at the corner of its saloon bar' (*ER75*, p. 49). The mixture of foppishness and dominance would have goaded Graham for class reasons. Waiting until 1992, six years after Graham's death, Donald Davie described him as 'a Clydeside proletarian, half-educated and bloody-minded'.[3] Perhaps. But encountering snobbish-ness like this, spoken or hidden, would try anyone's patience.

Graham's friend and patron Nancy Wynne-Jones explains that he was 'a gregarious but shy man [who] was unable to face the world without the support of a drink', although when he was drunk, says David Wright, he was 'useless as a human being' (*ER75*, pp. 53, 66). Tony Lopez, in his study *The Poetry of W.S. Graham* (1989), allows that '[m]any accounts of his behaviour indicate that he was comfortable only in the company of close friends'. In a characteristically deft manoeuvre Lopez manages to turn this to Graham's favour by arguing that '[his] continuing interest in the diffi-culty of communication, and in language as the subject of his later poetry, was thus by no means the theoretical matter that it is in academic literary studies' (Lopez, *PWSG*, p. 7). Drink and poetry go together perhaps, at least in the received idea of the inspired, inebriated bard. Lopez, though, suggests that something deeper may have been going on in Graham – that a social handicap became a vocational qualification.

'Five Verses Beginning with the Word Language', written around 1974, but never published in Graham's lifetime, show the persistence of his social unease and its intimate connection with questions of how to speak. 'O / Excuse me,' Graham apologizes, 'do you write poetry yourself?'

> But I know you do. Here we are among
> The great cats of stature in their literary
> Camouflage and all I can do is lay
> My head on the paper trying to speak and then
> Shift over to have my jungle-wounded head
> Easy against the flank of the yellow leopard.
>
>   (*AN*, p. 57)

He finds himself momentarily in a nightmare cocktail-party ('among the social beasts / Which quick assail me'[4]), intimidated and embarrassed, frightened and, as he admits, submissive in the end, seeking solace and rest 'against the flank' of one of the great cats. Trying to write has all the terrors of a roomful of strangers. You're pushed to 'make / Something of yourself which is not true' (*AN*, p. 57) – a self in language as false as the public self of a social gathering.

But Graham disqualifies himself from popular acclaim on grounds other than the merely personal. There is, for example, the vexed Scottish question. Douglas Dunn has pointed out that in his home country 'Graham has been less influential than a poet of his importance would at first lead you to believe' because 'he had the cheek to live somewhere else'.[5] Although Graham wrote often about Scotland and employed Scottish dialect words repeatedly, his residence in Cornwall has prevented him from being reclaimed as a Scottish writer.

Graham was himself hostile to the idea of Scottish writers writing exclusively in Scots and trying in that way to produce a national literature. He liked Hugh MacDiarmid personally but disliked his work (see *Nightfisherman*, pp. 63, 68–69). That stance may have done him no favours, especially early on. He was, it is true, included in *The Oxford Book of Scottish Verse* (1966) and *The Penguin Book of Scottish Verse* (1970); he was not, however, one of the *Twelve Modern Scottish Poets* in 1971, though he entered the ranks of *Twelve More Scottish Poets* in 1986, the year of his death.[6] On the other hand, Neil Corcoran devotes a section to Graham in his *English Poetry since 1940* (1993), the only other Scottish poet receiving similar treatment being Edwin Muir, MacDiarmid's 'traitor'. There are two chapters in Corcoran's book on Northern Irish poetry and separate discussion of Welsh poets – Dylan Thomas, Alun Lewis, David Jones and R.S. Thomas.[7] This is partly Corcoran's personal taste at work. Partly, though, it reflects the peculiar difficulty of being a Scotsman and writing in English.

Graham's Scottishness made him (and to some degree still makes him) less easily part of English literary culture than Welshness or Irishness would have done. You can after all write 'Scots' – a written dialect with a tradition that is largely intelligible to English readers and recognizably different. You can't write Welsh English or Irish English so easily; on the page, these Englishes are less distinct. To be Scots and part of English literature, then, you have to submerge yourself in it – to lose or at least suppress your Scottishness, assimilating completely or at least pretending to. And it is striking how both *Aimed at Nobody* (1993) and *Uncollected Poems* (1990) – volumes of uncollected work published after Graham's death – reveal a more Scottish poet than Graham himself had allowed to come through in the volumes published during his lifetime. Though *Implements in their Places* (1977) evokes Scotland vividly and tenderly, there were clearly many more poems located in Scotland, recalling it and using its words, that were left out. Earlier in Graham's career, the self-censorship had been still more marked. It's as if Graham was concerned not to put off an English audience. 'The Greenock Dialogues' is the most significant omission, but in *Aimed at Nobody*, there are also 'The Particular Object', 'As Told to Davie Dunsmuir' and 'The Conscript Goes' (*AN*, pp. 33, 35, 37–42, 59–61). In *Uncollected Poems* (pp. 24–25, 36), we find 'Alice Where Art Thou' and 'A Page About My Country':

> A word meaning an area and
> Here I see it flat pressed
> On my Mercator writing table.

Look I am looking at my sweet
Country enough to break my heart.
                    (*UC*, p. 25)

Yearning after Scotland and exiled from it, Graham could also feel unfairly neglected: when in 1970 the Scottish Arts Council finally gave him some financial help, an award of £300, Graham wrote: 'I am very pleased. It is a wee bit recognition from Scotland at last. I have always been a wee bit hurt (JOKE OR NOT JOKE?) that Scotland have [*sic*] never said anything about their exiled boy here, me' (*Nightfisherman*, p. 241).

Whether his absence from Scotland continues to harm his standing is more doubtful. According to Dunn the situation has been improving. Like Norman MacCaig and Edwin Morgan, Dunn says, Graham writes neither 'English English' nor 'Scots' but, as is the case with other writers coming after MacDiarmid, he makes 'a more tactful, perhaps a more experienced distribution of wondrous or otherwise exceptional diction'. All these poets began to be taken more seriously in the late 1980s and early 1990s, after suffering 'the malice, or silence, that destroys or prevents' a reputation.[8] Even so, W.N. Herbert, one of the most charismatic of the present evangelicals of Scottish literature, wrote in 1987 that 'W.S. Graham was, at the point of his death, the most important writer writing in England. That was because he was from Scotland.'[9] There is a hint of cheek and shame in this special pleading.

Graham's 'tactful [...] distribution' of Scottish words or forms persists, all the same, in declaring his distance from the original – both the place and its past. Parts of 'The Greenock Dialogues' reappear in the published poem 'Sgurr Na Gillean Macleod', which quotes and imitates 'The Skye Boat-Song'. Folk-song intervenes; Scottishness seems retrievable only as a lost, stylized past. Similarly, the poems that use Scots language most are 'ballads' – 'Baldy Bane' and 'The Broad Close', from *The Nightfishing*. They are odd ballads, though, Brechtian adoptions of a style rather than revivals of it. Ballads, Graham told Robin Skelton in 1958,

> must be more than just your own contemporary poetic experience expressed in the characteristic ballad 'voice'. The performer playing the Green King of the Wood must never for an instant let the audience get the idea that he thinks he really is the king. The disguise he uses to play the king must just be merely held before him, formal and apparent. In my own ballads one of the ways I attempted this was to lean round the disguise and grimace and speak 'personally' to the reader so that we became two intelligences or characters taking part in the action of the ballad.
>
>   (*Nightfisherman*, p. 157)[10]

All this is consistent with Graham's dislike of MacDiarmid's 'synthetic Scots'. It expresses too his consistent, often unfashionable wariness about the attempt to identify and continue 'Scottish poetry'.

For those to whom issues of mere personality and national identity seem inadequate in explaining literary phenomena, there are other possible reasons for Graham's marginal position. His 'bad luck' in being influenced by Dylan Thomas and then in choosing 'to write in a vein deeply counter to Movement norms' has become a traditional explanation. I want to consider another, simpler, explanation – that, perhaps, his poetry is not in fact very good. Doing so will help to bring out what it is exactly in his work that makes it so important.[11]

Hugh MacDiarmid, certainly, thought that Graham was simply not good enough. Reviewing Graham's first collection, *Cage Without Grievance* (1942), he opined: 'I cannot regard Graham's work as in any way answering to the crucial needs and possibilities of our time. It is not responsible work in this sense; it is an adolescent playing with the materials of great poetry.'[12] MacDiarmid, typically, was about half-right. The work was, and continued to be, playful, but it nonetheless answers to some basic human needs, above all the need to be heard.

There's no doubt, as MacDiarmid suggests, that Graham liked to play with the materials of great poetry, that he liked to mess with the big boys. His poem 'Dear Bryan Wynter', for example, begins:

This is only a note
To say how sorry I am
You died. You will realize
What a position it puts
Me in
                (*CP*, p. 255)

The lines evidently reprise William Carlos Williams's plum poem:

This Is Just to Say
I have eaten
the plums
that were in
the icebox

They manage nonetheless to twist a piece of whimsy into a moment of mocking self-regard. There are numerous other such echoes and allusions in Graham's work: the poems, like the man himself, are great practitioners of absorbency, poetic and alcoholic. 'At nine o'clock one morning,' recalls Sebastian Barker, 'he said, "Here I am, standing in your kitchen. You see this tumbler? It holds half a pint. I'll fill it to here with good Teacher's whisky, then up to the top with Coca-Cola. Now I'll drink it.'" (*ER75*, p. 90). He certainly liked to mix it, as he explained in his poem 'Approaches to How They Behave':

> I myself dress up in what I can
> Afford on the broadway. Underneath
> My overcoat of the time's slang
> I am fashionable enough wearing
> The grave-clothes of my generous masters
> (*CP*, p. 172)

In Joyce's *Ulysses*, Mr Deasy asks Stephen what an Englishman is proud of. 'I will tell you, he said solemnly, what is his proudest boast, *I paid my way... I paid my way. I never borrowed a shilling in my life.* Can you feel that? *I owe nothing?* Can you?'[13] Graham, born and brought up in a tenement building on the Clyde, who served his time as a draughtsman and as a journeyman engineer, could not feel it: he took whatever was offered. At several points in his life he lived in cottages lent by friends; he was reliant until 1974 on a monthly cheque for £25 from Robin Skelton in exchange for manuscripts. He was a man heavily indebted.

He owed most, poetically,[14] to Eliot, who greatly encouraged him in his work, and particularly in the composition of his long poem 'The Night-fishing', first published as a pamphlet in 1951. 'A nice letter from Tommy E.,' Graham told Moncrieff Williamson in 1950, 'saying thinks the N.F. is a whizz for sticking together and being a long poem.'[15] 'N.F.' is in fact stuck together with little bits from 'Tommy E.', beginning with an echo from 'The Dry Salvages': 'very gently struck / The quay night bell', and continuing with many reminders of the rest of *Four Quartets*. Eliot remained for Graham an important point of reference, a kind of marker buoy, bobbing up and down in his work, guiding him towards landfall and indicating routes for departure. Yet in a scene of strange underwater struggle in 'Implements in their Places' Graham dares to imagine Eliot locked up safely in a dead man's chest:

> I dive to knock on the rusted, tight
> Haspt locker of David Jones.
> Who looks out? A mixed company.
> Kandinsky's luminous worms,
> Shelley, Crane and Melville and all
> The rest. Who knows? Maybe even Eliot.
> (*CP*, p. 248)[16]

All the borrowing and the being influenced brought with them anxiety and self-doubt. Graham was always conscious of being, as he puts it in the magnificent 'The Greenock Dialogues', 'The boy made good' (*AN*, p. 37).

'What am I?' he once asked, 'Am I a poet? Or am I just a boy from Greenock?' He was a poet whose need for assurance and reassurance from others was perhaps even greater than his need for self-awareness. 'I should like a machine,' he once told Geoffrey Godbert, 'which, when I wake, will rub my head and say: "Good boy, good boy"'. Aye, there's the rub: above all, Graham wanted to be liked, he wanted to be patted; he is, in some ways, the poet as lap-dog.[17] Fortunately, though, he knew what he was like, and managed to turn his weakness into a strength.[18] He made his badge the mark of the beast, often referring not just to himself and to his poetry, but to language, as a 'creature', a creature that elicited both his affection and his contempt. And by 'creature', he didn't just mean the black dog, the enemy, the clawing depression of Keith Douglas's great unfinished poem 'Bête Noire':

> The trumpet man to take it away
> blows a hot break in a beautiful way
> ought to snap my fingers and tap my toes
> but I sit at my table and nobody knows
> I've got a beast on my back[19]

Graham's creature is a foundling and a friend, a suffering fellow-being. In 'I Leave This at Your Ear' the narrator delivers the poem, like a new-born infant or puppy, 'at your ear for when you wake, / A creature in its abstract cage asleep' (*CP*, p. 157), while in 'Slaughterhouse' he describes mysterious voices that 'hang / And drip blood in the sweet drains' (*AN*, p. 62). Critics and commentators have tended to emphasize Graham's belief in the poem as a constructed space, as an *inanimate* object, yet there is a strong sense throughout his work that the poem is not merely a device, or an instrument, or a tool, but a kind of imaginary being – a psychopomp, or a moon-calf.

At times what Graham refers to as 'the living, animal language' eludes his grasp and his capture, as in 'The Dark Dialogues' where language 'swings away / Further before me' (*CP*, p. 158) . At other times he seems to imagine the poem abducted, or at least adopted, by the reader:

> What does it matter if the words
> I choose, in the order I choose them in,
> Go out into a silence I know

Nothing about, there to be let
In and entertained and charmed
Out of their master's orders?
('Approaches to How They Behave', *CP*, pp. 169–70)

Nor surprisingly, one of his very best poems, 'Johann Joachim Quantz's Five Lessons', is all about tutoring and taming:

Good morning, Karl. Sit down. I have been thinking
About your progress and my progress as one
Who teaches you, a young man with talent
And the rarer gift of application.
                              (*CP*, pp. 222–23)

Similarly, one of his most disturbing, 'The Beast in the Space', has him cuffing a maleficent hound:

Shut up. Shut up. There's nobody here.
If you think you hear somebody knocking
On the other side of the words, pay
No attention. It will be only
The great creature that thumps its tail
On silence on the other side.
If you do not even hear that
I'll give the beast a quick skelp
And through Art you'll hear it yelp.
                              (*CP*, p. 147)

'Skelp' sounds nice and rough here (it means a blow, or a smack or a slap), but 'yelp' seems out of place. It is a mere rhyme, a piece of 'Art' only. Deliberately, I think, the word mocks the reader's and writer's involvement in this artificial business. More usually, the noise from Graham's artless art is much more like a sob, or a whimper. At one point in 'Malcom Mooney's Land' the narrator sidles up and asks, 'Have I not been trying to use the obstacle / Of language well?' (*CP*, p. 145), and in 'The Dark Dialogues' he sighs:

Only to speak and say
Something, little enough,
Not out of want
Nor out of love, to say
Something and to hear
That someone has heard me.
                              (*CP*, p. 160)

He could be a blatant beast: he wanted – he demanded – to be heard, and he had his methods.

There is, for example, an extraordinary amount of falling going on in the poems – from 'The Conscript Goes', to 'The Night City' (in which he falls into the arms of Eliot) and 'Enter a Cloud' ('Is there still time to say / Said I myself lying / In a bower of bramble / Into which I have fallen' [*CP*, p. 209]). Falling, though, seems not so much a means of encouraging philosophical or theological debate as simply a way of eliciting sympathy. Exploring the meaning of 'thrownness' or the paradox of the *felix culpa* take second place to something more importunate. 'Almost every child', according to Freud, 'has fallen down at one time or other and afterwards been picked up and petted; or if he has fallen out of his cot at night, has been taken into bed with his mother or nurse'.[20] Having fallen, Graham wanted to be picked up and petted.

But he also wanted to impress. Enthralled by Eliot, he brought philosophy into his poems.[21] Where some writers are content to have ideas on the level of language, Graham was determined to have ideas *about* language. He theorized about a world governed by language, in which language becomes the decisive metaphor through which we conceive of the self. Whether convincing or not, the advantage of this philosophizing was that it cleared away some of the excesses of his early work, which could be verbose and sloppy, stained by the influence of Dylan Thomas. His later poems have undergone a purging, or a process of pasteurization: they read as if they have been exposed to a high temperature for a short time. They are complex, yet not really difficult; entertaining, yet commanding.[22]

The great poem 'Listen. Put On Morning', for example, from *The White Threshold*, begins with a command, a bark, 'Listen', which reverberates throughout his work, and continues with a great rush of memories and instructions, leading towards a vision of apocalypse and renewal. 'The centuries,' Graham says, 'distil'

> One voice to talk to us.
> Yes listen. It carries away
> The second and the years
> Till the heart's in a jacket of snow
> And the head's in a helmet white
> And the song sleeps to be wakened
> By the morning ear bright.
> Listen. Put on morning.
> Waken into falling light.
>   (*CP*, p. 49)[23]

His poems are full of imperatives – 'Do not be frightened', 'Come down again', 'Remember I am here', 'Don't hurry away' and so on. One suspects, though, that for Graham the most important of all these repeated commands was the one to 'Listen'. 'Letter VII' from *The Nightfishing* ends by speaking to his love:

> My love my love anywhere
> Drifted away, listen. [...]
> Who hears us now? Suddenly
> In a stark flash the nerves
> Of language broke. The sea
> Cried out loud under the keel.
> Listen. Now as I fall.
>
> Listen. And silence even
> Has turned away. Listen.
> (*CP*, pp. 128–29)[24]

Tangled, multivalent phrases alternate here with urgent simplicity – the suppressed puns of 'nerves breaking' and 'crying out loud'; the unexpected meeting of 'stark' and 'flash'; these give way to 'Listen', just 'Listen'.

This is a combination typical of all Graham's work. It has been understood in terms of language – as representing Graham's struggle to escape the prison-house of the language which decides in advance what experiences we can describe or even have. But as Tony Lopez points out, this is not a dry exercise for Graham. Certainly, in 'Five Poems Beginning with the Word Language', he can condemn language wholesale:

> Language is when the speaker kills himself
> In a gesture of communication and finds
> Himself even then unheard. Or language is
> What people hear when they are unspoken to.
> (*AN*, p. 57)

Language is what happens when communication fails or breaks down, when people are '*un*spoken to'. It is the obstacle to as well as the medium of speech. To speak to someone is what Graham is always trying to do. The poems are as simple and profound as that. 'And why,' Graham asks in 'Pangur',

> have I
> Been put into this ridiculous
> Dream because I only wanted

To speak for once thoroughly
To another?

(AN, p. 10)

Or again in 'About the Stuff', another uncollected poem, Graham thinks of using a magnifying-glass to set things alight as an image of his desire to 'startle' the 'white paper' 'into a speaking flame'. He does not want to start a forest-fire or cause any trouble, he says.

> No, only it is I want
> To disturb the paper, to burn a sense
> Of a changed other person in
> On to the white of this public skin.

Indeed, he 'did not mean to speak' at all, 'but just / To lie down hidden away on the hill / Above Zennor' (AN, p. 30). '[T]horoughly' and 'burn a sense' both betray the passion of Graham's will to reach others and make the public world a personal place – to defeat the social beasts, not just by lying down beside them, hidden away or 'Easy against [their] flank'. Writing allows that, even encourages it. And he knows well enough how comforting it would be. The drive in his work, all the same, is towards others – towards hearing and being heard, speaking and listening.

Graham inscribed a copy of his *Collected Poems* to Nancy Wynne-Jones and her husband Conor:

> Dear Conor
> Dear Nancy
> Here is my book a kind
> of record of my life. Do not forget me.
>   W. S. Graham
>   X X

(ER75, p. 69)

'Do not forget me.' It is a basic instinct, and a noble request. It is matched by Graham's sense of himself as a bit of an anxious busy-body – not just self-pitying or artfully poignant but occasionally loud and attention-seeking. It is typical of Graham's comic touch that when he made a selection of his poems for Penguin in 1970, he placed 'Listen. Put on Morning', published in 1949, just before 'The Fifteen Devices' published that year. A self-deprecating piece about how he fashions an image of himself, partly for public consumption, partly to stay steady himself, 'The Fifteen Devices' ends by noticing the half-jolly, half-compulsive eagerness with which Graham encountered others:

My fifteen devices in my work
Shop of shadow and brightness have
Their places as they stand ready
To go out and say Hello.[25]

(*CP*, p. 176)

Notes

1 See Iain Sinclair (ed.), *Conductors of Chaos* (London and Basingstoke: Picador, 1996), pp. 209–22.
2 Julian MacLaren-Ross, *Memoirs of the Forties* (London: Alan Ross, 1965), pp. 183–85.
3 Donald Davie, review of Lopez, *PWSG*, in *Yearbook of English Studies*, 22 (1992), p. 365.
4 The poems are an earlier version of 'Language Ah Now You Have Me', published in *Implements in their Places*; these phrases are in both; see *CP*, p. 200.
5 Douglas Dunn (ed.), *The Faber Book of Twentieth-Century Scottish Poetry* (London and Boston: Faber and Faber, 1992), pp. xxxvi–xxxvii.
6 John MacQueen and Tom Scott (eds), *The Oxford Book of Scottish Verse* (Oxford: Clarendon Press, 1966), includes 'The Dark Dialogues', sections 2 and 3, plus 'Many Without Elegy'; Tom Scott (ed.), *The Penguin Book of Scottish Verse* (Harmondsworth: Penguin, 1970), includes 'Five Visitors to Madron'. Not a generous selection in either case. See Charles King (ed.), *Twelve Modern Scottish Poets* (London: University of London Press, 1971) and Charles King and Iain Crichton Smith (eds), *Twelve More Modern Scottish Poets* (London: Hodder & Stoughton, 1986). The latter selects from Graham's work: 'Listen. Put on Morning', part of 'The Nightfishing', section III, 'The Constructed Space', 'I Leave This at Your Ear', 'Loch Thom' and 'To Alexander Graham', which seem representative and not exclusively Scottish.
7 See Neil Corcoran, *English Poetry since 1940* (Longman Literature in English; Harlow: Longman, 1993).
8 Dunn (ed.), *Twentieth-Century Scottish Poetry*, pp. xxv, xxxv. Robert Crawford, *Identifying Poets: Self and Territory in Twentieth-Century Poetry* (Edinburgh: Edinburgh University Press, 1993), p. 159 gives the same impression as Dunn of new-found harmony and tolerance; Scotland's 'linguistic fluidity', he says, may now be seen to unite Edwin Morgan, Graham, MacDiarmid and Dunn himself.
9 W.N. Herbert, 'The Breathing Words', *ER75*, p. 102.
10 Graham said something similar about the ballads to Alan Clodd in 1954 – see *Nightfisherman*, pp. 138–39. 'Imagine a Forest' (*CP*, pp. 196–97) is a border ballad on the same theme.
11 David Punter, 'W.S. Graham: Constructing a White Space', in his *The Hidden Script: Writing and the Unconscious* (London: Routledge and Kegan Paul, 1985), p. 131. But, as Punter says, there is 'a limit to the accidental'. See above, Chapter 1, for a discussion of Graham's 'bad luck' in his career and critical reception.
12 Review first published in *The Free Man*; quoted in Lopez, *PWSG*, p. 11. Later MacDiarmid expressed 'admiration' for 'the way [Graham] has always set his "stout

heart to a stey brae'" in his 'undeflected – if almost unrewarded – devotion to his art of poetry' (*ER75*, p. 104).

13 James Joyce, *Ulysses*, ed. Danis Rose (London: Picador, 1997), p. 31.

14 Also financially: Eliot lent him £20 in 1950 (*Nightfisherman*, p. 124).

15 Quoted in *ER75*, p. 10; this letter is not included in *Nightfisherman*.

16 This is a cunning and typical moment because Graham's enjambement ('all / The rest') echoes and parodies Eliot's in *Four Quartets*, 'the rest / Is prayer' ('The Dry Salvages'). Eliot's phrase itself distorts Hamlet's 'The rest is silence' in the same way that Graham's lines echo 'Uncle Tom Cobbly and all'.

17 *ER75*, p. 89. Geoffrey Godbert, 'W.S. Graham', *Envoi* (1996), p. 91.

18 'Beholding Thee', a late uncollected poem, begins 'Beholding thee I run away across / The language shouting WOW WOW I BEHOLD THEE'. The poem rues this foolish, noisy cowardice and asks for help: 'Help me up from the shore. / Unoil my whiskers. What am I going to do / To be slightly patted on the head / By the human elements.' (*UP*, p. 32). The poet feels himself humiliated by his doglike desire to be liked and patted; he meets with condescension because he makes it too obvious that he wants a genuine encounter. As he wrote in the 1949 notebook, 'To show you *need* something from another person destroys any chance of receiving it' (*ER75*, p. 36). William Empson in 'Timon's Dog' (in *The Structure of Complex Words* [London: Chatto & Windus, 1951], pp. 175–84) thinks brilliantly about the implications of calling another person a dog.

19 Keith Douglas, *The Complete Poems*, third edition (London: Faber & Faber, 2000), p. 128.

20 Sigmund Freud, *The Interpretation of Dreams*, ed. Angela Richards, Penguin Freud Library IV (Harmondsworth: Penguin, 1976), p. 519.

21 In my view, the excellent, recent *Selected Poems* (London: Faber and Faber, 1996) was wise not to include Graham's famous philosophical pieces, 'What is the Language Using Us for?' and 'Implements in their Places'.

22 Sensibly, I think, the *Selected Poems* begins late on, with poems from Graham's fourth book *The White Threshold* (1949).

23 See Corcoran's fine discussion of this poem in *English Poetry since 1940*, pp. 48–49.

24 Graham returns to this passage in a later poem, 'Yours Truly', *CP*, p. 149.

25 The selection was for *Penguin Modern Poets 17: David Gascoyne: W.S. Graham: Kathleen Raine* (Harmondsworth: Penguin, 1970). 'Listen. Put on Morning' and 'The Fifteen Devices' are on pp. 112–15.

From **The White Threshold: 4**

Older stranger by stranger
I move towards you across
The strange sea borne in a gesture
Of the light word and the face
Turned to the heartbroke wall.
Beside and in the shade
Of my encountered arrival
From the caretaking dead,
This night I make my haul
From the twelve-discipled seas,
Filament from brother to brother.
This night the hill bothies
On the windbreak of Kintyre
Hear the downbearing sea
Break on the seashelled door.
Continually I am answered
By the selfseas for ever
Fed by the blinding air.

3

Graham and the 1940s

TONY LOPEZ

W.S. Graham and Dylan Thomas met in 1942 in Glasgow when Thomas stayed for a week in David Archer's house.[1] Archer, sometime bookshop owner and publisher of the Parton Poets (including David Gascoyne and George Barker as well as Thomas and Graham), was independently wealthy and a very generous patron to a whole crowd of Glasgow bohemians, as he had previously been in London when he owned and ran the Parton Street bookshop, the centre of the London poetry scene in the late 1930s. He moved to Glasgow to get away from the blitz, opened another bookshop and the Scott Street Arts Centre, and bought a large flat in Sandyford Place, Sauchiehall Street, where he allowed various artistic people to live and work for little or no rent: Jankel Adler, Helen Biggar, Douglas Campbell, Benjamin Creme, Robert Frame, Graham himself, and the actress and poet Julian Orde (a girlfriend of Graham's) were among those who lived in Archer's flat.

Graham had been moving around to avoid conscription. He had been at Newbattle Abbey College, near Edinburgh, where he got a year of formal education paid for by a trade union bursary; the college showed him a way out of the shipyards where he had served an engineering apprenticeship. It was in 1938 at Newbattle that he met his life companion, Nessie (Agnes) Dunsmuir, and they were eventually to marry in 1954. He had also been over to southern Ireland for a while, and had later worked briefly as a machinist in a torpedo factory in Fort Matilda, near Greenock; from there he moved to Glasgow and joined the Scott Street scene.

Robert Frame writes of Graham's time in the rent-free flat in Glasgow, of the poverty and hunger of their life there but also of the social freedom, the music, excitement and fun.[2] He remembers Graham's use of the scrubbed-wood kitchen table where he set himself up to write with his dictionary, his pile of Oxford classics and, tellingly, a pamphlet edition of Joyce's *Anna Livia Plurabelle*. He would play music from a small record collection as he worked: Richard Tauber's Mozart and Schubert, Sydney

McEwan and John McCormick. A particular favourite was the English tenor Heddle Nash; Graham himself had a fine tenor voice. Frame also describes Graham's working lists of interesting and striking words typed out in advance of his drafting of a poem, which he composed by inventing material to join the listed words together. The sense of the poem as a construction made of words (rather than a piece of self-expression) is very clear in the memoir, as it is also in the few brief critical statements that Graham made about his writing.[3] This working method and the company of various avant-garde artists also begins to explain the abstraction of Graham's early poetry, which is much more developed than it is in Dylan Thomas's work, from which Graham's is frequently seen to derive.[4]

Another important factor is Graham's enthusiasm for Rimbaud's *Illuminations*, which is strikingly registered in the earliest published Graham poems. In particular, the combination of mechanical and industrial imagery with aspects of the natural landscape in a compressed synthesis seems to be an effect he learned from Rimbaud, whom he read in the Rootham translation.[5] It is obvious, however, that the most important influence on Graham and his companions, in the early 1940s when his first books were being published, was the refugee Hungarian-Jewish modernist painter, Jankel Adler. Graham admired Adler for his artistic integrity and his complete commitment to his work as a painter.

Graham lived among artists all his life. Makers of fragmentation and abstraction in painting and sculpture were his daily companions right through his career. Some of them were his best friends and drinking companions who had what he was to call 'terrible times together': Robert Colquhoun and Robert MacBryde (known as the two Roberts), Johnny Minton, and later in Cornwall Bryan Wynter, Roger Hilton, Peter Lanyon, Alan Lowndes and Tony O'Malley. With Robert Frame and Benjamin Creme, the artists who made the Picassoesque illustrations for his first book *Cage Without Grievance* (1942), Graham assisted in running the Scott Street Arts Centre and organized a series of public performances, each incorporating music and each based on the work of an individual poet. Among them were readings of Blake and Rimbaud, an evening of contemporary poetry, including Graham's own work, and a dramatized performance of Eliot's *The Waste Land* with the different voices and characters portrayed by different readers. Some of the events were staged to incorporate audience participation, with different locations created by the use of screens, furniture and suspended canvas stretched into corridors to form a maze. Each section of the event would be in a different part of the construction and the performance included the conducting of the audience from place to place through the set.

It is clear that Graham's early conception of poetry was bound up with a wish for an integrated avant-garde art practice incorporating elements of drama, music, painting and what we now call installation and performance art, teasing and defamiliarizing at every turn. There is therefore a continuity between the modernist art scene in which Graham lived and the way in which he began to work as a poet. His early and much misunderstood experiments with radical disjuncture, unexpected word order and alliterative metres now seem almost inevitable products of such an environment, one that Graham actively sought out.

In 1942, Graham went from Glasgow to a residency in Kilquhanity, an experimental progressive school in Galloway, and there he met and had an affair with Mary Harris, one of the teaching staff. They went together in 1943 to stay in some caravans that her family owned at Germoe, near Marazion in Cornwall.[6] After a while Mary Harris went back alone to Scotland and their daughter Rosalind was born, though Graham did not meet her until many years later. Thus it was through Mary Harris that Graham moved down to the westernmost part of Cornwall and began to make a life there, though it was a fragile and unsettled existence for many years. In 1944 Nessie Dunsmuir went south to join Graham at the caravans in Germoe and they attempted to get some income by growing violets for the London flower market.[7] The scheme was not a success and the couple were, throughout their time in Cornwall, very hard up.[8]

The couple were visited by the painter Ben Nicholson, who took Graham to see St Ives and to meet Barbara Hepworth. In order to explain his enthusiasm for Ben Nicholson as a serious and important artist, Graham told Robert Frame 'he is like Jankel'. In 1944 or 1945 the two Roberts visited Nessie and Sydney, and also in 1945 Johnny Minton and Bryan Wynter both visited. The sculptor and writer Sven Berlin, who wrote the first book on the St Ives primitive painter Alfred Wallis, was in regular correspondence and visited several times.[9]

Meanwhile Archer's various enterprises in Glasgow had collapsed and the scene he had gathered around him moved to London to try to establish or re-establish themselves there. The poet Tom Scott has them at first staying in Julian Orde's attic flat in Highgate: Adler, who had an exhibition at the Redfearn Gallery; the two Roberts, who were soon to set up a studio together nearby; and Archer, who distributed folding money to poets and artists whenever he got a cheque.[10] Graham was moving around a good deal. He frequently hitchhiked up from Cornwall to meet friends and to conduct poetry business in those difficult and chaotic times: doodlebugs and V2s were exploding in London and in the Soho pubs there was a lively, if rather desperate, sense of gaiety. There was a great deal of heavy drinking in the Fitzrovia scene and Graham, who was from the outset a hugely ambitious poet, was also painfully aware of his humble background and ill at ease socially with the metropolitan Fitzrovia crowd. He found it difficult to meet people unless he had had a few drinks and his London trips turned into binges. In that, of course, he was conforming to type. Dylan Thomas and George Barker had established the public role of poets along these lines and Graham was good friends with both of them. Barker, like Graham, travelled between Cornwall and London; they had also been known on these occasions to share supplies of amphetamines.

Graham would often meet Dylan Thomas in the pubs where literary editors such as John Lehmann and Tambimuttu did business. This poem memorializes just such a meeting:

Incident in Soho

History – big word – being made
Outside the pub: armies in Normandy;
Planes with a load of damage overhead;
All London under fire from the enemy.

Masking the ordinary extraordinary,
There at the table where a small fat man
Talked with another, a Glaswegian,
I saw an unlike making of history.

Me, I didn't hear a word they spoke,
Was, so to speak, a deaf fly on the wall
When the small fat man took
His latest from his pocket; hands on table,

Read what he'd written. When he'd finished, 'Will
You let me see, because I couldn't hear?'
He gave it me, then turning to the other:
'Well Sydney?' The first reading of 'Fern Hill'.[11]

David Wright, the South African poet who settled in England, shows us Sydney Graham and Dylan Thomas together in a Soho pub in wartime, with Thomas, famous tearaway drunken Swansea poet, trying out what was to be one of his best-known poems on the 'Glaswegian'. It tells us something about Graham's and Thomas's relationship at that point, and Wright, with typical modesty, puts himself twice at the margins: once because of the literary importance of the two poets he depicts and again because of his own deafness, to poetry and to bombs. It also says something about Fitzrovia society at that time that Thomas could pull out and read his new poem, beginning 'Now as I was young and easy under the apple boughs', without undue embarrassment and without getting beaten up. John Heath-Stubbs similarly remembers Thomas in the Wheatsheaf reciting passages from what was to become *Under Milk Wood*, so evidently it was not unusual for Thomas to perform like this, being perhaps too drunk or too famous to worry about any disturbance of the peace.

Yet Thomas was undoubtedly a very canny judge of his audiences. Philip Larkin met him in Oxford in November 1941, when Larkin was an undergraduate student and treasurer of the Oxford English Club. As treasurer, Larkin went out to dinner with the speakers before the meetings and was one of those responsible for entertaining them afterwards. 'I remember,' Larkin said, 'we took Dylan Thomas to the Randolph and George Orwell to the not-so-good hotel. I suppose it was my first essay in practical criticism.'[12] Larkin was greatly impressed by Dylan Thomas's performance; he wrote to his friend James Ballard Sutton that Thomas was

> [a] hell of a fine man [... a] little, snubby, hopelessly pissed bloke who made hundreds of cracks and read parodies of everybody in appropriate voices. He remarked: 'I'd like to have talked about a book of poems I've been given to review, a young poet called Rupert Brooke – it's surprising how he has been influenced by Stephen Spender…'. There was a moment of delighted surprise, then a roar of laughter. Then he read a parody of Spender entitled 'The parachutist' which had people rolling on the floor. He kept up this all night – parodies of everyone bar Lawrence – and finally read two of his own poems, which seem very good.

Notice that Thomas is portrayed in this sketch of Larkin's as an ordinary bloke and also as a very worldly poet who is, as we learn from the jokes he makes and the parodies he reads, keenly aware of the dangers involved in the public role of the poet. He is in Larkin's sketch really the opposite of the bardic poet that the Movement writers later made him out to be. He reads only two of his own poems and these Larkin did not know. Larkin soon remedied his unfamiliarity with Thomas's poetry by borrowing the books from the Bodleian. According to Motion, 'Larkin was led to "soak" in Thomas's work and under its influence he "quite changed his style of writing". Within a week he had produced the derivative sonnet "Observation" (published by Amis in the Bulletin) and for the next several years Thomas's cadences and images swirled amongst those of his other idols'.[13] Later, for the writers of the Movement, Dylan Thomas was seen as the major poetic reputation that they needed to overcome. His *Collected Poems* was published in 1952 and it became the target for this new generation of writers to react against.

In this negative sense Dylan Thomas was crucial to the development of the Movement writers and his influence on them all continued to be very substantial. Blake Morrison documents adverse comment on Thomas by John Wain, Kingsley Amis, D.J. Enright and Donald Davie. He also shows that Amis's play *That Uncertain Feeling* parodied both *Under Milk Wood* and Thomas's poetry. Enright's poem 'On the Death of a Child' is a kind of revision of Thomas's 'A Refusal to Mourn the Death by Fire of a Child in London', while Larkin's poem 'I Remember, I Remember' revises Thomas's 'Fern Hill', as does Davie's poem 'A Baptist Childhood'.[14] By the 1960s, when Larkin wrote about this period he downplayed Thomas's influence, suggesting that it was Vernon Watkins's 1943 presentation of Yeats to the Oxford English Club that was the most important and formative of the early influences on his work.[15] I see no reason to doubt that Larkin was genuine in his proposal of Yeats as an influence on his younger self, but I wonder if that disclosure actually masks the real importance of an influence that by the 1960s he was less willing to admit.

Graham's third published book, *2ND POEMS* (the title's '2 N D' encodes 'To Nessie Dunsmuir'), was published in 1945 under Tambimuttu's imprint Editions Poetry London by Nicholson and Watson.[16] Also on the list were David Gascoyne, Lucian Freud, Nicholas Moore, Anne Ridler, G.S. Fraser, Ronald Bottrall, Graham Sutherland, Kathleen Raine, Henry Miller, Keith Douglas and Vladimir Nabokov. There was in wartime a good potential market for poetry but it was difficult to manage supply and demand because there was strict control of the very limited paper supply; warehouses were burning. Publishers who had stocks of paper could do business but new firms could not get a permit to get started. So opportunities were limited and Graham had done well indeed to get Archer and Tambimuttu to publish his work. Recently a copy of *2ND POEMS* with Graham's own annotations has come to light, and it is clear from that copy that Graham was judging his own progress by how far he had gone beyond his early influences of Rimbaud, Thomas and Gerard Manley Hopkins, which were replaced in his eyes by the Joyce of *Finnegans Wake*.

He was attempting to alter his reader's expectations of meaning by manipulating word order. He stressed what he called the 'Anglo-Saxon components of English', something he had developed a feel for when reading Pound.

'His Companions Buried Him', from *2ND POEMS*, shows some of the impact of these changing influences on Graham's work. It also suggests the perhaps surprising kinship between Graham and Larkin at this stage in their careers.

His Companions Buried Him

Always by beams of stars (and they disclose
India Africa China Asia then that furry queen)
I see Earth's operator within his glade
Gloved in the fox of his gigantic hour.

The first ship cast to perish wintered blood
Found beachbergs on the flesh. Another tongue
Flooded what law the planet's bowline hung
Where sun and moon go up the blinded shipping.

The second ship cast to perish bruised on brain
Tethered to hydrogen, explored the island.
Popular as are its people, the land they found
Disguised its landscape with a wagtailed sand.

The third ship cast to perish perished hard
On land rigged round with sea on speaking sea.
Each word was word and end of it away
With all its travels for ever almost O.

Always by beams of stars (and they disclose
That furry queen who saunters on night's boards)
I see Earth swing within its own explorer
Who dangles each star lighting up his map.[17]

This exploration poem is structured by means of a near-repeat of the first stanza in the last, and also by the pattern in the middle three stanzas beginning 'The first ship', 'The second ship' and so on. Each is numbered for an imagined ship's voyage and 'cast to perish' in various ways. In the character, 'Earth's operator', Graham portrays God in the guise of a crane operator in a Clydeside shipyard, hiding in a glade and making all the visible world appear and disappear, grow and develop 'by beams of stars' – by the magic energy that allows us to see and know the world.

'The furry queen' turns up again later in Graham's writing (in *Malcolm Mooney's Land*, published in 1970) and is most likely a private and loving title for Nessie. The annual fair and parade in Helston, Cornwall – a kind of traditional West Country carnival and day of misrule – is known as the Helston Furry, so that Nessie may be thought of here as a May-queen, the queen of the Furry. I think that 'gloved in the fox' continues this sexy, furry, private language, as the word 'foxglove' is suggested by being unpacked. Both parts of the word are made visible, so that the language seems active and already coded with meanings, which the reader discovers, as it were, after the event. The doubleness of this language is full of the private coded meanings of love talk.

For Graham the title, which he noted as 'a phrase which seemed to occur so significantly and frequently in northern exploration accounts', signified a heroic explorer, someone like Nansen or Scott, who dies far away from his home.[18] These figures were types of male heroism and heroism is their function in the poem, by contrast with the furry queen, who comes at night.

The poem adopts radical shifts in scale, learned I think from Auden's *The Orators* (1932) with its shifting viewpoints of aviators and secret agents. In the Graham poem dangling stars become a dangling lightbulb as the imagined hero looks at his explorer's map and sees the territory displayed in miniature. There is a kind of formal identity in replication, as the shape of the lightbulb is picked up in 'planet's bowline', as if the earth were tied up with a rope, and also 'tethered to Hydrogen', which suggests a balloon or airship. The shifts of scale move from continents 'India China Africa Asia', to the planet as an imagined island, to a ship in a ballad, to a lightbulb suspended above a map.

The first ship (stanza 2) has elements of Nansen's voyages and perhaps the 1912 *Titanic* disaster with its 'beachbergs' and 'blinded shipping'; the second ship (stanza 3) appears to enact the discovery of a particular island that remains unknown to us, a different culture whose difference is experienced as 'disguise'. Here the 'wagtailed sand', like 'gloved in the fox', compresses the name of the waterside bird, 'wagtail', into the movement that names it and the place where it may be found. The third ship (stanza 4), 'rigged round with sea on speaking sea', seems to exist in a ballad like Coleridge's *The Rime of the Ancient Mariner* or some much older sea shanty, 'for almost ever O', from which that poem is derived. Graham's poem is turned in on itself, an exploration of the language of exploration, figuring at another level (and with what Graham saw as Joycean wordplay) the exploration of otherness in sexual love.

Larkin's title poem sequence from *The North Ship*, published the same year as *2ND POEMS*, has a good deal in common with 'His Companions Buried Him'. The first poem in the sequence, 'Legend', is an exploration poem that develops out of the first line of the Christmas carol, 'I saw three ships':

Legend

I saw three ships go sailing by
Over the sea, the lifting sea,
And the wind rose in the morning sky,
And one was rigged for a long journey.

The first ship turned towards the west,
Over the sea, the running sea,
And by the wind was all possessed
And carried to a rich country.

The second turned towards the east,
Over the sea, the quaking sea,
And the wind hunted it like a beast
To anchor in captivity.

The third ship drove towards the north,
Over the sea, the darkening sea,
But no breath of wind came forth,
And the decks shone frostily.

The northern sky rose high and black
Over the proud unfruitful sea,
East and west the ships came back
Happily or unhappily:

But the third went wide and far
Into an unforgiving sea
Under a fire-spilling star,
And it was rigged for a long journey.[19]

As in Graham's poem, here the stanzas that follow the first one begin 'The first ship', 'The second ship', 'The third ship' in sequence, and again as in Graham's poem the first stanza is closely echoed in the last (though in Larkin's poem it is the last line of the first stanza that is almost exactly repeated, together with the metrical pattern of the stanza as a whole). Larkin's poem is also tied together with a refrain second line, 'Over the sea, the lifting sea', 'Over the sea, the running sea' and so on. The rhymes (*abab*) also create a more sustained pattern throughout the poem. Overall, the Larkin poem feels just as formulaic and literary as Graham's, its origins lying closer perhaps to Yeats than to Joyce. Though they both make quite sparing use of nautical language ('rigged' appears in both poems, 'bowline' in Graham's and 'anchor' in Larkin's), the scenery remains pretty conventional in both, albeit rather more crowded and exotic in Graham's poem.

Larkin's sequence of poems also imagines northern exploration: his first imagined ship goes west, the second east and the third, whose journey is followed through the sequence, travels ever further northwards. It leaves behind the 'darkening sea' of 'Legend' where the 'decks shone frostily' to reach in the sequence's second poem a cold dream of death; it goes on from there to a fortune-teller who tells of a dark girl's kisses, to a blizzard (like a girl's thick hair) and then finally to entrapment by a woman who has 'ten claws'. The end of Larkin's voyage into the imagination is a sexual liaison full of cosmic fireworks: 'More brilliant than Orion / Or the planets Venus and Mars'. In a way that prefigures much of his later, deliberately downbeat and colloquial writing, the sexual encounter proves to be a trap. Graham's and Larkin's poems both recall Coleridge's *Ancient Mariner*. The sense of guilt in Coleridge's poem is matched by Larkin's 'recurrent dream' and 'waken[ing] / Increasingly to fear' (in '65°N'). The formal patterning of poetry is harnessed by both Larkin and Coleridge to figure 'natural' repetitions – in the waves, the tides, dawn and dusk – and for Larkin's fantasy self there is a analogous, recurring dream of death from sheer cold. One might say that as a whole the sequence *The North Ship* resembles Coleridge's poem in being a fear-filled sexual fantasy in which the unknown is translated into an imaginary geography that is at first forbidding and later entrapping.

Both Graham and Larkin reinvented themselves as poets, making drastic changes in their styles of writing, so that these early poems would not seem typical of either of them at their best. Yet they reveal the common ground (in neo-Romanticism and post-Symbolism) shared by writers who are often thought of as opposites; they disrupt, in other words, the literary history written by the Movement, which has been in part responsible for Graham's comparative neglect.[20] For Larkin, it was after the effort of writing two published novels and one unfinished novel that he began to write the poems for which he is now so widely known. On 11 April 1942 he wrote: 'What a poet has to do is create a new language for himself. And more – it has to be a good one. Pound, for instance, is shit. Likewise Joyce, if you can call him a poet.'[21] By the time he came to write the poems of *The Less Deceived*, Larkin was established in his career as a university librarian, a career in which he achieved a great deal. After Wellington public library he went to Queen's University, Belfast, to Leicester and then to Hull. He was caught up in institutional concerns, the reorganization of library services, the building of a new library, university politics and funding battles. He would never write another post-Symbolist voyage poem.

Graham went in precisely the opposite direction, living an insecure existence well outside the bounds of middle-class respectability. He and Nessie moved in early 1947 to a cottage in Mevagissey, near St Austell, Cornwall, and continued to live together as an unmarried couple in a bohemian scene. Here Graham wrote many of the poems collected in *The White Threshold*. In 1947, they were at 26 Cliff Street – a house loaned to them for some months by the novelist Frank Baker. Kathrine Talbot, writing of her life with the painter Kit Barker (brother of the poet, George) remembers among the artists living in and around Mevagissey Louis Adeane, poet and publisher's reader who lived a little way inland; the poet Derek Savage, his wife Connie and their children; and the American poet Douglas Newton and his wife, the writer Mary Lee Settle.[22] Adeane and Savage are both described by Talbot as pacifists. Also in the area were Ben Nicholson, Bryan Wynter, Susan Lethbridge, David Wright, David Haughton, George Barker and his girlfriend Cass. George Barker and Michael Asquith stayed in Mevagissey for some time and David Archer (who was chasing the suntanned fishermen) stayed for the whole summer of 1947. When Frank and Kate Baker returned with their two sons, Nessie and Sydney moved to a smaller cottage nearby.

Mevagissey was at that time a small 'unspoilt' fishing village with narrow streets and hardly any traffic. These incoming residents must have seemed very exotic. Their unconventional lifestyles were tolerated by the locals in a way that would not have been possible in much of provincial England. The writers and artists managed to live on very little money because the rents for sail lofts and small fishermen's cottages were very low and they could always beg fish when they had nothing else to eat. The fishermen themselves were used to irregular incomes and hard times. It was in 1947 that Graham was asked out as fourth hand on a fishing boat from Mevagissey. He had had some experience on boats on the Clyde when he was growing up, and he took to the work. He went out on fishing trips with the crew on and off during the next few years.

By the end of the 1940s, Graham's poetry took him America to try his luck there. He made contacts in America through the Columbia professor Vivienne Koch, who had written an early review of his work. He had met her in London and she visited the Grahams in Mevagissey. It was through her efforts that he got an Atlantic Award from the Rockefeller Foundation which enabled him to travel to the United States. Nessie and Graham split the money when they separated – she went to Paris and he went to stay with Vivienne Koch in New York, giving a series of lectures on British literature at New York University and touring around giving poetry readings. *The White Threshold*, his first book with Faber and Faber, appeared in 1949 and in 1950 Graham was back in London, again staying with Vivienne Koch, who was working on a book about Yeats. He had several meetings with T.S. Eliot at this period.

By 1954, however, Graham was back in the far west of Cornwall, once more with Nessie, and the couple married in that year. From March 1956 they lived at the old Coastguard Cottages at Gurnard's Head, a few miles along the coast, west of St Ives, and later moved to Gulval, near Penzance. Soon after that they went to live in a small cottage in nearby Madron, owned by the painter Nancy Wynne-Jones, which she let them have rent-free. In Madron they were near some of the major St Ives painters – Peter Lanyon, Bryan Wynter, Roger Hilton and Patrick Heron. These friends and the artistic community of St Ives became the enduring context of Graham's work for the rest of his life.

Like Larkin's in a way, Graham's writings after the 1940s developed towards greater lucidity. Also, and again arguably like Larkin, beneath the radical changes of style a continuity remains. Graham was, first of all, always much more ambitious for poetry than the other neo-Romantic writers who came to prominence in the 1940s. He consistently works in and towards long poems. Secondly, the voyage of exploration and self-discovery in 'His Companions Buried Him' remained the single most important theme of his career and was developed throughout his work. It began with *The Seven Journeys* (1944), the first book he wrote and the second to be published. The title poem of *The White Threshold* is a con-frontation with the unknowable sea, and the poem remains there at the edge, reproducing the conflict of endurance and destruction in nature, translating it into human and linguistic terms. That book also reconstructs the Clydeside community in which Graham grew up and stresses its distance from the power centre of London, with its standard English and its remote authority. 'The Nightfishing', which for many readers is

Graham's major achievement, depicts a voyage out into the sea, and seeks to establish a view of the self as a shifting and retrospective construction made out of life-experience and work. At the poem's centre is a constructed silence, an experience of aloneness out at sea and under the constellations at night. This pause, just before the silver herring are gathered in with the nets, manages to communicate a spiritual awareness that is post-Homeric and post-Christian – loaded with Christian meanings but also located within ordinary work experience. It is a remarkable achievement that is much more substantial than anything foreseen in Graham's poems of wartime. Yet 'The Nightfishing' is a 1940s poem. Graham was working on it in Mevagissey in 1947, and included it in his readings in America in 1948–49. In 1950, when he met Eliot to discuss his work, Eliot had read 'The Nightfishing' and was very impressed by its structure as a long poem. It was first published in 1951, in the journal *Botteghe Oscure*, Rome and as a separate pamphlet. The book of the same title was published in 1955 by Faber and Faber in London and by the Grove Press in New York. (In the same year, the Marvell Press produced Larkin's *The Less Deceived*.) Voyaging continued to be central to Graham's work in his two later collections – *Malcolm Mooney's Land* (1970), whose title poem is an imaginary voyage into frozen wastes, and *Implements in their Places* (1977), whose fragmentary forms are full of vestiges of all the voyaging that has gone before.

The White Threshold now seems to be a key stage in Graham's development of voyaging as one of his principal concerns. When it was written, the title poem was certainly Graham's most ambitious work to date, summing up his previous experiments and working to clarify his identity as a poet. Having grown up in the shipbuilding town of Greenock on the Firth of Clyde and having subsequently lived for some years right next to the sea in Cornwall, he had been attempting to communicate the terrible power and beauty of the sea and to harness some likeness of its irreducible presence in his imaginative definition of the self. He was interested to establish authenticity in this approach, to deny a purely descriptive purpose, and to insist upon a poetry of philosophical enquiry. According to Vivienne Koch (who probably worked in collaboration with Graham on her critical essays on his poetry), Graham's 'increasing purposive drawing on sea imagery' was successful because 'its resources for ambiguity' were 'grounded in an authentic knowledge of the sea itself'.[23] The very power of translating the sea into language was what he was after in 'The White Threshold', but his purpose was to apply such an imaginative energy in order to explore the most urgent moral and ethical questions in poetic form. In this ambition for poetry and in the way that it was realized, Graham sought to inherit from Pound's and Eliot's modernism. The result is a poetic composition in the grand manner, surely conceived as a performance piece to be read aloud. It has a highly wrought and sumptuous linguistic surface and a wide range of poetic and musical effects that are obvious once they are voiced.

The principal effect at the outset is the loading of lines, wrenching the language away from normal sense and creating a powerful impression of synthetic self-containment. The declarative use of rhyme and repetition, the rising alliterative and syntactic patterning, alternates between the five-line stanzas and the single lines between them. Words are spliced, substituted and rent apart: 'all ways', 'all mighty', 'seabraes', 'seabent', 'rudimental', 'maiden- / Headed', 'foamthatch', 'sheerhulk', 'heartlit'. One result is to create a sheer crashing loudness which is intended to re-enact the crashing of the white threshold itself. The poem makes a kind of primitive identification between breaking wave rhythms and the physical basis of verse rhythms in pulse, heartbeat and sexual arousal. All the conventional imagery connected with wave, foam and surf is employed here, so that the threshold of the title stands between various binary oppositions: male and female, consciousness and drowning, faring and homecoming. What is surprising, in this kind of composition, is the scale of Graham's subsequent development of the poem through changes in metre and tone.

After the first section's staged drama of self against ocean there is in the second section a more measured progress along an imaginary shore landscape, steady in four-stress metre and quieter tone, developing into the recognizable scene of a night-time clifftop walk near the site of a crashed warplane. The third section itself splits into three points of view, contrasting versions of female and male histories (Nessie and Sydney Graham's), with a third voice unveiled as other to both these two. This three-way contrast of voice is created out of industrial scenery of mining and shipbuilding, further locating the poem in the war economy.[24] The fourth section, written in what was later to become Graham's characteristic three-stress metre, is a quieter evocation of the night-time off the west coast of Scotland, an imaginative recreation of trawling:

This night I make my haul
From the twelve-discipled seas,
Filament from brother to brother.
This night the hill bothies

On the windbreak of Kintyre
Hear the downbearing sea

At this stage the Christian imagery of the net, 'Filament from brother to brother' from 'the twelve-discipled seas', seems to add a huge sense of dimension and repetition to the bereavement that drives the poem in this section: 'the humancrowded song / Of the lamenting sea', 'his young life broke through', 'And bright air of each death' (*WT*, p. 59; *CP*, pp. 81–82).

It is in the fifth section, written in regular rhymed and half-rhymed iambics, that we meet the image of Christ discovered as a continuity with earlier myth: 'Good Phoebus youth nailed on the bleeding branches'. This is coupled with an increasingly explicit attack on the way in which Christianity is harnessed by the state:

I'll hold you off your sacrifice even for
The martyr in burning cities brother sister
All of the elemental founded churches' error.
[...]
                    A fallen force
Across the cleft cathedrals in the furnaced city.
Endeavour burns its gases.
                    (*WT*, p. 61; *CP*, pp. 82–83)

The logic of a morality based on sacrifice, though it appears to be passive, accommodating and cooperative, is here identified as what makes warfare possible in a modern state whose economy and total production are geared to war. The poem thus includes profound and uncertain critical work on the ideology of the war era and should be understood as a poetic exploration of the most difficult issues arising in that time. The Christian framework of social recovery and consolation is challenged in Graham's poem as complicit in the industry of mass slaughter. Graham, from a quite different background and intellectual position, is working through some of the same concerns that Eliot addressed in his *Four Quartets* (1943). 'The White Threshold' is a substantial and significant achievement in twentieth-century English-language poetry, even though it has been overshadowed by the major poems that Graham wrote later in his career. It is certainly one of the most significant poems published in the 1940s, and the volume as a whole responds, as few others do, to the impact on civilians of the Second World War.

Notes

1 For a fuller account of Graham's work see Lopez, *PWSG*. This version, however, has benefited from discussion with Michael and Margaret Snow, who were at the time preparing their edition of Graham's letters for publication. I am most grateful for their generous help, including access to Graham papers.
2 Robert Frame, 'W.S. Graham at Sandyford Place', *ER75*, pp. 60–65.
3 The most developed statement by Graham about poetics is 'Notes on a Poetry of Release', *Poetry Scotland*, 3 (1946), pp. 56–58; reprinted in *Nightfisherman*, pp. 379–83.
4 I discuss relations between the work of Thomas and Graham in more detail later.
5 Arthur Rimbaud, *Prose Poems from Les Illuminations*, trans. Helen Rootham (London: Faber and Faber, 1932).
6 Marazion is on the south coast of Cornwall, a few miles east of Penzance and due south of St Ives.
7 See David Brown, 'Chronology', in *St Ives 1939–64: Twenty-Five Years of Painting, Sculpture and Pottery* (London: The Tate Gallery, 1985), p. 102, and *Nightfisherman*, pp. 62–65.
8 Nessie worked in St Ives hotels for many years, and their financial position eased only much later in 1974 when Graham was awarded a Civil List pension.
9 Sven Berlin, *Alfred Wallis – Primitive* (London: Nicholson & Watson, 1949).
10 Tom Scott, 'W.S. Graham in the Forties and Fifties', *ER75*, pp. 57–59.
11 Previously unpublished; copyright the estate of David Wright.
12 Andrew Motion, *Philip Larkin: A Writer's Life* (London: Faber and Faber, 1993), p. 45.
13 Motion, *Philip Larkin*, p. 71.
14 See Blake Morrison, *The Movement: English Poetry and Fiction of the 1950s* (Oxford: Oxford University Press, 1980), pp. 145–53.
15 Philip Larkin, 'Introduction', *The North Ship* (1945) (London: Faber and Faber, 2nd edn, 1966). The introduction was written for the second edition.
16 W.S. Graham, *2ND POEMS* (London: Editions Poetry London/Nicholson & Watson, 1945).
17 Graham, *2ND POEMS*, p. 12; *CP*, pp. 32–33.
18 W.S. Graham, annotated typescript, 'Nine Poems for a Poetry Reading', National Library of Scotland, Edinburgh, access no. 2793.6. For Graham's reading of Nansen, see *Nightfisherman*, p. 141.
19 Larkin, *North Ship*, p. 44.
20 See Lopez, *PWSG*, pp. 10ff
21 Larkin to James Ballard Sutton, 11 April 1942, quoted in Motion, *Philip Larkin*, p. 75.
22 See Kathrine Talbot, *Kit Barker, Cornwall 1947–1948: Recollections of Painters and Writers* (St Ives: The Book Gallery, 1993). Mevagissey is about 40 miles east of the Marazion and St Ives area.
23 Vivienne Koch, 'A Note on W.S. Graham', *Sewanee Review*, 56.4 (1948), pp. 665–70. See also her 'Review of *Cage Without Grievance*', *Sewanee Review*, 54.4 (1946), pp. 699–716; 'The Technique of Morality', *Poetry Quarterly*, 9.4 (1947), pp. 216–25; and 'Review of *The White Threshold*', *Sewanee Review*, 59.4 (1950), pp. 664–77.
24 Nessie Dunsmuir's poems echo in Graham's phrases in this section of the poem:

compare his 'pits and wheels / Unwinding in diving cages' (*CP*, pp. 79–80) with 'Raith Pit' and 'Stanis Pit', in *Nessie Dunsmuir's Ten Poems* (Emscote Lawn, Warwick: The Greville Press, 1988), pp. 6, 8: 'Behind my head the falling sun / reddens the rim of the pit's dark wheels', 'The cage falls like a guillotine', 'Into the morning wind / the pit-wheels whirr and grind'.

The Nightfishing: 5

So this is the place. This
Is the place fastened still with movement,
Movement as calligraphic and formal as
A music burned on copper.

At this place
The eye reads forward as the memory reads back.
At this last word all words change.
All words change in acknowledgement of the last.
Here is their mingling element.
This is myself (who but ill resembles me).
He befriended so many
Disguises to wander in on as many roads
As cross on a ball of wool.
What a stranger he's brought to pass
Who sits here in his place.
What a man arrived breathless
With a look or word to a few
Before he's off again.

Here is this place no more
Certain though the steep streets
And High Street form again and the sea
Swing shut on hinges and the doors all open wide.

4

'Roaring between the lines': W.S. Graham and the White Threshold of Line-Breaks

ADAM PIETTE

W.S. Graham is clearly a poet influenced by Wordsworth's way with lines. In Book XIII of the 1805 *Prelude*, the poet contemplates the sea of mist surrounding Snowdon, in particular a breach in the sea through which the sound of rushing water can be heard:

> a blue chasm; a fracture in the vapour,
> A deep and gloomy breathing-place through which
> Mounted the roar of waters, torrents, streams
> Innumerable, roaring with one voice!
> (1805 Bk XIII, ll. 56–59)[1]

Wordsworth, as Christopher Ricks has shown, is the principal innovator after Milton in the use of line-break white space.[2] Here Wordsworth tropes the space to figure a sublime breathing-place full of roaring voice. For Graham, the white space was a 'welcome-roaring threshold', where the voices of poet and reader both 'go down / Roaring between the lines'.[3] When we roar together, our voices become animal, natural like the seas and rivers, but also echoing with resounding sounds. Hearing Graham's roaring white space echo with Wordsworth's 'roaring with one voice', our own voice resounds within the threshold of the line-break, as though accompanied by many voices.

I have preferred the term 'line-break' to 'line-ending' mainly because it more closely suits Graham's modernist technique. Modernist poets who write free or accentual verse, in that they discard the metrical regularities that had policed the line for ear and eye, will be more likely to deploy the endings of their lines as breaks. As James Scully observes, in his 'Line Break', modernist and postmodern free verse consciously breaks sentences: 'the sentence has been broken to release meaning'.[4] What I hope to demonstrate, however, is that in Graham's work the line-break is used as a means towards the imagining of measures of continuity between modernist and Romantic practices, by sensing ways in which the break can at the same time work as a move across the difficult air of the 'curious necessary space' beyond and between the lines.[5]

Line-breaks in free verse are a contested issue, for it has been impossible to work out whether something like significant enjambement occurs in the form. It is complicated by its prehistory in the French Symbolist tradition. Clive Scott's extraordinary monograph on *vers libre* argues that the shift from liberated verse to free verse after the death of Hugo had nothing to do with increased attention to enjambement. Rather it depended on a recognition by French poets, learned in the new science of experimental phonetics, that French is not a syllabic language at all, but is accentual, has sense-accents like English.[6] And, though Scott does not make this explicit, it was through translation of English models, in particular Laforgue's translations of Whitman, that the *verlibristes* found a technical means to express this new sense of language. It is a curious irony that it was principally American poets who introduced free verse form into English poetry, as though you needed the French to bounce Whitman back, via translation, into their modernist imaginations. But the effect of this translation was a considerable resistance, taken as a whole, to the idea of enjambement in free verse. The French had, again in general, preferred to synchronize phrase units and syntax with the line. But, in time, mainly through the practice of Eliot and Williams, poets sensed that they had lost a real resource. The French poets had serious reasons to demote enjambement in free verse: enjambement was identified with Hugo's liberated alexandrines, this being the principal means of shifting the caesura. I hope this article will show how a technically accomplished writer of free and rhythmical verse in the modernist tradition deploys enjambement again with the express purpose of both modernizing it and linking it back to the lost resources of the Romantic blank verse line.

Lineation defines the free or rhythmical verse line as poetry to the eye. Without the line-break, without the typographical white space, we could not see the clauses as poetic lines.[7] Neither, perhaps, could we hear them. Reading out free or rhythmical verse is a hard job precisely because the poet must indicate line-breaks without so much as pausing. Good poets, in my experience, have a version of the French convention of slightly lengthening the last vowel sound in any line to signal, however faintly, that the line-break is happening. Free or rhythmical verse, then, needs the white threshold of the starboard space beyond and between the lines in order to be poetry. W.S. Graham was more than usually conscious of this essential defining distinction, for he heard strange roaring white noise, a confusion of just-absent voices and the sounds of transformation occurring within that strange white space: 'I heard voices within / The empty lines and tenses' ('Letter V', *N*, p. 52). Part of the sense of these lines is that they challenge readers to hear them as vocal. This would mean imagining the dead poet's breath uttering the lines and tenses. It would therefore entail imagining the poem's language imperceptibly pausing at the line-break, voicing, as it were, the emptiness of the white threshold beyond and between the lines. And this means that we must become alerted to line-breaks by significant enjambement. If we do not hear this imperceptible vocalization of the line-break, then the lines are potentially voiceless, not poetry, not a poet's voice, not a poem.

But the co-presence of line-break and enjambement could not be a continuous practice in free or accentual verse in English. It would be foolish to demand that we hear the white space as voiced at *every* line-break. Poets of Graham's calibre will tend to give readers a break either when it matters, or at least often enough to remind them that this is poetry. If the free verse or rhythmical verse poet were to allow prose syntax to dictate the line-breaks throughout the poem, it seems to me that Graham would argue that the poet fails, technically, to do his or her job. This crucial point is made by Jon Silkin in his critique of H.D.'s imagist free verse. For Silkin, there must be some active intersecting of the prose syntax of a sentence in a free verse poem with the lines' rhythm and lineation to create an 'enacting line-break': '[Herbert Read] has understood the necessity of intersecting the three components, rhythm, syntax and lineation in active (free verse) cooperation'.[8] This means that the poem must have noticeable enjambement to make the three components work for both ear and eye[9] – again, these enjambements must occur either at important moments, or at least often enough to mark the poem out as poetry. The line-breaks I concentrate on in Graham's work are, almost invariably, moments of important enjambement, what Hartman referred to as 'significant conflict'.[10]

I will be looking primarily at the 1940s work, for it was during this period that Graham acquired a quasi-mystical understanding of what it means to print words on a white page. This understanding is hardly a theory, and it cannot be said that Graham had any specific philosophical or critical theorist in mind when developing his own prosodic poetry of release. That said, I will be reading his 1940s poetry in the light of comparable thinking about poetics in the work of Mallarmé and Heidegger.

Graham had studied philosophy at Newbattle Abbey College under John Mack, concentrating on the pre-Socratics. This is already an indication that he was in Heideggerian territory, since Heidegger championed the pre-Socratics as the forgotten source of true Being. He was also rereading philosophy prior to the composition of 'The Nightfishing' in 1946–48. As Tony Lopez notes of the reading Graham did at this time, specifically in relation to the coherence of subjectivity 'as a problem requiring examination through performance in language': 'He read the Pre-Socratics, the Existentialists, Sartre and Heidegger, and no doubt much more'.[11] As Lopez has also shown, Graham held firm in his 1940s work to a mystique of language that is remarkably Heideggerian, particularly in the emphasis on the phenomenological situating of the poetic voice in an abstract printed territory that lies somewhere between the abstract spirit of the language and the ordinary language of the people (Lopez, *PWSG*, pp. 109–10).

What is remarkable about Graham's poetry is its anticipation of Heidegger's later writings. For Graham, the page becomes a terrain shared by two time zones, the time of creation by the poet, and the time of reading, the strangeness being that the poet, by inscribing her voice upon the white space, enters into a space between, a threshold liminal both to her own real surroundings and to the reader's imagined environment. This liminal terrain is a space of language for Graham, necessarily, and is therefore constructed. It is where a radical 'turn' takes place. It is this emphasis on the turn that rhymes so remarkably with Heidegger's theory of *Kehre*, the moment of *Ursprung* that transforms *Dasein*, at once a turning back (*Rückkehr*) and a turning into (*Einkehr*). As Joseph Fell puts it in his remarks on Heidegger's 1957 *Der Satz vom Grund* (*The Principle of Reason*), 'the turn is the movement through *apparent* nothingness to a "forgotten" and "cancelled fulness"'.[12] The turn takes place at a juncture, for Heidegger, a juncture of sensing, thinking and naming, 'a juncture (*Fuge*) of the imperceptible and the perceptible […] in naming, language accomplishes this juncture'. This juncture is where, Heidegger argues in his 1957 *Hebel – der Hausfreund* (*Hebel – Friend of the House*), the word crosses 'the play-space between earth and the heavens', a place held open by language.[13] I hope to demonstrate the common ground between Graham's phenomenological poetics and late Heidegger, to show how deeply and intuitively Graham had understood and anticipated the linguistic turn implicit in Heidegger's earlier practice.

As his work on German poetry (Stefan George and Trakl) shows,

during the post-war years Heidegger turned to language as phenomenological environment, and was concerned to show how language speaks
itself, how writing or speaking in a poem might better be construed as an
act of listening to what language has to say. Writing, in Heideggerian
terms, is an exercise in the approach to this phenomenological voice of
language by the poet's voice, a severing of the normal ways in which we
believe language to operate as personal expressiveness and communication
between human beings. This would mean that the voices we hear within
the empty lines and tenses of poetry should not be so easily identified with
the human, embodied voice of the historical person. Rather, the voices are
some strangely liminal amalgam of the supernatural spirit of the language,
and the posthumous (absent) presence of the poet as printed voice.

Graham's 'Notes on a Poetry of Release', published in *Poetry Scotland*
in July 1946, rhymes astonishingly with Heidegger's poetics. There is the
same emphasis on language as environment: 'With words my material and
immediate environment I am at once halfway the victim and halfway the
successful traveller. There is the involuntary war between me and that
environment flowing in on me from all sides and there is the poetic
outcome' (*Nightfisherman*, p. 379). This is very close to Heidegger's
complex representation of the double nature of language in terms of a
voyage along language's own road, language as at once a forcefield of
words that seems to speak through us as we listen to ourselves speak, and a
human arena of expression which reveals itself as our own.[14] And Graham,
like Heidegger, sees the environment of language as Heraclitean: 'Each
word is touched and filled with the activity of every speaker. Each word
changes every time it is brought to life. Each single word uttered twice
becomes a new word each time. You cannot twice bring the same word
into sound' (*Nightfisherman*, p. 380). This rhymes with Heidegger's
reading of the early Greeks, in particular his 1951 paper on Heraclitus and
Logos, which interpreted early Greek Being as essentially an act of
presencing of language in a lightning flash of speech.[15]

What distinguishes 'Notes on a Poetry of Release' from Heideggerian
theory is its emphasis on word order and word position. Poetry releases
the energies of language most powerfully as a set of *lines*, what Graham
calls 'those adventures along those lines of words'. It is as lines that the
poem can release 'the sudden affection of the language':

> Though do I move along words in a poem when, after all, as I am at the last
> word and look back I find the first word changed and a new word there, for it
> is part of the whole poem and its particular life depends on the rest of the

poem. The meaning of a word in a poem is never more than its position. The meaning of a poem [...] is brought to life by the reader and takes part in the reader's change. Even the poet as a man who searches continually is a new searcher with his direction changing at every step.

> For ever as the seeker turns
> His worshipping eyes on prophetic patterns
> Of shape arising from all men
> He changes through, he shall remain
> Continually stripped and clothed again
> (*Nightfisherman*, pp. 382–83)

Graham mimes the change of first word by position, and the searcher's change 'at every step' with the quotation's turn at the line-break: 'as the seeker turns / His worshipping eyes'. This change is Heidegger's *Kehre*, the double-natured break that is both radically a break and a transformative turning into, creating what Stephen Cushman calls phenomenological prosody.[16] The turn across the line-break anticipates Heidegger on the tearing break that occurs at the threshold of Dif-férence in his 1950 Bühlerhöhe lecture, 'Die Sprache': 'the tearing is the hyphen which, like a first trace suddenly opening up space, signs and joins together that which has been held apart in Dis-junction'.[17] Heidegger does not talk openly about line-breaks, which raises the question as to the influences colouring Graham's identification of Heideggerian *Kehre* with line-ending white space. This is important, for, as I shall show, in technical terms, the sudden affection of language takes *place*, for Graham, at the defining junction point between the clause and the line in a poem, at the silent and visible white threshold of the page space to the right of the text.

Though it is clear that Graham may very well have made the identification himself by strenuous technical study of poets (particularly Wordsworth, Hopkins, Eliot and Yeats),[18] it was Mallarmé who most radically identified such spaces of exchange with the white space of the page around print. In his essay 'Le Mystère dans les lettres', Mallarmé argues that *symboliste* typography would seek to emphasize the relationship between print and white page. Though we may dismiss the white space between title and first line, we are forced to acknowledge the unarbitrary nature of the subsequent white spaces generated by the modern artist's typographical technique:

> When we read, the white space between title and first clause on a page may be said to be the defining condition of the page's inherent *ingenuitas*, or noble candour, a candour that forgets, as it were, the too-distant title above. After

the first line has been read, however, even the least little break into print, disseminating each word and vanquishing the vagaries of chance, then the white space returns, as if without fail, a white space no longer gratuitous but now clearly and surely meant. It is a white space which concludes that there is nothing beyond at the same time as it authenticates its own silence.[19]

This apotheosis of the relations between poetic line and surrounding white space was put into hard practice in 'Un Coup de dés jamais n'abolira le hasard'. In his preface, Mallarmé argued that the expanses of white space in the pages were there to emphasize the rhythm of the individual free verse clauses, but behind this technical purpose lay a hallucinatory idealism of the sheer fact of print on paper. The white spaces are where the 'paper intervenes'. They are the defining condition of the free verse clauses, or 'prismatic subdivisions of the Idea'. And, most radically, they are there to stress the evanescence of the vocal selfhoods brought into fitful life by each clause:

> The paper intervenes each time an image, of its own accord, ceases or departs, leaving room for the succession of other images. And since the clauses are free verse lines and not regular lines or acoustic units as of old – rather, prismatic subdivisions of the Idea, appearing for an instant for the length of time of their convergence, in an exact staging of the mind – the text as clause will make itself known in a variety of different locations on the page, with a varying distance from or proximity to the latent main thread, according to inherent truth conditions.[20]

This is not the time to enter into the complex history of the typographically free verse line, since Graham did not himself follow Mallarmé in the practice of free-floating clauses in oceans of white space. What does make Graham post-*symboliste* is his attachment to Mallarmé's cult of white paper space.

In the 1949 notebook published in *ER75*, Graham develops his theory of the white space. Poetry is where 'impulse, like electricity, crossing the space, leaves its signature'. The poem, as such, is 'a created space, a constructed solitude' set on 'a silence of a certain shape' ('From a 1949 Notebook', *ER75*, p. 24). As William Carlos Williams puts it: 'What else is verse made up of but "words, words, words"? Quite literally, *the spaces between the words*, in our modern understanding, which take with them an equal part in the measure.'[21] This space is the white space of the page constructed by the presence of what Graham calls '"NONSILENCE"' (*ER75*, p. 24), i.e. the words on the page as 'movement of the mind' (*ER75*, p. 24).[22]

The first indication of this cult is in the last line of 'No, Listen, for This I Tell' from *Cage without Grievance* (1942): 'We fall down darkness in a line of words',[23] a line separated from the rest of the poem by a stanza break, and emphasized by being cut short, as it were – for the rest of the poem is in quatrains. The fall is a fall into pure poem, beyond the human: 'This drop no man descends / To death or depth of meaning.' Death is the space where the poet's printed voice, the voice of 'no man', is listened to for depth of meaning.[24] The darkness is the blackness of the print on the page, the fall both the accidence of each line, and the descent of the reading eye to the bottom of the page, the bottom of the poem – thus the appropriateness of a fall just below a stanza break. But we do, I think, harbour grievances about the cagey inhuman wiliness of this, about the cage of technique trapping the voice. Graham is buttonholing the reader ('No, listen!') and making a song and dance about the empty act of descanting on the darkness of ink.

We find him looking to nature for a proper equivalent for the act of writing, not just to furnish readers with a make-believe simile, but in order to ground the metaphysics of writing in the real working world he knew – this I take to be an important revision of a potentially inhuman phenomenology and symbolism of the voice, as advocated by Heidegger and Mallarmé. He found the analogue in writing about the sea – not simply because of the crowded tradition of analogies between the sea and the unnameable sublime ('that other fond / Metaphor, the sea'[25]), but because he did know it in real space and time. As his 1949 notebook reveals, in relation to a draft of 'Witch Rime', he was intent on achieving a poetry that merges the abstract with the 'nonabstract', as he was in crossing free with metrical verse: 'A poem of say 6 stanzas of 3 lines of say 4 iambics fairly formal and decisively knit. The statement philosophical and rather "abstract" so that it might montage creatively with a prosaic prose *non*philosophical *non*abstract running between the stanzas aggressively irregular like some Yeats chorus lines' (*ER75*, p. 28). And it was within the sea's real 'nonphilosophical nonabstract' spaces and times, with its substantial liminal zones between shore/boat and inhuman element, that the pursuit of language could really *take* place.[26]

In 'Continual Sea and Air', we hear this emphasis on the sea as real place (*CP*, p. 37). The sea, the poem argues, saves people from 'death in air' in wartime because it feeds them, through merchant shipping and fishermen, and protects them, with the Navy and the difficulty of distance represented by the sea for enemy bombers. It is not then necessarily merely a place where we fear to die. It nurses 'the liveman's trade', not the merely inhuman depths of meanings of his earlier work. Graham, with this new perception of the sea as deliverance from death in wartime, came to a different perception also of the craft of writing:

> The long outline
> Leans over waving houses, new marine
> Green man to be.

The line of poetry becomes, visually, the horizon line of the sea seen over the houses of the fishing village. Just as the fact the sea seems to be above the houses makes them wave like its waves, so the line of poetry leans over the word 'houses' and makes it wave with the poem's wavy rhythms. The fishing village, for a moment, in and across the line-breaks, becomes marine, its people green sea creatures because so defined by the protective element. Similarly, poetry, by incorporating the real circumstances of fishing ports in wartime within its textures, transforms the inhabitants into the 'green man', the 'me' of the lyrical, liquid rhythms and acoustics of the printed poem. But it does so like the sea, for poetry also loves and preserves from evanescence.

It is *The White Threshold*, however, that inaugurates Graham's metaphysics of the line-break. The 1949 title poem is rich in broken run-on lines, as Graham gestures towards an identification of the white threshold with the white space beyond the line-ending: 'from the deep heart / Drowned'; 'speak / up famous fathoms'; 'my air / Breathed'; 'well / Worth'; 'trinket gone / Down' etc. (*CP*, pp. 77–83). Certain motifs begin the work of the identification. The position of 'threshold' at the line-ending ('the welcome-roaring threshold'; 'the threshold sea') is accompanied by an equally insistent line-end position of 'heart'. This aligns heart-beat with the sea threshold to make a point about the identity of the sea's liminality and the pause in the voice.

There are some puns on line-break that work too: 'His young life broke through / The bloodbolts of his heart'; 'Hear the downbearing sea / Break on the seashelled door'. This is backed up by a persistently self-conscious use of 'across' to signal the move of the voice across the white threshold of death and of the page space ('self seawork across / The rudimental waste').[27] The line-ending is the shore: note the repetition of 'Very end then of land. What vast is there?' after double space – this vast is where the poet speaks to the dead of the war.

The meditation on the wartime dead at sea and in the blitzed cities was,

Graham felt, an act of communication between the living and the dead. Since the dead died at sea and on land, it is also, appropriately, an act of communication between land and sea. Both acts of communication can only take place within the sacred space of language at its radical threshold, the free verse line crossed with rhythmical verse, the poet's I-voice merging with the voices of the crowds of dead, the rhythms of language beating with the rhythms of a human heart. All these thresholds are enacted (not just symbolized) by the poem's attempt to cross the land–sea threshold with the line–white space threshold.[28]

To my ear, this is an attempt rather than a triumph simply because Graham's writing is so unsure of itself. The lines are crowded not just by the dead, but by awkward solecisms, tactlessness of touch:

> Here as man's heir
>
> Weirdly put out as what the night invents me,
> I see the crowds.
>
> (Section 5, *CP*, p. 82)

These not untypical lines veer towards the ungrammatical, the brokenly inarticulate, mainly because there is such a strain of high Romantic overstatement about the prophetic I-voice, and an unconvincing display of humility. How can he be at once the clairvoyant seer of the dead, heir to man, Hamlet of the night of the imagination, and a mere weird sister, an invention of Gothic language? Graham is squirming against the humble role his heart tells him ought to be the part played by poet-as-witness, secretly wishing to relish the visionary power he thinks is his rightful inheritance. His poetic ego is put out (as in 'in a huff'), just as the syntax collapses into ugly, overcrowded lines. Worst of all, the gains painstakingly won in the exploration of the technical possibilities of identifying line-breaks with white thresholds are thrown away in the clumsy, hollow and meaningless move over the stanza break – man's heir is put out, one is tempted to say, like the annoying cat at night.

The gains were powerfully garnered, though, with 'The Nightfishing', that extraordinary journey into the outer reaches of sea and language. The poem narrates a herring fishing trip at night out to sea, with the poet as one of the crew. It brings together technical and obviously experienced descriptions of the work of a Scots fishing boat somewhere among the Isles[29] with heady metaphysical meditations on selfhood, language and writing. The nightfishing trope is meant to work on both sides of the equation, with equal weight being given both to the practical work of catching herring and to the act of inscribing words on the page: '[Fishing for herring at night] is the physical activity which the poem represents as a continuous logic throughout and which, I hope, makes that which is less a physical statement, more valid to believe.'[30]

What is so useful for Graham in the trope is less the more obvious cultural echoes (Christ's disciples and their *pêche miraculeuse*, Ahab and the whale, the Old Man and his marlin, etc.) than the happy coincidences that marry modernist poet and fisherman: both seek a catch in a simultaneously liquid and recalcitrant medium; both involve a journey out and a return home; both sift through the shifting, treacherous signs of the world for directions; both know their vessels, line of poem and boat, leave an immediately vanishing trace in wake and word; both are hard-headedly practical in their technique and visionary, mythical and hieratic in retrospect; both involve crafts, lines, waves, turns and a play of surfaces and unseen depths. Nightfishing is most appropriate, for Graham, because the play of the fishing boat's white wake on black sea is a felicitous inversion of the black wake of print on the white page.

The poem is also adeptly superstitious in its faith that there could be a serious purpose in constructing a taxonomy of uses of line-breaks. The white space is, according to a first set of associations, both 'far out' beyond the lines and 'within' the lines. As such, it can be taken to figure both the distant region of the dead, and the closely-inward dead voices within the self:

Now within the dead
Of night and the dead
Of my life I hear
My name called from far out.
        (*N*, Section I, p. 15)

The inversion of black night and white space is announced in these early lines. The poem is heard, like one's name called from the echoing spaces of Hades, *within* the dead, as within the lines. To read within the lines is only odd if we forget that the starboard space is both between the lines and an arbitrary space inside the sentence sound. These twin senses (dead far out and within the voice) are confirmed later when the quay bell strikes 'the held air like / Opening the door' (*N*, Section I, p. 16) – the white space is a held air where we can communicate with the distant dead – and with the lines 'a stranger's breath / From out of my mouth' (*N*, Section I, p. 16) – the held air is also the strange breath of the inner voice. The combination of these twin senses occurs at the line-break, for it is principally at the line-break that held air is combined with breath to create the release Graham defined as essential to his poetry: 'a construction of release to accomplish a courageous, other air to breath'.[31]

Graham brings out a second set of associations for line-endings: the white space is technically where the 'turn' of enjambement takes place, but can be imagined, again obscurely and superstitiously, to be the space where the 'I' of one line dies to become another 'I', the voice of the next line:

> I turned out
> Into the salt dark
> And turned my collar up.
> (*N*, Section I, p. 16)

Again the white space is figured as the 'salt dark' outside the self, in particular the dark sea ('I am befriended by / This sea which utters me'). It is within this dark white space that enjambement (a turning out of the voice into the next line) becomes that other turn, the turn of trope, or transformation (the self, in the turn from line to line, is transformed into its next manifestation).

Graham likes the pun on 'turn' in the poem, since a fishing boat crew spends so much of its time turning out and in ('I'm one ahead of [the dead] / Turned in below'), the boat itself is constantly turning ('The hull slewed out through / The lucky turn' [*N*, Section I, p. 17]), and there are the turns in the winds' direction ('The winds slowly / Turn round on us and // Gather towards us with dragging weights of water' [*N*, Section III, p. 24]). The working cycle of watches and repose on the boat coupled with the boat's own turning movements across and through the sea against turning winds gives a solid material basis for the potentially arcane and pretentious overreading of tropes and enjambements. The sea cannot just be the space of phenomenological utterance and selving – it must work as the sea. Hence Graham's insistence that the sea is a real place: 'The sea as metaphor of the sea' (*N*, Section III, p. 8), recalling Wordsworth's 'Into the sea, the real sea' (1805 *Prelude*, Bk XIII, l. 49).

The puns on 'turn' are backed up by a sustained play on line-break and on run-on lines. The paradox is that where the voice breaks off, it also runs on. Graham grounds these puns again securely in the real world of nightfishing: the nets and their ropes are run out; breaking occurs when fish break the surface of the water ('It's right for shooting, / Fish breaking the oiled water'), when dawn breaks ('rising to break wide up over the /

Brow of the sea'). Both line-break and run-on occur in another couple of lines about dawn breaking over the sea:

> It is that first pallor there, broken, running
> Back on the sheared water.
>   (*N*, Section III, p. 20)

The break of light on the dark water is seen, as it were, in the break of the line – Graham has inverted his inversion ('The night and day both change their flesh about / In merging level'). But the mystery of the line-break is that it is also where the line runs back on to the next line, like the light of dawn on the waters.[32] As our eyes move across the white threshold of the page, our reading mimes the mysterious ways Graham hears the lines of poetry crossing from dark language into the poem: 'What measures gently // Cross in the air to us'. But, as if to counter the inhuman mystification of language-idolatry involved in this Heideggerian move, he insists that the white space is also where he is, where his human voice and name resides: 'It is me named upon / The space which I continually move across' (*N*, Section III, p. 22). The crossing of the human with the inhuman, the abstract with the 'nonabstract', takes place at the poem's crossing points, shadowing, as it were, the other fusions that take place technically in the poem, such as the fusion of free with metrical rhythms.[33]

The next set of meanings turns on the line as black print on the white page. As I have shown, Graham has inverted this relation within the poem, as in the line (just before a stanza break) 'My eyes let light in on this dark' (*N*, Section II, p. 18), where the white page becomes 'this dark' and the print is 'light', the poem as a whole a 'script of light'.[34] The white wake behind the boat is also the line of print: 'as we go / Running white from the bow' (*N*, Section II, p. 18). The inversion holds the two worlds of sea and poem together, as though on either side of a negative's membrane. The white spacing, since it defines the line as a separate trace of the voice, is also used self-consciously to figure spatial relations between manifestations of the voice and scene:

> night rises stooped high over
> Us as our boat keeps its nets and men and
> Engraves its wake.
>   (*N*, Section III, p. 19)

Here the three levels – of night, boat and wake – are mimed by the spatial relationship of line above line. Each line is also figured as an engraving of the voice's 'wake' (a Joycean pun that works up the death–rebirth motif). The boat writes a white line on the black surface of the sea – 'The keel in its amorous furrow / Goes through each word' (*N*, Section III, p. 19). The poet writes black lines on the white surface of the page. Each line is at once a trace of the self's manifestation that dies at its line-ending, and a motion across the space into its next self.[35] The white space is, in this sense, a breathing-place where the memory of one line, its acknowledgement according to Graham, mingles with the forward movement into troped transformation:

> At this place
> The eye reads forward as the memory reads back.
> At this last word all words change.
> All words change in acknowledgement of the last.
> Here is their mingling element.
>
> (*N*, Section V, p. 29)

Thinking hard about how the acknowledgement of memory of one self might mingle with the next manifestation of soundlessly vocalized printed voice, Graham found an apt figure in the technical ways in which a line-break is at once an end and a beginning:[36]

> Yet not a break of light
> But mingles into
>
> The whole memory of light

The white space is here a break of light, where memories of the previous line mingle into the memory of the whole poem – this compared to the ways 'the unfolding water / Mingles its dead' (*N*, Section III, p. 23).

Graham is acutely aware, perhaps fanatically so, that the printed self is a thing of words. Its manifestation and transformations, since they can be said only to occur on the printed page, are quite literally only a matter of lines and white spaces.[37] As such, to communicate living, changing human presence, i.e. a living voice, to the reader in this black and white medium may be as difficult as to imagine oneself communicating with the dead, or with one's own dead selves. The issue is complicated by the conventions of poetry whereby the poet's voice may not even have the luxury of being vocalized by the reader.

The space starboard to the line concentrates all these difficulties. It is not sounded. It is, as Mallarmé wrote, a blank proof that 'there is nothing beyond at the same time as it authenticates its own silence'. The creation of an authentic 'I'-voice on the white space of the page depends partly on a faith in the invisible reader naming the voice 'W.S. Graham', hearing his voice soundlessly cross the space within the lines. Because the white space defines the lines as lines of poetry, they define the voice as a poet's. The poet knows that this white space is a sign of simple blank lack of presence – Sydney Graham is not here. But it may authenticate its silence by being heard as a voice of courage, of heartedness. The printed voice is a lack and hearted, a mere line of dead print against a white ground, and a named self moving across the real world, a heart-beat rhythm and the simple absence of recognizable human self in posthumous poetry.

> So I have been called by my name and
> It was not sound. It is me named upon
> The space which I continually move across
> Bearing between my courage and my lack
> The constant I bleed on.
>   (*N*, Section III, p. 22)

As Graham wrote in 'Letter V', anxieties about the poet–reader contract are anxieties about survival as print immortality, and those anxieties turn on the impossible but necessary superstition that something or some voice is going on within the lines. The reader must hear his or her own voice mingle with the voice of the departed, must listen to the faint roar of those two voices roaring between the lines:

>   Cast in this gold
> Wicklight this night within
> This poem, we two go down
> Roaring between the lines
> To drown. Who hears? Who listens?
>
> I entered. Enter after
> Me here and encounter
> Dimensions of a grave.
>   ('Letter V', *N*, p. 52)

This is a hard invitation to accept – we are invited into the black sea of the page's white space to drown and meet a dead poet in his grave – but it is an invitation, also to hear, to listen to the only selves that do survive beyond the grave, the voices of poems possessing our inner voice, at the strange *Kehre* of their juncture and release.[38]

This is spooky poetry, a poetry of roaring voices that are not sound, of selves as lines, of herring boats that are made of ink, of liminal zones that are merely where paper intervenes, of mystical spaces that are flat as the surface of a page. It is a poetry that senses the chilling nature of the posthumous poetic voice, 'said and fixed and dead' on the page in little lines of print, a by-product of the 'lonely meanings' that 'are read / Into the space we make'.[39] 'This is no other place / Than where I am, between / This word and the next.' But it is also poetry that asks for simple acknowledgement that Sydney Graham is there, somehow, on the other side of language, a poet of nerves and heart and sudden affection who was once in the world, 'real and / Particular'[40] upon the real unabstract sea, but who is now living, at once roaring and silent, between, within and across his turning, breaking, running lines, there at the white threshold, his only home.

Notes

1 William Wordsworth, *The Prelude: A Parallel Text*, ed. J.C. Maxwell (Harmondsworth: Penguin, 1972), p. 512.

2 This article is by way of tribute to, and acknowledgement of, Christopher Ricks's fine essay on line-endings in Wordsworth, 'William Wordsworth 1: "A Pure and Organic Pleasure from the Lines"', in his *The Force of Poetry* (Oxford: Clarendon Press, 1984), pp. 89–116. Many of the observations I make with regard to Graham's line-break technique echo Ricks's findings. The definition of the line-ending as constituting 'an invisible boundary', 'pregnant silence' and 'potent absence' (pp. 90, 99); the 'silent self-referring metaphor' of the white space (p. 97); the nuances created by the resolution of the line-ending's 'flicker of hesitation' (p. 98); Wordsworth's intuition that this white space could be made mimetically to represent intersections 'of time and the timeless' (p. 103), states of mental pause and suspension (p. 104), ideas of ends and beginnings (p. 107), the 'felicities of space' (p. 110) and freedoms of breath (p. 116): all these considerations have not only influenced me in this article, but have also informed, it seems to me, by the direct route from Wordsworth's practice, Graham's own sense of the line-break.

3 From 'The White Threshold', *CP*, pp. 77–83 and 'Letter V', *N*, p. 52.

4 James Scully, 'Line Break', in Robert Frank and Henry Sayre (eds), *The Line in Postmodern Poetry* (Urbana and Chicago: University of Illinois Press, 1988), pp. 97–131 (120).

5 'The Beast in the Space', *CP*, p. 146.

6 Clive Scott, *Vers Libre: The Emergence of Free Verse in France 1886–1914* (Oxford: Clarendon Press, 1990).

7 Cf. Charles Hartman, *Free Verse: An Essay in Prosody* (Princeton: Princeton University Press, 1980), p. 11: '*Verse is language in lines*. This distinguishes it from prose'.

8 Jon Silkin, *The Life of Metrical and Free Verse in Twentieth-Century Poetry* (Basingstoke: Macmillan, 1997), pp. 44, 45.

9 This is particularly the case in short-line non-metrical verse, as Stephen Cushman has observed: 'In nonmetrical verse short-line enjambments determine lineation directly, unlike their metrical, long-line counterparts. They have the immediate power to influence the grouping of successive words into successive lines. This grouping of

successive elements (words) and events (lineations) becomes the basis of prosody in non-metrical verse' (Stephen Cushman, *William Carlos Williams and the Meanings of Measure* [New York: Yale University Press, 1985], p. 22).

10 Significant conflict occurs in free verse counterpoint: 'the primary form of counter-pointing arises with line-sentence disjunctions, which produce enjambments and caesurae' (Cushman, *William Carlos Williams*, p. 25).

11 Tony Lopez, 'W.S. Graham: An Introduction', *ER75*, p. 20. The 1940s might seem early for British appreciation of Heidegger. Nevertheless, the high profile of French existentialism immediately after the war combined with the extraordinary popularity of phenomenology after Husserl would make it odder if a philosophically inclined intellectual such as Graham had *not* been aware of Heidegger. As Waelhens remarks in his study *La Philosophie de Martin Heidegger* (Paris: Editions de l'Institut Supérieur de Philosophie, 1942), phenomenology was 'the dominant philosophical movement' (p. v). As Waelhens points out, Sartre's immensely popular *La nausée*, published in 1939, 'expresses with unmatchable force and clarity the central experience of all of Heidegger's philosophy' (Waelhens, *Heidegger*, p. 367, translation mine). Riding the wave of French existentialism (e.g. Mairet's 1948 translation of *Existentialism and Humanism*), Werner Brock's collection of essays, *Existence and Being*, was published in 1949(in English), popularizing Heidegger by comparing him to Sartre and outlining the debt to the pre-Socratics. And of course, it was Werner Brock who had first popularized Heidegger in his 1935 *Introduction to Continental German Philosophy*. Even hard-line analytic journals such as *Philosophy* were grudgingly acknowledging the interest in existentialism in the 1940s. F.H. Heinemann was asked to do a survey of philosophy in Germany in 1949, and began it with the sentence: 'Existentialism is one of the most talked of topics of our time' (F.H. Heinemann, 'Philosophy in Germany', *Philosophy*, 24 [1949], pp. 261–65 [261]); Heinemann foregrounds the influence of Heidegger's combination of existence and ontology (pp. 261–62). In the same issue, H.B. Acton surveys philosophy in France, and it is clear that French existentialism is the only horse running: Acton reviews Kojève on Hegel, Merleau-Ponty and de Beauvoir as members of the 'Sartre circle' (H.B. Acton, 'Philosophy in France', *Philosophy*, 24 [1949], pp. 77–81 [80]).

12 Joseph P. Fell, *Heidegger and Sartre: An Essay on Being and Place* (New York: Columbia University Press, 1979), p. 127.

13 Quoted from Fell, *Heidegger and Sartre*, pp. 224, 225, 407.

14 Cf. in particular Heidegger's 1959 Berlin lecture 'Die Sprache'.

15 Cf. 'Logos (Heraclitus, Fragment B 50)' in Martin Heidegger, *Early Greek Thinking*, trans. David F. Krell and Frank A. Capuzzi (New York: Harper & Row, 1975).

16 See Cushman, *William Carlos Williams*, p. 22.

17 My translation from the French 'La Parole', in Martin Heidegger, *Acheminement vers la parole*, trans. J. Beaufret, W. Brokmeier and F. Fédier (Paris: Gallimard, 1976), p. 30.

18 Perhaps Eliot most of all. In his 1949 notebook for *The Nightfishing*, published in part in *ER75*, Graham copies out lines from 'Burnt Norton': 'Words, after speech, reach / Into the silence' ('From a 1949 Notebook', *ER75*, p. 24).

19 Stéphane Mallarmé, 'La Mystère dans les lettres', in *Oeuvres Complètes*, ed. Henri Mondor and G. Jean-Aubry (Paris: Gallimard Pléiade, 1945), p. 387 (translations from Mallarmé are my own).

20 Stéphane Mallarmé, 'Un Coup de dés jamais n'abolira le hasard', in *Oeuvres Complètes*, p. 455.
21 William Carlos Williams, 'Measure', *Spectrum*, 3.3 (Fall 1959), p. 155.
22 Graham was, in effect, constructing a transcendental prosody, as defined by Justus Lawler, who sees enjambement as a gesture of freedom, a breaking of limits, a transformation through union with something outside oneself: 'The human subject suddenly experiences the overcoming of limitations and an expansion into something beyond those limits' (Justus George Lawler, *Celestial Pantomime: Poetic Structures of Transcendence* [New Haven: Yale University Press, 1979], p. 74).
23 'No, Listen, for This I Tell' (1942), *CP*, p. 23.
24 Cf. C. Day Lewis's 'The Conflict': 'where we used to build and love / Is no man's land, and only ghosts can live / Between two fires' (in Michael Roberts and Anne Ridler [eds], *The Faber Book of Modern Verse* [London: Faber and Faber, 1951], pp. 270–71).
25 'The Dark Dialogues', I, *CP*, p. 158. W.H. Auden was, interestingly enough, working out his own abstract idea of the sea in the US. In *The Enchafèd Flood*, he produces a list of attributes of the sea according to Romantic symbolism: it is a wilderness where the individual is 'free from both the evils and the responsibilities of communal life'; it is a lonely place of alienation; it is the 'Alpha of existence, the symbol of potentiality'; it is a 'primitive potential power', a site of freedom and solitude (W.H. Auden, *The Enchafèd Flood, or The Romantic Iconography of the Sea* [New York: Random House, 1950], pp. 16–20).
26 He had always been interested in sea poetry, but there seems to have been a sea-change for him after he had read, in 1945, Ben Nicholson and Sven Berlin's 1928 *Horizon* essays championing the primitivist artist and fisherman Alfred Wallis. For more about this, cf. Graham's letters to Sven Berlin in *Nightfisherman*, pp. 51–52, 81–83.
27 There is a possible allusion to *The Waste Land* here: 'The wind / Crosses the brown land, unheard' ('The Fire Sermon', ll. 174–75).
28 For a semi-explicit statement about the sea as symbol in *The White Threshold*, cf. letter to Edwin Morgan, 14 April 1949, *Nightfisherman*, p. 92.
29 Mor Light, the Black Rosses and Skeer are references to general seascape features: lighthouse, promontories, rocks.
30 'From a 1949 Notebook', *ER75*, p. 35.
31 Letter to David Wright, 26 May 1945, *Nightfisherman*, p. 46.
32 Graham acknowledges a debt here to Hopkins, a debt paid in the naming of the line-break as a form of outrider: 'The boat / Rides in its fires' (*N*, Section III, p. 18); '[those swells] outride us in a slow follow / From stern to stem.' (*N*, Section III, p. 19) These recall Hopkins's 'With a mercy that outrides / The all of water' (*The Wreck of the Deutschland*, stanza 33).
33 Section I's verse paragraphs use a mixture of two- and three-beat lines with trochaic/iambic trimeter/dimeter. Section II alternates six-line and four-line stanzas; these cross iambic tetrameter with three-beat lines. Section III's 38 8-line stanzas merge iambic pentameter with four-beat lines, each stanza ending with an iambic dimeter. Section IV alternates four-line and two-line stanzas and is more formal. It has trochaic trimeter in the quatrains, and anapestic dimeter in the two-line sections (two-line ending in trochaic trimeter). Section V is freer, in three-beat lines with occasional

four-beats. The last section's 11 three-line stanzas (structured 3/5/3), pararhyming *aaa*, cross four-beat lines with iambic tetrameter.

34 *N.*, p. 22. This is another remarkable anticipation of Heidegger: '[The word of language] gives light and illuminates or clarifies in a script' (*Hebel – der Hausfreund*, quoted in Fell, *Heidegger and Sartre*, p. 224).

35 Again, a possible debt to Eliot, especially his 'Marina', where the old voice on his boat is pitched between memory and forgetting across blank space: 'I made this, I have forgotten / And remember'.

36 'East Coker' is clearly an important poem for Graham, particularly the lines on the dawn wind on the sea which interrogate the human presence of the 'I'-voice across the ending and beginning of each line: 'Out at sea the dawn wind / wrinkles and slides. I am here / Or there, or elsewhere. In my beginning'.

37 What Robert Graves called 'the substance of mere words' ('Lost Acres') and Laura Riding the 'reality of paper' ('The Map of Places'); see Roberts and Ridler (eds), *Modern Verse*, pp. 223, 233.

38 'The various voices are his poem now' (Sidney Keyes, 'Glaucus', in Roberts and Ridler [eds], *Modern Verse*, p. 420).

39 Quotations from 'The Constructed Space', *CP*, pp. 152–53.

40 'The Dark Dialogues', 4, *CP*, p. 165.

From **The Dark Dialogues: 4**

So to begin to return
At last neither early
Nor late and go my way
Somehow home across
This gesture become
Inhabited out of hand.
I stop and listen over
My shoulder and listen back
On language for that step
That seems to fall after
My own step in the dark.

[...]
See how presently
The bull and the girl turn
From what they seemed to say,
And turn there above me
With that star-plotted head
Snorting on silence.
The legend turns. And on
Her starry face descried
Faintly astonishment.
The formal meadow fades
Over the ever-widening
Firth and in their time
That not unnatural pair
Turn slowly home.

This is no other place
Than where I am, between
This word and the next.
Maybe I should expect
To find myself only
Saying that again
Here now at the end.
Yet over the great
Gantries and cantilevers

Of love, a sky, real and
Particular is slowly
Startled into light.

5

Abstract, Real and Particular: Graham and Painting

RALPH PITE

In 1956, Graham moved to the St Ives area of Cornwall where he lived the rest of his life. He had lived there before, in a caravan at Germoe between 1943 and 1947, and at Mevagissey in 1948–49. During these earlier stays, he had made contact with several artists connected to the St Ives school: Ben Nicholson, Sven Berlin and Bryan Wynter. The last of these became a close friend. When he settled in Cornwall permanently, Graham became part of a loose-knit artistic community which included (as well as Wynter) Terry Frost, Michael Snow, Karl Weschke, Alan Lowndes, Nancy Wynne-Jones and, most importantly perhaps for Graham's development, Roger Hilton and Peter Lanyon.[1] Graham's contacts in Glasgow and London during the 1940s also included many painters, including Robert Frame, Robert Colquhoun, Robert MacBryde and, most intimately, John Minton, who stayed in Germoe for six weeks in 1944.[2]

1956 was an interesting time to be in and around St Ives. Roger Hilton, who had trained in Paris and worked in London, was himself 'becoming drawn to Cornwall' and spent Christmas 1956 there visiting Patrick Heron. More frequent visits followed over the next few years.[3] Around the same time, Heron's own work shifted significantly: in 1955–56 he made a 'decisive move into non-figurative abstraction' in which he had 'to do without the pretext provided by a subject'.[4] Bryan Wynter's paintings also changed around 1956, losing their (albeit indirect) references to the Cornish landscape and becoming 'a kind of visual flux, a surface on which the eye found it difficult to rest so that, if it were not rebuffed, it would be compelled to push deeper and come to terms with the forces underlying the painting'.[5] For both Wynter and Heron, personal factors were involved in these changes in style. Heron had bought the house, Eagle's Nest in Zennor, he had long dreamt of and started to live there all the year round; Wynter had inherited money and could enjoy greater artistic freedom as a result. He had also started to experiment with mescalin.[6]

Both artists were also responding, however, to other painting. Contemporary reviewers saw French *tachisme* – a post-war form of abstract painting in which the paint was applied in small, blotlike touches – as a clear influence on their new work, while the famous 1956 Tate exhibition 'Modern Art in the United States' also had a considerable impact. The exhibition brought Abstract Expressionism (the work of de Kooning and Pollock among others) to Britain for the first time, making the new movement much more powerfully available to those, including Heron and Wynter, who were already aware of it.[7]

Abstraction had been connected with St Ives artists since before the war, in the work of Nicholson and Barbara Hepworth, and the school they helped establish, which included Peter Lanyon among its younger members. However, the new abstraction, which developed after the war and came to prominence after 1956, tended to move away from the mathematical precision and cool formalism generally characteristic of pre-war abstract art and still pursued by Constructivists such as Victor Pasmore.[8] Lanyon said in 1961 that his war-time experiences had left him 'with a complete rejection of pure abstract painting' and a new fascination with '[t]his country here, and its stone, and its oldness'.[9] Hilton too turned from the austere abstraction of his 1952–54 paintings towards allowing 'references to atmosphere and seasonal change, and even to the figure'.[10] Adrian Lewis says that Hilton's work after 1956 'took on a more fluid quality of drawing, opening forms into a more relaxed spaciousness, often infused with earth-browns or atmospheric blue-greys, while titling became more evocative. Colours and rhythms are absorbed from this new environment [Cornwall], though still deeply internalised in terms of bodily sensation [...] and mental states'.[11] Hilton himself wrote in 1958: 'In much painting today we are being given paint which is delightful but which has not been put to the sterner but ultimately more rewarding task of presenting something other than itself so that itself becomes transfigured in the process.'[12]

Abstract Expressionism may have contributed to this new mode of abstract art in which expression and figurative reference returned. So too may the CoBrA school, founded in Europe in 1948. CoBrA sought a form of painting that was 'neither abstract nor figurative' but in some way both 'abstraction and new representation'.[13] Earlier in the 1950s, Hilton had been in close contact with Constant Nieuwenhuys and Stephen Gilbert, both connected to the CoBrA group. Hilton may have been responsible for bringing their ideas to Heron, Lanyon and Wynter in Cornwall, while the landscape emphasis of St Ives painting had a reciprocal impact on him.

The French movement known as 'Lyrical Abstraction' was probably also influential in St Ives, though more perhaps in Lanyon's work than in Hilton's. Work of this school 'bore reference to nature without describing it; it was sensitive, not to things, but to the effects which those things produced – walls, rippling water, the bark of trees, waves, sky, nebulae, mud'.[14]

Critics, notably Neil Corcoran and Tony Lopez, have suggested that Graham's work after his move back to Cornwall echoes the interests of modernist painting in St Ives: 'Hepworth's idea of a work that breaks the subject-object relation of the artist to the world, is paralleled in Graham's portrayal of a fragmented self, constituted through experience'.[15] Corcoran emphasizes how the art and the poetry both draw attention to their medium, making language or paint the focus and the problem of the work: '[Lanyon's, Hilton's and Wynter's] move away from figuration towards self-reflexively "painterly" values, towards a primary concentration on the material itself and the material's behaviour, undoubtedly influenced Graham's own linguistic experiments'.[16] The painters' own commentary on their work suggests that their form of abstraction did not in fact involve a 'primary concentration on the material itself'. Hilton and Lanyon explicitly reject that version of abstraction. Equally, although these critics claim to identify common ground between art in St Ives and Graham's poetry, it is common ground shared with other important influences on Graham. Modernism in general, as Lopez recognizes, questions and problematizes subject–object relations. Likewise, Eliot, Joyce and Beckett – three of Graham's most powerful literary influences – all differently draw attention to language as a medium.

It may be that the presence of so many St Ives painters among his friends simply kept Graham focused on these characteristically modernist forms and hence on his modernist precursors. On this view, Cornwall makes Graham into a late modernist by contrast with his contemporaries – the Movement, the Group, Expressionists such as Ted Hughes, confessional poets – who were more decisively rejecting or departing from modernist positions. Maybe, one might think, it held him back. Maybe it was another piece of 'bad luck'.[17] I would say, though, that Cornwall and St Ives had a beneficial and more specific influence. The distinctive brand of abstraction among the painters Graham met contributes to Graham's peculiarity as a modernist writer. The poet shared with the painters a concern with work in which abstract and figurative meet; that is, in which the medium (paint or language) encounters 'something other than itself' – a landscape or the selfhood of the artist or the 'effects which [...] things produced'.

Graham wrote to Roger Hilton soon after they met in 1956:

> The strange thing is this, Roger, I found when I returned here that your pictures and 'timbre of voice' of your painting has affected me more strongly than I had realised. In the same way that one sees influences of contemporary abstract painting in Landscape and in News photographs in newspapers lying upside down etc., that particular kind of graphic disturbance which is your 'voice' in painting suggested itself more and more in things.
>
> (*Nightfisherman*, p. 154)[18]

Graham is writing here (13 December 1956) after a period of '[p]rofound melancholy', brought on, he says, by worse than usual poverty and Nessie's being ill. He had recently written 'Hilton Abstract' – dated 13 November 1956 in one manuscript (see *Nightfisherman*, p. 154) – and in the letter he addresses Hilton very fondly, inviting back down to Cornwall his 'love-chasing abstract boy'. This phrase joins urgency with cool, the adolescent's hot blood with aloof intellectuality, philandering with unworldliness. It repeats, that is to say, the tension and contention of post-war abstract art.

These preoccupations are dwelt on by the poem itself. It begins:

> Roger, whether the tree is made
> To speak or stand as a tree should
> Spreading its branches over lovers
> And moving as the wind moves,
> It is the longed-for, loved event,
> To be by another aloneness loved.
>
> (*CP*, pp. 168–69)

'Hilton Abstract' questions and returns to 'quick and slow'. In stanza 2, Graham writes:

> Hell with this and hell with that
> And hell with all the scunnering lot.
> This can go and that can go
> And leave us with the quick and slow.
> And quick and slow are nothing much.
> We either touch or do not touch.

The phrase comes back again at the end:

> Yet the great humilities
> Keep us always ill at ease,
> And in keeping us they go
> Through the quick and through the slow.

Sometimes addressing Hilton, sometimes seeming to speak for him or express in words what his paintings 'voice', and sometimes apparently arguing with him, 'Hilton Abstract' tries to reconcile the 'shout and whimper', the desperate 'love-chasing' that underlies all efforts to communicate, with the discipline that in poetry constructs time into an orderly sequence and in painting either accurately represents objects or expresses their inner being – making the tree 'speak' or 'stand as a tree should'.

Stanza 2, seeming at first to attack the high-flown rhetoric of the first and its high-minded conclusion, turns out to make the same point. It is as if Graham imagines Hilton's impatient dismissal or, imagining it, internalizes it, pre-empting the rejection. The abstract artist rejects convention, figuration, commercial success; if he is Hilton, he is an 'artist of the astringent' – difficult, irascible, testy, as various friends and acquaintances report. Getting rid of the superficial and faddish, the 'scunnering lot' of rubbish that surrounds art, allows you back to the self-discipline that is its essence.[19] Yet this too achieves little: the work touches us or it doesn't; it makes it possible for alonenesses to touch each other or it fails to do so. This is more fundamental still than the 'quick and slow' of artistic skill.

'Abstract' is a recurring word in Graham's poetry and his other writings too. In his 1949 notebook he remarks:

An abstraction blooded, as a man by thought: 'It must be abstract' Stevens

Last stanza of IT MUST BE ABSTRACT

(*ER75*, p. 32)

The first sentence – 'An abstraction blooded […]' – is also from Wallace Stevens's poem 'It Must Be Abstract', which is the first section of 'Notes toward a Supreme Fiction' (1942). The poem's last stanza tells the aspiring writer, the 'ephebe', that his or her subject must be inglorious and generic, 'The man / In that old coat, those sagging pantaloons':

It is of him, ephebe, to make, to confect
The final elegance, not to console
Nor sanctify, but plainly to propound.

In the notebook, Graham goes on to quote lines from earlier in Stevens's poem:

Perhaps there are moments of awakening,
Extreme, fortuitous, personal, in which

We more than awaken, sit on the edge of sleep,
As on an elevation, and behold
The academies like structures in a mist.[20]

Stevens joins plainness and elevation: a heightened state of awareness in which the preordained fades away and direct perception takes over. The equivalent of this direct perception is a principle of candour, propounding others as if they were laws of nature – laws that, nice or nasty, must be accepted.

This is a Romantic position, echoing Keats's 'The Fall of Hyperion' and Yeats's 'rag-and-bone shop of the heart'. Graham takes from it the paradox of a 'blooded' abstraction – the sense, in other words, that ideas and institutions, words even, must be used and gone beyond. They must be blooded – maimed for the job – and brought into contact with the ordinary for two reasons: firstly, so that they do not become academic merely, and secondly, in order that the ordinary can be propounded and beheld.

Graham's comments on 'The Nightfishing' in 1955, soon after it was published in his collection *The Nightfishing*, enforce the poem's attention to the reality of the sea: 'If it made somebody seasick [...] I would be pleased' he wrote to Alan Clodd. To Charles Causley, a few months later, he remarked more seriously 'I wanted to write about the sea and make it a grey green sea, not a chocolate box sea. [...] I wanted to use those kinds of very physical phenomena in whatever real action was represented. Because although I wanted to write about the sea it was not the sea only as an objective adventure (if there is such a thing) but as experience surrounding a deeper problem which everybody is concerned with' (*Nightfisherman*, pp. 141, 144). 'The Nightfishing' is arguably Graham's most Eliotian poem and he also writes about it in terms reminiscent of Eliot's aesthetics. Realizing specific objects as fully as possible provides a way of going beyond them into 'a deeper problem', 'another intensity'. The particular words reach into a universal silence.

Edwin Morgan has written strikingly about the silence at the centre of 'The Nightfishing' and the difficulty Graham found in 'stitching together the outer and inner demands of the poem'.[21] However one feels about this, Graham's own work changes after 1955. He includes in the letter to Alan Clodd a draft of what became 'The Constructed Space' (stanzas 1 and 2 of the finished poem, plus the end of stanza 3). 'Don't be frightened,' Graham wrote, 'at the bareness and prosaicness of this section. It is meant to be as "abstract" as I can make it, unvisual in its images and suggesting no real place or atmosphere' (*Nightfisherman*, p. 143). In pages from a notebook that he sent to Bryan Wynter, Graham recalls both 'Hilton Abstract' and 'The Constructed Space' in formulating a similar position with greater authority. He sent the notebook in November 1958 but may easily have written in it earlier.

> And I remember this. I remember that always somewhere under the live and speaking idiom of the Voice in poetry there is the count, the beats you can count on your fingers. Yes always under the shout and whimper and the quick and the slow of poetry there is the formal construction of time made abstract in the mind's ear. And the strange thing is that that very abstract dimension in the poem is what creates the reader's release into the human world of another.
>
> (dated 19 November 1958, *Nightfisherman*, p. 162)

Again, in 1966, he wrote to Ruth Hilton (who was by then divorced from Roger Hilton): 'Art expression is a voice between two things. Abstract formality and the very human gesture. And one doesn't work without the other.' The terseness of this may be in part the result of his ongoing disagreement with Hilton over the role of form. 'Roger's adoption [...] of the beat disorder is apparent', he told Ruth at the same period (*Nightfisherman*, pp. 195, 197). Earlier, and probably thanks in part to Hilton's presence, Graham seems to have moved forward by reversing the relation between the external object and abstract pattern.

Abstract works of art were defined by Herbert Read in 1948 as those which, 'though they may start from the artist's awareness of an object in the external world, proceed to make a self-consistent and independent aesthetic unity in no sense relying on an objective equivalence'.[22] Graham after 1955 seems to think of the process as going in the opposite direction: starting with bareness, prosaicness, the unvisual, with the abstract pattern of verse, he establishes communication between one human world and another. Like Patrick Heron at the same period, he decided 'to do without the pretext provided by a subject' but in order, in his case, to reach the subject. And Graham's phrasing in '*release* into the human world of another' (emphasis mine) shows that he assumes a continuity between this way of working and his approach in the 1940s – he published 'Notes on a Poetry of Release' in 1946. Such a continuity is confirmed, I think, by the resemblance between his remarks in 1955 and the passages from Wallace Stevens he adopted for himself in 1949.

'The Constructed Space' concludes by affirming that the self becomes present to the other via the establishment of something purely abstract – a pattern, a space, a silence:

I say this silence or, better, construct this space
So that somehow something may move across
The caught habits of language to you and me. [...]
Here in the present tense disguise is mortal.
The trying times are hastening. Yet here I am
More truly now this abstract act become.

(*CP*, p. 153)

'Disguise is mortal' in two contradictory senses: it is temporary and it belongs to the human condition. Disguise *will* pass at last and yet its passing is a trial to us because we are wedded to it. Graham places against this paradox the 'abstract act' which provides an escape from both the thrill and the fear of losing your disguise and being exposed to another person. You can be 'More truly' yourself and be more vulnerably present: 'here I am' simply and undisguised. That is possible because you have 'become' the abstract act, in a phrase whose elliptical syntax also implies that 'now this abstract act [has] become'. Its completion coincides with your truly appearing. And becoming truly present occurs in the pause established by the density of the last line. The 'trying times' are no longer 'hastening' here; they cannot. The 'I' that has, despite disguise and disease, finally 'become' stands still, fully visible in its constructed, abstract space.

The thought here extends Graham's reaction to Hilton's paintings – his finding that their 'timbre', their 'particular kind of graphic disturbance [...] suggested itself more and more in things'. Their artistic peculiarity reveals Hilton, as if he has 'become' the abstract act, and this 'something' seems to 'move across' to Graham so that he begins to see it elsewhere – 'in things'. If an artwork's value depends solely on whether 'We [...] touch or do not touch' ('Hilton Abstract') then Hilton's art succeeds. It allows Graham not only to sense the artist but to respond as well; it allows both painter and viewer to touch and be touched in equal measure.

Despite the success of 'The Constructed Space' and its popularity, 'Hilton Abstract' is the poem more characteristic of Graham because of its unease about the relation between the 'blooded' and the 'abstract' – an unease it shares with Hilton.[23] Hilton insists on painting's 'sterner but ultimately more rewarding task' to go beyond 'paint which is delightful'; paint, he says, must be 'transfigured in the process' of 'presenting something other than itself'. His terms are severe and grand – 'astringent', as Graham put it. In 1961, Hilton is more emphatic and absolute: 'I see art as an instrument of truth, or it is nothing':

One must express oneself. There are situations, states of mind, moods, etc., which call for some artistic expression; because one knows that only some form of art is capable of going beyond them to give an intuitive contact with a superior set of truths. The direct imitation of life or nature cannot express the complex human situation which exists for us all today.[24]

In his contribution to Lawrence Alloway's influential collection *Nine Abstract Artists* (1954), Hilton described the artist as 'like a man swinging out into the void'. In his 1961 essay, 'The Confrontation of Medium and Idea, Remarks About Painting', Hilton repeats this heroic and mystical idea of the artist: 'The artist's job is to arrange a meeting between paint and idea; in doing so, particulars will be transfigured into universals'. Paint is the 'language' or 'form' in which the idea ('a feeling, an intuition or an obsessional image') is incorporated: 'without the battle between [these two] and the final sinking of each sovereignty in a common wholeness, there can be no art'.[25]

Uncompromising and brutally serious, Hilton elevates the artist into a prophet or seer and at the same time rejects anything pretentious or fey: transfiguring particulars into universals or reaching an intuitive contact with a superior set of truths, these are nothing more than '[the] artist's job'. The 'delightful' is nothing beside the true and the transfigured and, furthermore, Hilton denies that anything less than the transfigured is art at all. Where paint and idea do not intersect, 'there can be no art', he says; art is truth-revealing or 'it is nothing'. So, as Graham said, ventriloquizing his friend, 'Hell with this and hell with that / And hell with all the scunnering lot. / This can go and that can go'. An abstract art, for Hilton, that does not make these or equivalent demands on itself falls radically short. Maybe self can express itself more truly through the abstract act of painting; characteristically, though, Hilton insists that it absolutely must do so. It is not a cherished possibility so much as an essential prerequisite.

His paintings reflect that urgency in their restless variety, their 'confrontation' between massive blocks of colour and hectic scoring. Alan Bowness observed in 1963 how Hilton's 'rambling, groping, scribbling line makes a sharp contrast with the flat plain areas of colour'.[26] This effect is particularly marked in paintings from the late 1950s and afterwards – in, for example, *October 1956*; *Grey Day by the Sea, March 1959*; *Large Orange, Newlyn, June 1959*; *The Long Walk, 1959*; and *March 1960 (Grey, black and white)*. It produces an extraordinary, fierce restlessness amidst calm. Rothko's plangent serenity and Pollock's feverish dances of being both seem decorative by comparison or, in Hilton's terms, merely 'delightful'.

Bryan Wynter's paintings from around the same time – such as *The Interior* or *Prison* from 1956 – are similarly hectic but, as the titles suggest, more inward. Less aggressive to the viewer than Hilton's, they give the impression that Wynter is addressing some problem of his own – some sense of confinement or inner chaos. The palette is more muted and harmonious, the units of colour smaller and the composition busier. The comparison brings out how strongly Hilton seeks to make a personal impact on the viewer (and on himself), how resistant he is to prettiness, first of all, and, connected with this, to both impersonality and privacy.[27]

Graham shares Hilton's suspicion of abstract acts and his commitment to them. He steps back, however, from Hilton's conscious severity, partly as if he cannot live up to such expectations and partly like Sancho Panza eyeing Don Quixote askance. 'Hilton Abstract' suggests this manoeuvre, I think. 'We either touch or do not touch' ends stanza 2 and stanza 3 begins:

> Yet the great humilities
> Keep us always ill at ease.
> The weather moves above us and
> The mouse makes its little sound.
> Whatever happens happens and
> The false hands are moving round.

This is not 'the void' of Hilton's artist, nor is it 'contact with a superior set of truths'. The ordinary that surrounds us and the false that often controls us are 'the great humilities', disrupting our ambitions and, in their own way, providing the 'something other than itself' that art must both confront and touch. This seems to be the point of Graham's concluding lines:

> Yet the great humilities
> Keep us always ill at ease,
> And in keeping us they go
> Through the quick and through the slow.
>   (*CP*, p. 169)

These trivial, sometimes nasty things disturb us, breaking the artistic reverie, and in doing so they inhabit and revive 'the quick and slow' of form, which is nothing much in itself and only valuable, Graham implies, when these experiences 'go / Through'.

Hilton's comments on his painting suggest that he would probably not disagree with this in substance. The tone, though, is very different. Similarly, Graham has a slightly different take from Hilton's on the pitfalls of

form. More confident perhaps than Graham, Hilton rejected complacency
and faddishness. His writing and painting both suggest someone still
convinced that good work was possible, that it could and would reach the
new perceptions he claimed for it, and that he as an artist could pull this
off. He wrote to Terry Frost, at the period when he was leaving pure
abstraction and Constructivism behind:

> I have taken so much against the people who are making constructions (for
> the most part because they cannot paint anyway) and cliquey people in
> general that it won't do them any harm to let them know that I can do a bit of
> bad expressionism as well as the next man. Don't worry any more about
> architecture or construction. For myself I have decided that it is all nonsense.
> The adventure of painting is far from finished. Painting must be given back its
> soul.[28]

Graham's letters to Hilton in the 1960s, encouraging and reassuring him,
suggest that the latter was not always as buoyant as this.[29] Nonetheless,
Hilton remains convinced about the value and power of painting. It is a
talent, which some people simply lack, and it is a calling. He, Hilton,
must carry it on.

Peter Lanyon's work after the Second World War pursues, as Hilton
would later, a 'complete rejection of pure abstract painting'. This leads
him, however, towards uncertainty about painting itself. Canvasses such
as *Porthleven* (1951) and *St. Just* (1952–53) developed out of constructions,
lino-cuts, drawings, painted glass. His *Built-Up Coast* (1960) and others
from the same time combine several media – ceramic tile, stained glass,
wire, mirror and oil on masonite. Instead of turning from Constructivism
back to painting, Lanyon aims at combining the two. His painting after
the war, he said, 'had completely changed', and it is characteristic of him
to sound both tentative and dogged. He does not present himself as
rescuing the old medium. He struggles instead to stop the medium – its
traditional expectations, its authority – from overwhelming him and
obscuring the personal vision of landscape that he was trying to convey. In
these areas, he often overlaps with Hilton, yet there are differences – in
self-image, in self-presentation and, most importantly, in relation to
painting itself. Lanyon sounds more fearful that painting will stop him,
rather as Graham expresses the fear that language will entrap him.

Likenesses between the latter two emerge in how they describe their
work. Lanyon remarked in conversation that he thought of a painting as
'something surfacing, like a man's face, very old and deep roots, coming
up, as it were, through my feet into my own bones and then physically

interpreting it back into painting [*sic*], but I couldn't do it with the direct representation of a single viewpoint. In fact, I couldn't see my country from outside.'[30] Graham remarked about 'The Nightfishing' and his experience of looking back at it: 'I can see it and be curious about its eccentricities and the various strands which suddenly emerge to the surface to become for a moment an ephemeral objective correlative before they sound again' (*Nightfisherman*, p. 141). Perhaps this is only a coincidence: Graham describes a sudden event, a momentary crystallization out of 'various strands'; Lanyon presents a more gradual process in which 'something' enters him and forces him to the task of 'physically interpreting it back into painting'. All the same, a sense of artistic passivity is common to both, coupled with a feeling that the poem or painting rises out of obscurity to the surface which is the art-object itself. Hilton's artist 'swinging out into the void' is not so very far away from these ideas, yet Lanyon and Graham both sound more reliant on what happens and on what the form or medium allows. This, ultimately, might not be very much.

'Hilton Abstract' was first published in 1957, 'The Constructed Space' in 1958. Graham next published a sequence, 'The Dark Dialogues', in 1959 and that, apart from the publication of one old poem without his knowledge, was the last that was heard from him until 1966 when another sequence, 'Malcolm Mooney's Land' appeared.[31] Both sequences end in a similar movement. Repeating lines from near the opening, the last stanza of 'The Dark Dialogues' runs:

> This is no other place
> Than where I am, between
> This word and the next.
> Maybe I should expect
> To find myself only
> Saying that again
> Here now at the end.
> Yet over the great
> Gantries and cantilevers
> Of love, a sky, real and
> Particular is slowly
> Startled into light.
>   (*CP*, p. 165)

'Yet here I am / More truly now' seems echoed in 'This is no other place / Than where I am', although in a more defeated tone. There is nothing out of the ordinary about this, Graham suggests, but also nothing deceptive or deceitful. The sequence of words gives you only and fully him – him alone. These lines, though, are themselves an echo within the poem and Graham registers in that repetition the feeling that language, as he puts it in 'Malcolm Mooney's Land', 'freezes round us all'. As soon as he says something, it feels as if he's 'only / Saying' it. The place where he feels he most truly is becomes, almost at once, a mere habit of speech and mind, a familiar, unconvincing claim. And Graham is rueful about this. He wishes he could more peaceably expect and predict this unavoidable let-down, which comes all the more wearily after the writer has made so much effort to speak truly to another and to himself. The effort seems useless and the collapse of language into itself confirms isolation: 'find myself only / Saying that again' can divide syntactically in two ways – at the line-end and earlier, between 'myself' and 'only'. Graham can find himself only saying something and find himself alone as he repeats himself.

The last five lines miraculously counteract this slide into disappointment. Within the space made by love something real and particular is able to appear. The 'great / Gantries and cantilevers' against the sky recall Graham's Clydeside home (remembered earlier in the sequence). By adding 'Of love' to them, though, Graham takes these loved objects over for a moment, suggesting that his writing has constructed a space – effortfully and even with a comically disproportionate amount of labour. Through that work of trying to speak to and touch another / himself, the sky is 'slowly / Startled into light'. Something does emerge and it is surprisingly 'Particular'. Gantries and cantilevers seem, on the face of it, more particular than the sky. The line-structure and cadence – 'a sky, real and / Particular' – suggests that particularity coming to be recognized. The specific remembered objects – gantries and cantilevers – reveal themselves as metaphors; the sky, vague and easily symbolized, becomes just itself. 'Here now at the end' we 'find [itself] only'. 'Startled', however, contains Graham's sense of how and to what extent solitude is overcome and dialogue achieved. The sky seems to have been dragged blinking into the light; it seems modest before our gaze and reluctant. Love has actively provoked this and love sympathizes with the sky's (the other's) sense of being exposed.

'The Dark Dialogues' is, arguably, Graham's most abstract poem. With 'Hilton Abstract' and 'The Constructed Space' it dates from the period when Graham was most excited by Hilton's way of proceeding in painting. Its ending, moreover, shares with Hilton and Lanyon the conviction that an abstract process can lead to the disclosure of something 'real and /

Particular'. Graham goes on – distinctively, I think – to suggest a loving intimacy between the subject and the 'something other than itself' for which it searches.

'Malcolm Mooney's Land' follows, as I have said, a similar pattern. The speaker addresses 'Elizabeth' in the last verse-paragraph, mentioning 'the boy', perhaps their son. It isn't clear. 'Tell him a story', the speaker says:

> Tell him I came across
> An old sulphur bear
> Sawing his log of sleep
> Loud beneath the snow.
> He puffed the powdered light
> Up on to this page
> And here his reek fell
> In splinters among
> These words. He snored well.
> Elizabeth, my furry
> Pelted queen of Malcolm
> Mooney's Land, I made
> You here beside me
> For a moment out
> Of the correct fatigue.
>
> I have made myself alone now.
> Outside the tent endless
> Drifting hummock crests.
> Words drifting on words.
> The real unabstract snow.
>   (*CP*, pp. 146–47)

Using the same metre as 'The Dark Dialogues', this last section of 'Malcolm Mooney's Land' echoes its downcast loneliness. 'Maybe I should expect / To find myself only / Saying that again' becomes, more starkly, 'I have made myself alone now.' He has willed it and can do so successfully because language is endlessly manipulable, providing no route out of (or for) the trapped self. So, the bear can be imagined and comically described but its 'reek' comes over only in 'splinters' – in fragments and frozen solid. Elizabeth is addressed but she has been made up – hallucinated in a delirium the speaker has fostered in himself by using 'the correct fatigue'. Words do not construct a space between people that can be crossed, they drift on top of each other, an empty obstacle. Consequently, the 'real unabstract snow' is a threatening, sinister presence. 'Outside the tent' (of self and the self's language), the snow is definitively other to the abstract structure and patterns of language. It cannot be made up nor denied nor brought into a relationship with the speaker. It is death, waiting in the wings for the trapped explorer. It is the fact of others – present, threatening, beyond our control.

Letters between Graham and Roger Hilton in the late 1960s suggest that 'Malcolm Mooney's Land' partly originates in the slow disintegration of their friendship. 'Clusters Travelling Out' (first published in 1968) seems likewise related to Hilton, who had been a prisoner of war and was imprisoned for drunk driving in 1966. He was in prison for six weeks before being referred to hospital (see *Nightfisherman*, pp. 201ff.). The link to Hilton and Graham's disagreements with him is confirmed by the poem's hostility to abstraction; no longer is the process of abstract art able to bring about an insight into superior truths, as Hilton claimed. Quite the opposite. 'Yet here I am / More truly now this abstract act become' sounds despairingly satirized by the last lines of 'Malcolm Mooney's Land', where 'Words drifting on words' face 'The real unabstract snow'.

'The Dark Dialogues' reveals a closer, more affectionate relation to Peter Lanyon. In section I, Graham mentions

Wanton with riding lights
And staring eyes, Europa
And her high meadow bull
Fall slowly their way
Behind the blindfold and
Across this more or less
Uncommon place.

In section IV, these figures reappear:

See how presently
The bull and the girl turn
From what they seemed to say,
And turn there above me
With that star-plotted head
Snorting on silence.
The legend turns. And on
Her starry face descried
Faintly astonishment.

As the poem moves here towards its close, Europa and the bull, 'That not unnatural pair / turn slowly home' (*CP*, pp. 158, 165). Graham wrote the poem in 1956–58; Lanyon produced a series of *Europa* paintings in 1953–54. Europa in the myth was a beautiful girl, loved by Jupiter, who disguised himself as a white bull and carried her away to Crete. Ovid tells the story in the *Metamorphoses* and Titian painted the *The Rape of Europa*, a picture that follows Ovid's version very closely. The myth was Christianized – Jupiter is Christ, rescuing the soul (Europa) and taking it to heaven (Crete). It was seen by Frazer as a solar myth (Europa as Moon, Jupiter as Sun) which celebrated the interlunar day when sun and moon were married. Jung read it as one of many myths in which the animal passions, represented by the bull, were accommodated by the self – accepted and, by that method, controlled.[32] Graham would have been interested by these mythical possibilities – from his love of Joyce and his excitement at Robert Graves's *The White Goddess* (see *Nightfisherman*, p. 84). Still 'The Dark Dialogues' suggests his separating himself and his work from these mythical figures, who inhabit a realm above and beyond him. They turn to their home, he to his – the 'Gantries and cantilevers' of Clydeside.

Lanyon stands in the wings of 'The Dark Dialogues' in other ways too: Graham's elegy for him, 'The Thermal Stair', is placed just before it in *Malcolm Mooney's Land*, separated only by 'I Leave This at Your Ear'. In the elegy, Graham tells his friend to 'Sit here on the sparstone / In this ruin'; in 'The Dark Dialogues' he urges the other to 'Stand still by the glint / Of the dyke's sparstone'. And, more significantly, in 'The Thermal Stair', the poet's and painter's 'job is Love / Imagined into words or paint to make / An object that will stand and will not move'. The 'Gantries and cantilevers / Of love' fulfil this agenda, which retrospectively ('The Thermal Stair' was written later) Graham links with Lanyon.[33]

Lanyon's *Europas* draw on myth and on Titian, bringing figures from high art into earthier, rougher forms and thereby drawing the painter himself back to home. They are part of his encounter with and resistance to pure abstraction. So, they continue his struggle to find a form of landscape painting that could be true to his experience of place. They are closer to Hilton than is Lanyon's later work and in dispute with him.[34]

Lanyon's feeling that he 'couldn't do it with the direct representation of a single viewpoint' gives rise to the Cubist elements in his paintings from the early 1950s. Later on the same concern led to the extraordinary evocations of flying over and through a landscape that are achieved by his last paintings: *Ground Sea*, *Thermal*, *Calm Air* and *Glide Path* among others. Painterly features in these – an abstract patterning internal to the medium and representing its energies – cannot be separated from their realization of how it feels to glide. Lanyon took up gliding partly in order to develop this view of landscape and he died in a gliding accident in 1964.

Flying does not liberate Lanyon's eyes and mind from their attachment to earth; he does not join Europa among the stars. Instead, he is still connected to, fond of and inseparable from the ground as he climbs the thermals and sweeps down from their heights. Graham's late poems are similarly full of attachment to particular places – Zennor, Madron, St Gurnard's Head. These are places Lanyon painted – his *Zennor Storm* (1958) is one of his masterpieces – and Graham writes about them too with Lanyon's sense that the abstract spaces of the air lead us back to earth:

> Above the spires of the fox
> Gloves and above the bracken
> Tops with their young heads
> Recognising the wind,
> The armies of the empty
> Blue press me further
> Into Zennor Hill.
> ('Enter a Cloud', *CP*, pp. 209–10)

Notes

1　See *Nightfisherman*, pp. 10, 152.

2　See Frances Spalding, *Dance Till the Stars Come Down: A Biography of John Minton* (London: Hodder & Stoughton, 1991), pp. 73–79, and, for Graham's letters to Minton, *Nightfisherman*, pp. 19ff.

3　Adrian Lewis, 'British Avant Garde Painting 1945–56, Part 2', *Artscribe*, 35 (June 1982), pp. 16–31 (18).

4　Mel Gooding, *Patrick Heron* (London: Phaidon, 1994), p. 95.

5　Lewis, 'British Avant Garde Painting', p. 22, quoting Bryan Wynter, *Notes on my Painting* (Zürich: Charles Lienhard Gallery, 1962).

6　'Although he habitually spent holidays in Cornwall, Heron was based in London until 1955' (Margaret Garlake, *New Art New World: British Art in Postwar Society* [New Haven and London: Yale University Press, 1998], p. 164).

7　Garlake discusses the influence of the exhibition on Lanyon's 1956 paintings and their 'more gestural approach to paint handling' (Garlake, *New Art New World*, p. 177); see also Frances Spalding, *British Art since 1900* (London: Thames and Hudson, 1986), p. 174.

8　Anna Mozynska points out that abstraction had from the beginning been divided between such mathematical formalism and 'the more intuitive, subjective and expressionist attitude of Klee and Kandinsky' (see her *Abstract Art* [London: Thames and Hudson, 1990], p. 98).

9 Peter Lanyon in conversation with Lionel Miskin, c. 1961; quoted in Lewis, 'British Avant Garde Painting', pp. 18–19n.

10 Spalding, *British Art since 1900*, p. 174. The catalogue to Hilton's 1958 exhibition, *Paintings 1953–1957* (ICA), states in its chronology that Hilton's one-man exhibition in 1954 was 'neo-plastic with expressionist overtones', noting that 'at this time Hilton approached construction but rejected it' (n.p.).

11 Lewis, 'British Avant Garde Painting', p. 18.

12 Roger Hilton, 'Statement', in *Paintings 1953–1957*, n.p.

13 Jean-Michel Atlan, one of the CoBrA artists, writing in 1950, quoted in Mozynska, *Abstract Art*, pp. 138–39.

14 Michel Ragin, 'Lyrical Abstraction from Explosion to Inflation', in his *Art Since Mid-Century: The New Internationalism: Volume 1: Abstract Art* (Greenwich, CT: New York Graphic Society, 1971), pp. 72–94 (80–81).

15 Lopez, *PWSG*, p. 9.

16 Neil Corcoran, *English Poetry Since 1940* (London and New York: Longman, 1993), p. 50.

17 See David Punter, 'W.S. Graham: Constructing a White Space', in his *The Hidden Script: Writing and the Unconscious* (London: Routledge and Kegan Paul, 1985), pp. 131–32 for a discussion of Graham's career and its supposed misfortunes.

18 The letter is dated 13 December 1956, from Gurnard's Head. The Grahams had moved there in March. The preceding letter in *Nightfisherman* is dated 7 February 1956. It is not clear how long Graham had been out of touch with Hilton, though it sounds like a matter of some months ('Nessie's had flu twice in the last 2 months', Graham tells him). It seems too that their last meeting was in London so that 'I returned here' means to Cornwall after a visit with the Hiltons to the capital. As often, Graham is writing a thank-you letter of sorts.

19 'Scunnering' is a Scots dialect word meaning 'sickening' or 'disgusting'. The manuscript version reproduced in *Nightfisherman* reads 'fucking' instead. 'Scunnering' moves the stanza closer to Graham's voice and further from Hilton's.

20 Wallace Stevens, *Collected Poems* (London: Faber and Faber, 1955), pp. 385, 386, 389. Graham quotes these lines accurately, except for the stanza break .

21 See above, Chapter 1. See also his 'The Sea, the Desert, the City: Environment and Language in W.S. Graham, Hamish Henderson, and Tom Leonard', *Yearbook of English Studies*, 17 (1987), pp. 31–45, where Morgan describes the still centre of the poem as 'a too conscious abreption from the story for the reader to be other than slightly suspicious of it' (p. 35).

22 Herbert Read, *Art Now*, quoted in *OED*, 'abstract', *pple* and *adj*, def. 4d.

23 'The Constructed Space' is included in the selection from Graham's work in Charles King and Iain Crichton Smith (eds), *Twelve More Scottish Poets* (London: Hodder & Stoughton, 1986); it is also reprinted in *Nightfisherman*, p. 378, placed at the end of the book as a kind of elegy.

24 Cited in *Roger Hilton: Paintings and Drawings 1931–1973*, Serpentine Gallery exhibition catalogue (London: Arts Council of Great Britain, 1974), n.p.

25 Cited in David Nicholson, 'Roger Hilton', *Artscribe*, 34 (March 1982), p. 34.

26 Alan Bowness, 'Roger Hilton', *Cimaise*, 63 (January–February 1963); cited in *Roger Hilton: Paintings and Drawings 1931–1973*, n.p.

27 It is consistent with this that in the late 1960s and early 1970s, when Hilton started to produce his cartoon-like gouaches, Wynter painted quiet abstracts, often in yellows, with fluid forms.

28 Quoted in Lewis, 'British Avant Garde Painting', p. 18.

29 See *Nightfisherman*, pp. 201–06, 230–33.

30 Quoted in Lewis, 'British Avant Garde Painting', p. 19n.

31 There is also a big gap in *Nightfisherman*: between a letter written from Iceland (24 February 1961) and a letter to the *TLS* (21 January 1965) protesting about the unauthorized publication of Graham's poem 'In Memoriam – Burns Singer' (*Nightfisherman*, p. 189). *Nightfisherman* is a selected edition, so perhaps other letters exist from this time, but it certainly seems to have been a difficult period for Graham. 'Malcolm Mooney's Land' suggests this; 'I've been very low creatively,' Graham wrote in September 1965, 'but in the last month or two the muse seems to be becoming cuffed […] into some respect for me' (*Nightfisherman*, p. 193). Tom Scott's inclusion of parts of 'The Dark Dialogues' in *The Oxford Book of Scottish Verse* (Oxford: Clarendon Press, 1966) may have cheered Graham (see *Nightfisherman*, pp. 190–91).

32 See J.G. Frazer, *The Golden Bough: A Study in Magic and Religion*, third edition, 10 vols (London: Macmillan & Co., 1930–36), IV, pp. 71–73, and C.G. Jung, *Man and His Symbols* (London: Aldus Books/W.H. Allen, 1964), pp. 138–39, 147–48.

33 See *CP*, pp. 155, 159, 165.

34 Perhaps there is a politics to these paintings as well: a desire for Europa/Europe to re-establish itself on its own ground rather than being swept up in Jupiter's/the United States's *Pax Americana*.

Implements in their Places: 35–38

35

Language, you terrible surrounder
Of everything, what is the good
Of me isolating my few words
In a certain order to send them
Out in a suicide torpedo to hit?
I ride it. I will never know.

36

I movingly to you moving
Move on stillness I pretend
Is common ground forgetting not
Our sly irreconcilabilities.

37

Dammit these words are making faces
At me again. I hope the faces
They make at you have more love.

38

There must be a way to begin to try
Even to having to make up verse
Hoping that the poem's horned head
Looks up over the sad zoo railings
To roar whine bark in the characteristic
Gesture of its unique kind.
Come, my beast, there must be a way
To employ you as the whiskered Art
Object, or great Art-Eater
Licking your tongue into the hill.
The hunter in the language wood
Down wind is only after your skin.
Your food has stretched your neck too
Visible over the municipal hedge.
If I were you (which only I am)
I would not turn my high head
Even to me as your safe keeper.

6

Syntax Gram and the Magic Typewriter: W.S. Graham's Automatic Writing

MATTHEW FRANCIS

W.S. Graham's unpublished writing is, arguably, an attempt to escape from the fixity and impersonality he associates with printed text, to bathe in the sea of language without freezing to death in the Arctic of the completed poem. That is one of the reasons why there is so much of it. The late unpublished writing constitutes almost an alternative oeuvre to the poems of *Malcolm Mooney's Land* and *Implements in their Places*, one whose creative energy and radical technique represents a remarkable avant-garde challenge to the institution of literature.[1]

The late Robin Skelton's archive of Graham manuscripts, now in the Library of the University of Victoria, Canada, contains one item of exceptional interest. It is a copy of the book *Toward the Well-Being of Mankind* by Robert Shaplen, which Graham has defaced with graffiti-like annotations and by pasting in prose manuscripts of his own (I use the word 'manuscripts' to include typescripts, which the vast majority of them are).[2] It is these pasted-in pieces that I want to consider in this essay. The dates that Graham habitually wrote on the manuscripts, often incorporating them into the text or using them as part of a heading as one does with a letter, reveal that they were written between 1967 and 1973. Shaplen's book was used as a convenient medium for transmitting the manuscripts to Skelton, who was paying Graham a small regular income in exchange for them. Graham also sent some of the material in the form of letters to his friend Ruth Hilton.[3]

These prose manuscripts are, for the most part, experiments with automatic writing, and represent an exceptionally frenzied spell of creative activity. Many phrases and images that eventually appeared in his last two collections were generated in this way. Whatever its degree of intrinsic literary interest, automatic writing was a significant factor in the production of the late poetry. Graham's word for his pieces of automatic prose was 'clusters', and it is the term I shall use in referring to them. One of the results of his commitment to the technique of automatic writing is the poem 'Clusters Travelling Out' . But 'Implements in their Places' owes still more to the clusters, both in its use of automatically generated phrases and images and in its fragmented structure. Clusters, then, have become 'implements', implying that Graham has fashioned useful objects out of naturally occurring formations. The poetry seems to be both adopting and refashioning the automatic prose, making it public and more impersonal, a practical implement more than an intimate cluster.

This difference suggests that the clusters demand a different approach from Graham's other works, a more speculative, biographical and Freudian reading than his published poetry ever welcomes. What follows is an attempt to uncover the private workings of the clusters. I want to suggest their importance to the poems they helped Graham to write and, at the same time, I want to preserve their distinctiveness as a separate body of work, requiring a reading of their own. In my view, although (perhaps because) Graham was never a confessional nor even a straightforwardly autobiographical poet, the clusters are deliberately self-revealing and self-exploratory beneath the disguise of a secret language.

Graham's employment of automatic writing techniques places him in a tradition, originating most importantly in Surrealism. Graham's work is similar to that of the Surrealists, yet not derived simply from them. Joyce's impact is also considerable. The technique of automatic writing pre-supposes an agency that will take power away from the conscious mind and thus make possible meanings that are unknown to it. Critics and artists have frequently identified this agency with the Freudian unconscious. For Graham, however, the agency was more often understood to be language itself, regarded as an entity possessing superhuman powers. To see exactly what Graham was attempting and achieving in this part of his output, we therefore need to look at the kind of automatic writing he produced – how similar it is to Surrealist texts, how close to Joyce, how Freudian and in what way.

The Surrealist André Breton's method of making contact with the agency was to write as quickly as possible:

> I resolved to obtain from myself [...] a monologue spoken as rapidly as possible without any intervention on the part of my critical faculties, a monologue consequently unencumbered by the slightest inhibition and which was, as closely as possible, akin to *spoken thought*. It had seemed to me, and still does [...] that the speed of thought is no greater than the speed of language, and that thought does not necessarily defy even the fastest moving pen. It was in this frame of mind that Philippe Soupault [...] and I decided to

blacken some paper, with a praiseworthy disdain for what might result from a literary point of view.[4]

For Breton, writing rapidly like this is the best way of obtaining unmediated access to what he calls neither 'the unconscious' nor 'language' but simply 'thought'. He regards speech as having privileged access to thought because it is faster than writing, so the speed of writing is an attempt to negate this distinction and thus 'express [...] the actual functioning of thought'.[5] His formula for doing this is: 'Write quickly, without any preconceived subject, fast enough so that you will not remember what you're writing and be tempted to reread what you have written.'[6]

Whether it is permissible to correct what has been written in this way is a point on which Breton is not entirely clear. He praises Soupault because 'he constantly and vigorously opposed any effort to retouch or correct, however slightly, any passage which seemed to me unfortunate'. On the other hand, in a footnote, he observes that 'one is at the mercy of [...] outside distractions' and suggests that the automatic text may contain 'obvious weaknesses' which must be blamed on such distractions.[7] This is a possibility he takes into account in his instructions for novices in the technique: 'If you should happen to make a mistake – a mistake, perhaps due to carelessness – break off without hesitation with an overly clear line. Following a word the origin of which seems suspicious to you, place any letter whatsoever, the letter "l" for example, always the letter "l", and bring the arbitrary back by making this letter the first of the following word.'[8] Breton accepts, then, the possibility that automatism will not always be successful. Something – conventional patterns of thought, or the conscious mind – may intervene in the transaction between writer and writing agency.

How, though, is the writer to know that the work produced is indeed the authentic product of this agency, unaffected by such interventions? For Breton, the test of authenticity is the quality that most readers would acknowledge as the distinguishing feature of Surrealist texts, 'their *extreme degree of immediate absurdity*'.[9] In the spontaneously generated sentence that instigated his own experiments, this absurdity took the form of an incongruous image: 'There is a man cut in two by the window'.[10] Graham's automatic writing, too, as we shall see, is characterized by both absurdity and rapidity of composition.

Graham's clusters show signs of a feature that has been identified by J. Gratton in the writings of Breton as 'runaway': 'a creative *élan* [...] an

impulse which thrives on critical moments of deflection, or even dis-
location, yet releases an urge towards flux and sheer uninterruptedness'.
This is 'an agent of *radical continuity*'.[11] Flux was always an important
theme in Graham's poetry. It is manifested in the narrative shifts of a
poem such as 'The Nightfishing', which moves continually between
present and past tense and between first and third person, and in his use of
the imagery of water, particularly the sea.[12] In the clusters, flux is a feature
of the syntax – not for the first time, for he used unorthodox syntax
sporadically throughout his career, in poems such as 'The Dual Privilege'
and 'Enter a Cloud', but more consistently and daringly than anywhere
else in his work.[13] In this respect, he is taking 'runaway' further than the
Surrealists themselves took it, for their writing is, in general, grammati-
cally well-formed. Graham's dreamlike distortions of words and syntax
derive more closely from *Finnegans Wake*.

Joyce, listed by Graham as one of the major influences on his poetry,
was arguably the greatest and most durable influence of all.[14] Although
the Surrealists were the pioneers of automatic writing, Graham always
seems to have associated the practice in his own work with an attempt to
imitate Joyce, his literary hero. Explaining one of his manuscripts from
the 1950s, he wrote (with a grammatical and orthographic carelessness
itself reminiscent of the clusters): 'Automatic prose, part of which seem to
me a little comic when it is not being to self-consciously punny. Rejoyce.'[15]

Throughout his life, Graham wrote letters in a playful, punning style
imitating *Finnegans Wake*. The linguistic exuberance of these letters forms
a link between the early poems and the clusters: 'Thus Tom Mick a Muse-
meant for yews elf use Jams Joss – BUST IN HELL WARLID. Thus
double in boy mucks goo. Ruskin wee day illso. O mush as end glims nigh
so snorely noire arain the chummies' gabbles slooping bemoth an
a'sternlauft. Lay mint. Sick cloth to Waly Greymoo.'[16] Graham was also
obsessed by the activity of dreaming – Joyce's justification for his use of
language in *Finnegans Wake*. Many of Graham's late poems ('Greenock at
Night I Find You', 'To Alexander Graham' and 'To My Wife at
Midnight', for example) describe dreams. They do so in a lucid, almost
oversimplified style and the clusters can be seen as the dark side, the
unconscious, of that style. In the poems, Graham could no longer indulge
to the full his love of wordplay because in them he was doing his best to
communicate with the reader. 'We want to be telling // Each other alive
about each other / Alive' (*CP*, p. 193), Graham asserts, in the face of all the
obstacles to communication that the poems so brilliantly explore.

Nonetheless, the dream language he learned from Joyce continued an important, submerged existence in the clusters.

The clusters' syntactic flux often allows us to picture the process by which they came into being. The following sentence, for example, is very characteristic of their dynamics: 'I can hear anything while father's ego sleeps bear his bones in my bones' ('Clusters', 21 March 1967). This suggests that he intended to write 'I can bear anything', but struck the wrong key on the typewriter ('B' and 'H' are adjacent on the keyboard); on noticing his mistake, he added the word at the point he had already reached, producing a change of direction by using the word in a different sense. This deliberate adoption of chance events recalls Breton's instruction to use the letter 'l' after a mistake, in order 'to bring the arbitrary back'.

The appearance of so much of this material in greatly changed form in later poems shows in addition that Graham often used automatic writing as a starting-point for further work. This approach, too, is typical of the Surrealists. As Anna Balakian points out: 'These "Surrealist texts", as they are called, must not be taken for poems. They are just a means of developing or enriching poetic consciousness.'[17] Indeed, Graham actually applied the method to poems he was already working on. In one manuscript, following an attempt to write a passage of verse that eventually became Implement 51, he writes 'try it in clusters', and immediately switches to unpunctuated prose ('Clusters', 21 March 1967).

Most pages of the clusters begin with a title typed in capitals, which is, given the nature of the exercise, a starting-point rather than a summary. André Breton and Paul Éluard had made use of titles to stimulate writing in their joint text *L'Immaculée Conception*.[18] If, as I suspect, this is a coincidence, it nevertheless demonstrates the extent of Graham's imaginative attunement with the movement Breton and others had founded some forty years earlier.

These titles are of importance because they show the techniques he followed in the clusters themselves. They use unnatural syntax, which sometimes seems compressed, and place capital letters in a prominent position. The effect is reminiscent of a newspaper headline, and this impression was not lost on Graham, who parodied such a headline in the heading of one page:

CHINKS OF HOPE IN THE PALL OF GLOOM CHINKS OF GLOOM IN THE PALL OF HOPE   SELFSHRINKING HEADS SHARES OF MARG ACHIEVE NEW CEILING   New low for low me.

('Clusters', 15 March 1967)

The gist of this is an analogy between financial and personal depression. The headline style re-emerges several paragraphs later in the line 'ARTICULATED TRAILER LIFTS IMPEDIMENTED MAN OF 48' ('Clusters', 15 March 1967). The 'impedimented man of 48' is Graham himself, whose 48th birthday was in November 1966, and who saw art as an 'impediment' to human relations and himself as maimed or 'Graham-strung' (*CP*, pp. 143, 155, 'Clusters', 13 March 1967). (There is also a connection with a knee injury he suffered falling off a roof.[19]) The 'articulated trailer' is his automatic writing, with its changes of direction (articulation) and continuity (trailing), which has made him feel better. 'Articulated' also means 'verbalized', and this punning account of text as articulated flux occurs also in 'The Nightfishing', in the phrase 'my ghostly constant is articulated' (*CP*, p. 98).

Headings like this provide further clues to Graham's working methods. The parody headline 'CHINKS OF HOPE' suggests that he took real or stereotypical texts and rearranged them in various ways, using the resulting combinations to generate ideas. Michael Riffaterre has argued that such modifications are a definitive device of poetry. In his terminology, the original phrase is referred to as a 'hypogram' and the type of modification used here, in which elements of the hypogram are rearranged, is called 'scrambling'.[20] There are many examples in the clusters of something similar to this scrambling technique.

The heading of one page reads 'SOMEWHERE BEGIN MUST WE BEGIN HEADTAIL TO TELL SOMEWHERE' ('Clusters', 22 March 1967). Clearly, Graham has started with the phrase 'WE MUST BEGIN SOMEWHERE', an admission that he is so far devoid of ideas. He has reversed this to produce 'SOMEWHERE BEGIN MUST WE'. Then he has added another 'BEGIN' to produce a question ('MUST WE BEGIN') which fights against the initial (reversed) assertion while coexisting with it in the same sentence. Following this he has added a word descriptive of his method: 'HEADTAIL'. Then he has taken the second part of this compound word as a pun and used it to generate a familiar phrase 'TAIL [TALE] TO TELL'. Finally, by adding another 'SOMEWHERE' to the end, he produces a vague impression of a palindrome. These peculiar wordgames act as a kind of prompt to him, suggesting a possible direction for the rest of the piece. In this case, the phrase that counts is 'TAIL TO TELL', since it suggests to him the idea of writing a story, which he goes on to do.

An elaborate example of scrambling including reversal occurs in a piece without a heading. It begins with the following sentence: 'ITeenthirt March Four Two Seven away put started across which luminous sand know never shall' ('Clusters', 13 March 1967). 'Teenthirt' inverts 'thirteen', at the level of syllables rather than letters or words. Inverting the other numbers, however, does not complete the date, since there are three of them. The month 'March' itself has suggested a pun, to which it is possible that two of the three numbers refer. The four and the two may belong to a march rhythm of 1-2-3-4, while the seven is what remains from the date 1967.[21] The sentence is a condensed and scrambled form of the date 13 March 1967, and the statement 'I march away across which luminous sand I shall never know.' The phrase 'put started' fits rather more awkwardly: Graham has 'started' his cluster and his hope may be to 'put' it 'across', though equally, since it is private, he may be merely putting it 'away', as the sentence suggests when read the other way round.

A phrase that confirms once and for all Graham's reliance on the technique of inversion occurs on an undated page: 'Poet young A was Maharg'. It is significant, I think, that this inverted form of the poet's surname resembles the M- names of Samuel Beckett's novels, Murphy, Molloy, Moran, Malone and Mahood. Beckett was another writer listed by Graham as a major influence on his work.[22] Certainly the spare style and existential comedy of Graham's late poems seem to owe a great deal to the trilogy, as many critics have noticed.[23] *Molloy*, *Malone Dies* and *The Unnamable* gradually move from the confident characterization of tradi-tional fiction to a refusal to fix identity in words – a refusal epitomized by the shifting names of the hero of the last volume.[24] This process must have been fascinating for a poet who, as the rest of this essay will make clear, was himself engaged in an endless quest for a name that would establish a full identity for him in the impersonal world of text.

The inversion 'Maharg', together with the fact that Graham used a distorted form of the name 'SYDNEY GRAHAM' in the heading 'SYNTAX GRAM AND THE MAGIC TYPEWRITER', suggests that the parody-headline discussed earlier, 'SHARES OF MARG ACHIEVE NEW CEILING', is more complex than it appears ('Clusters', 21 March 1967). 'MARG' is the inverted form of 'GRAM', or Graham. A new ceiling for his inverted self, the one that exists in the clusters, is, we are told, a 'new low for low me'. The world of the clusters is a looking-glass world, for Lewis Carroll, as well as Beckett, is a presence in them. The 'Maharg' piece ends with an evocation of the inverted spirit of Madron, the Cornish village where Graham lived: 'Nordam's a backward place.

Her towers are deep. Her ups are furred with the softest down. Her beasts are bosom-slaps. Gnirps si gnimoc. LLEWERAF. Oireehc' ('Clusters', no date). This inversion is associated with text in Graham's published work, too, as in 'Approaches to How They Behave', where he states: 'Backwards the poem's just as good', or in 'Untidy Dreadful Table' where he tells the reader, 'Of course I see you backwards covered / With words backwards from the other side' (*CP*, pp. 173, 198). The conceit underlying this is that the writer is behind or underneath the words on the page and therefore 'on the other side / Of language' (*CP*, p. 181).[25] To write is to submit to a reversal or scrambling of identity in order to permit oneself to become readable. By turning his name backwards, Graham attempts to make himself a suitable inhabitant of the textual world. This is no doubt one reason for his claim, in poems such as 'Five Visitors to Madron' and 'The Secret Name', that his name does not belong in his work: the only appropriate form would be Maharg (*CP*, pp. 184, 232).

The clusters are full of puns, which are, in effect, another form of scrambling. The punning technique Graham favoured is paronomasia, the distortion of an original phrase that can still be deduced by the reader. One might describe the trope as a process by which words are made to differ from themselves, retaining the context and memory of their original shape while acquiring a new one. In the space of this difference, new meanings are created. Puns of this kind are classified by Freud in his study of jokes as 'modification jokes'. An Italian example he gives is 'the well-known cry "*Traduttore – Traditore!*"' (translator – traitor). They have an obvious similarity to Freudian slips of the tongue or pen, and to mis-hearings or misreadings.[26]

A typical Graham paronomasia is the phrase: 'Sign me a right in the pillow of cloudy night. By day a fire-distinguisher' ('Clusters', 13 March 1967). The idea of a sign suggests a passage from Exodus 13.17: 'And the Lord went before them by day in a pillar of cloud, to lead them the way; and by night in a pillar of fire, to give them light'. Graham distorts and condenses the passage even as he transcribes it, writing 'pillow of cloudy night' for 'pillar of cloud by night' and then apparently remembering that the pillar of cloud appeared 'by day' and adding this phrase as an afterthought. Since, according to the principles of automatic writing, he is forbidden to go back and change anything, he must assign the fire to day instead of night. The pillars of cloud and fire are examples of signs, and the phrase 'sign me a right' (or 'aright') is the poet's request for such a sign. By transforming 'pillar' to 'pillow', he changes the signs seen by the

Israelites in the desert into another kind of sign, a dream. The reassign-
ment of cloud to night is appropriate both for the vagueness of a dream
and the white fluffiness of a pillow. But this reversal has left him with the
rather undramatic image of a pillar of fire by day, which would be difficult
to distinguish against its sunlit background, and this unsatisfactory image
overdetermines another paronomasia, 'extinguisher'/'distinguisher'.

When the passage finds its way into the published poem 'Implements
in their Places', however, all traces of the process that generated it have
been removed. The two pillars have been separated, leaving the 'pillow of
cloudy night' on its own in Implement 17 and the 'extinguisher'/
'distinguisher' contrast, reapplied to stars and birds, in Implement 46:

> Sign me my right on the pillow of cloudy night.
> (*CP*, p. 240)

> By night a star-distinguisher
> Looking up through the signed air.
> By day an extinguisher of birds
> Of silence caught in my impatient
> Too-small-meshed poet's net.
> (*CP*, p. 247)

The shared origin of these two verses remains detectable in the theme of
signs and in the contrast between day and night which still structures
number 46.

Another punning technique is the portmanteau, which Graham owes,
like paronomasia, partly to Carroll and partly to Joyce.[27] The portmanteau
fuses two source-words into an object-word, which, in most cases, did not
previously exist. 'Childhood', for example, is not a portmanteau word,
although it looks like a fusion of the words 'child' and 'hood' (and
Graham experimented with splitting it into these components by the use
of line-breaks; see *CP*, p. 162). In one passage, he lists the denizens of a
verbal circus, many of which are portmanteau animals. 'Paragriphons', for
example, are a cross between griffins and paragraphs, 'elephantinies' are
tiny elephants, 'donkrses' are formed from 'donkeys' and 'arses' (overdetermined by a hidden pun on 'ass'), and 'zebracorns' from zebras and
unicorns ('Clusters', 21 March 1967). The attraction of these animals is
that they exist only as words, so that to invent them is to inhabit a
wonderland or looking-glass world of language.[28] Indeed, some of their
constituent animals are themselves mythical beasts, such as the unicorn
and the griffin, the latter already a cross between an eagle and a lion.

Overall, then, Graham's automatic writing technique in the clusters appears to be related to Breton's advice to 'bring the arbitrary back'. Whereas Breton recommended doing this by putting down a letter at random, Graham tended to do so by rearranging the letters, syllables or words of whatever he was planning to write, and using the resultant absurdity to generate a writing temporarily liberated from conscious planning. A phrase from one of the clusters, when unscrambled, gives us a rather touching portrait of the writer at this quixotic task: 'my hear can back to back killing echo' ('Clusters', 13 March 1967). 'Back to back', like the 'HEADTAIL' we have already considered, must be a metapoetic description of his inversion technique, for the three words that precede it, when reversed, read 'can hear my'. The only possible object to be found for this sentence-fragment is 'killing echo'. He was, after all, using a typewriter. The echo of his keys must have been a reminder that he was alone, engaged, not in a dialogue with another human being, but in a bizarre attempt to converse with the language itself.

Indeed, the clusters reveal, perhaps more clearly than any of his other writings, his devotion to a superhuman language, which he equates with community and femininity. In a passage of lucid expository prose buried among the clusters he wrote: 'The thing is to find or create (in this case the same thing) a language, a timbre of thought or voice, which I will live in. It will never be adequate except for its moment but it will be the nearest to my soul speaking and as I change so it shall' ('Clusters', 19 March 1967).[29] Language cannot be personal because it transcends the personal, because individuals participate in it rather than creating it. As Maurice Blanchot has pointed out, if automatic writing puts us in touch with language, it does so only at the expense of our individuality and hence of the power to speak.[30] But for Graham this transcendence is analogous to the way a community transcends the personal. The nearest he can come to personalizing language, therefore, is to create a home for himself in it, somewhere he can live, just as an individual's relationship to the community is defined geographically as a home.

The theme of language as both the cause of a fall from an Edenic original community (the working-class Clydeside of his childhood) and a possible means of redemption from that fall can be traced throughout Graham's work, and I have done so elsewhere.[31] It derives in his case from a deep sense of guilt at having abandoned the values of his home and family to become a writer. The poems exist in a constant state of tension between a logocentric belief that writing can never offer the human satisfactions of speech and a persistent conviction that it can be justified in communal terms, as an act of love. It is in the clusters, however, with their improvisatory character, that Graham tries hardest to abolish the difference between writing and speech and thus to take his place in a community of language as loving and immediate as the speech-based community of his mythologized childhood.[32]

Language, then, is a form of community that Graham strives to turn into a home. The focus of a home for him is the mother, and therefore to create a home in language is to discover a mother. Graham found precedents for this maternal presence within language, as Tony Lopez has shown, in the traditional concept of the Muse, particularly as expounded by Robert Graves in *The White Goddess*.[33] In one of the clusters, this figure is invoked as follows: 'Cuntess Muse, her stays enlocked stitched wornout to the gloves of Astra Khan. As little cistern closets mingle to big sea sewers so rushed thundering negativwards his last fake frantic experients in keeping mum. Is the word?' ('Clusters', 15 March 1967). The C[o]untess, with her aristocratic yet carnal title and astrakhan gloves, is also a celestial tyrant ('Astra Khan' as in Genghis Khan). Language is both a formidable restraint ('stays enlocked') and a frayed and tattered material ('stitched wornout'). In the next sentence, language is represented by the sea, as it is in 'The Nightfishing' and related poems. The relationship of the individual utterance to the system, of *parole* to *langue* in Saussure's terms,[34] is that of a river to the sea it flows into, but this fairly conventional analogy is given a scatological turn so that the sea is also a sewer filled by the products of individual 'little cistern closets'. There is a pun here, characteristically involving kinship: the 'little cistern closets' and the 'big sea sewers' are sisters.

It is true, of course, that utterances modify the language, but the reverse flow was more important to Graham, since he was deliberately trying to open himself to the promptings of the personified language, to become the voice of the Muse. In his case, therefore, the river flows 'negativwards' (one reason for his cult of inversion). 'Mum', the maternal muse, may be a kept woman, but does he have the 'experients' to keep her? These 'frantic experi[m]ents' are his attempts to do so, but in the silence of writing ('mum is the word') he is forced to rely on the dubious meanings of words isolated from the personal context of speech, leaving him with an unfinished question: 'Is the word?'

A sentence in an earlier piece also equates maternity and language: 'Fluxy mother me utters to abridge us time again' ('Clusters', 13 March

1967). Language is fluid, feminine, generative and dominating – a fluxy mother. Her offspring, the poetic utterance, on the other hand, does not inherit these qualities; it is, as so many of Graham's poems complain, static, frozen on 'the dead-still page' behind 'the Art barrier of ice' (*CP*, pp. 174, 150). If *langue*, the entity with which he is trying to communicate in automatic writing, is feminine and equated with the mother, Graham identifies the other term of this binary opposition, *parole*, with the masculine and the son. In a passage probably written on the same day as the 'Cuntess Muse' cluster, we read: 'What are you frightened for it's all language. We're in it somewhere. Lines and spaces. Good boys all deserving doubtful favours' ('Clusters', no date). 'We're in it somewhere' repeats a claim made in his most important piece of theoretical writing, the essay 'Notes on a Poetry of Release', that 'the shape of all of us is in [the] language', except that that 'somewhere' demonstrates the perplexity of the poet as he tries to find his home in this daunting community.[35] Graham's ultimate model of a community is always the family, or rather his own family. Hence the 'good boys', for his family was one with two boys. The phrase 'good boys all deserving doubtful favours' is of course an adaptation of the mnemonic for the lines of a musical stave. He is comparing language, a system of differences, with music, a system of intervals or 'lines and spaces'. We may surmise that it is the spaces he is frightened of. Language's favours to 'good boys' are doubtful because it has, in Saussure's formulation, 'no positive terms'.[36] Indeed, if the lines of the stave are equated with boys, we can go further and suggest that the spaces represent not just difference but femininity.

The combination of sex, music and language continues: 'Suffle your molecules all guys between Madhoven fucks Cecilia's daughters who lose their keys in the shoe-string band. It's gramar as wolf kills us better. Melt predicate unparsable with which us cares for laughs.' The guys (lines) are between the girls (spaces). The shuffling of the molecules is the process of rearranging words in which Graham is currently engaged. Madhoven, the Madron equivalent of Beethoven (who is perhaps mad) has sex with the daughters of Cecilia, the patron saint of music, who have lost their phallic keys. Grammar is also 'grandma', the wolf in Little Red Riding Hood, who kills 'us', no doubt the same 'us' who are 'in it somewhere'. Language is the matriarch that kills and swallows the individual. The last sentence really is 'unparsable' and a predicate missing a subject. Presumably it is grandma who has eaten the subject and melted the predicate, leaving the sentence unparsable.

In these examples, we see that the feminine language in which Graham is trying to find a home is associated with anxiety as well as longing. Language is a Big Bad Wolf, a Cuntess Muse. This anxiety about the feminine is a familiar theme of psychoanalysis, and an investigation of the clusters reveals a thinly disguised castration symbolism. I have suggested that the uttered 'me', the *parole*, is masculine and identified with Graham himself. It is also identified with the male genitals, seen as isolated from the body to which they belong. Words, in Graham's shifting terminology, are 'molecules', 'clusters', 'implements', 'particles', all terms that could be taken as euphemisms for the male genitals. This last word occurs shortly after the passage we have just looked at: 'somewhere our belonging particals believe'. This phrase was later used in the couplet that opens and closes 'Implements in their Places':

Somewhere our belonging particles
Believe in us. If we could only find them.
(*CP*, pp. 236, 254)

The word 'particles' refers to linguistic fragments, and is also a diminutive suggesting a possibly rather pathetic smallness.

Remembering, however, the prevalence of portmanteau words in the clusters and that this passage has its origins there, I would suggest that the word in this instance is overdetermined by a similar wordplay: Graham treats it as if it were constructed from a combination of 'parts' and 'testicles'. (Indeed, the phrase 'private particles' appears in a cluster of 22 March 1967.) Suddenly this rather cryptic complaint makes sense. The poem is cut off from the poet like genitals cut off from the male body. To be in language offers the fantasy of being reunited with the mother, but the price paid for such pleasurable union is absorption into a feminine system of differences, one's lines swallowed by female spaces, a good boy receiving extremely doubtful favours. Once again, the union takes place in that mysterious 'somewhere', a home the poet can never find because he has been cast out from it. Graham's claim that he is 'maimed' or 'impedimented' can now be seen to be something more than a Romantic assertion of the stigma of genius. It is clear that there is a degree of neurotic guilt behind this imagery, and that his quest for a union with the language is also a quest for a reunion with his home and mother, and between the separated parts of his own self.

The themes of exile and castration are linked in the clusters. Separation is both Graham's crime (he has rejected his upbringing by leaving home and becoming a writer), his punishment (he feels deprived of human contact) and his hope of redemption (language may provide him with an alternative home, though one that will never be truly satisfactory). In terms of the castration metaphor, the text is isolated from its author like separated genitals, but it may still be able to achieve a kind of remote sexual contact with the reader. Graham's descriptions of words often imply that they have a subhuman life of their own, reminiscent of the mischievous independence sometimes ascribed to the penis in popular culture. Words are beasts, as in the following passage:

> These words (Who they were? The beasts!) recorded it past me, the blemish thus now this is so them now each paticle agog for changing into light not fast enough for finishing events of their own. Language or silence illmannered leave me for saying my own piece alone to share another. Whose fragments afloat in memory's distorting distortions of space still carry kindly an echo of their original? Speaking's for putting down nerve-end highjinks somersaulted arestoelbow in a destined oner.

('Clusters', 21 March 1967)

This passage anticipates the exclamation 'the beasts!' in Implement 52 (*CP*, p. 248). Words are animated, made into independent agents, by writing. The problem ('blemish') here is that the words are not being put down fast enough to take over entirely. They change into light, that is, become visual rather than aural, but do not succeed in 'finishing events of their own'. Separated from the body of language, the particles are 'fragments'. Exiled to the space of the page, they suffer 'distorting distortions' like those to which conventional syntax is subjected by Graham's own automatic prose. There is another buried sexual metaphor here, one familiar from Derrida's deconstruction of Rousseau: writing ('saying my own piece alone') is analogous to masturbation, speech to sex ('to share another').[37] Graham's description of speech ('nerve-end highjinks somersaulted arestoelbow') has a definite sexual charge.

So far I have written as if the Oedipal theme of the clusters were entirely represented by Graham's frustrated longing for his mother. But the Freudian family romance is, at the least, a triangle, and castration anxiety is usually directed at the father rather than the mother. One manifestation of the father in the clusters, as elsewhere in Graham's work, is God, who turns up in an inverted disguise in the sentence: 'To say what to who for reason such as why in the name of Dog' ('Clusters', 15 March 1967). The same Dog/God, inverted by writing and possessing the phallic, animal qualities of Graham's verbal beasts, appears in the published poem

'Dear Who I Mean' as a 'quick brown pouncing god' (*CP*, p. 152).[38]

As Freud remarked, the fear of the outraged and castrating father is complicated by the son's love for him.[39] In 'Notes on a Poetry of Release', Graham showed a certain pride in the fact that 'my history has my eyes and mouth and a little likeness of my father'.[40] His guilt separates him from his father as well as his mother, and it is his father who punishes him, at least in his fantasies; however, since the guilt is of heterosexual origin, it is also something father and son have in common, a bond between them. The automatic prose of 21 March 1967 (a particularly productive day) contains the seed of some of this later writing: 'I can hear anything while father's ego sleeps bear his bones in my bones for ever beside the horde unlimited stretching back to the branivin lizards bottled in the ouzo marches.' I have already discussed the correction Graham made here. Perhaps he found the idea of a son bearing his father too feminine, however, for he removed it from the version that eventually appeared in Implement 7:

> My father's ego sleeps in my bones
> And wakens suddenly to find the son
> With words dressed up to kill or at
> The least maim for life another
> Punter met in the betting yard.
>   (*CP*, p. 237)

This Oedipal theme of conflict and equivalence between father and son is also present in Graham's ballad 'The Broad Close' (*CP*, pp. 129–34). Words are the son's weapon against the father, but the permanence of writing means that the latter is never really dead. Words are both castrated 'particles' and penetrating 'implements'. Whatever violence the son may carry out against the father, the latter is always preserved in the 'magic medium' of language, as if by bottling (*CP*, p. 192). The only way back to the family is through language with its permanent traces of 'the horde unlimited', the millions who have spoken, written and modified it before. The 'branivin lizards', whatever they may be, are bottled in ouzo, a drink often mentioned in Graham's manuscript poems inspired by holidays in Crete, which explore the possibility of rediscovering his family through a community that reminded him of the Greenock of his childhood.[41]

Paradoxically, then, writing, because of its permanence, is a link to the father, offering a substitute for heredity. But what precisely is preserved? The father's recognition of his son is symbolized by the passing on of his name. For Graham, naming is problematized in the realm of writing, a shadowy place haunted by shifting pronouns where numbers are more appropriate. This theme continues a little later in the passage:

> Only let me begin a new life ignorant of an old other. Make me twig No. 999955 on the greatest oak in a forest of terrible thousands. But save me from life as a dressing-table leg. Make me a puffball, healthy and true, but save me from the chopsticks of the Red Guard. Make me forget to stir the lentil pot of my moral broth. Make me make. Make me make me.

In this passage, which anticipates Implement 59 with its discussion between numbered twigs, he is trying to find his name in the linguistic wood (*CP*, pp. 250–51). In the automatic writing, I would suggest, he is communing with his Muse, the personified spirit of language, and it is not surprising, therefore, that the words should have the form of a prayer. He asks to forget his 'old other' life, the world of Greenock, and begin a new one. He will be satisfied, he says, with being a number. What he asks is not to be cut off, a fate that combines alienation and castration: 'Save me from life as a dressing-table leg'.

Graham's ambivalence about communities in general and his own place in them is shown by the phrase 'save me from the chopsticks of the Red Guard'. This clearly started out as 'save me from the chop', and the fact that the line ends at this point on the typescript gave Graham the idea of a trick enjambment. The 'chop' he is frightened of needs no further explanation, but the 'chopsticks of the Red Guard' are somewhat more difficult. He is afraid both of being turned into chopsticks (as he is of becoming a dressing-table leg) and of being eaten. The transformation of the word allows him to make a connection to another image of a depersonalizing community, Communist China, famous for its enormous population and with a reputation for treating that population in a mechanically systematic way – associated, that is, with numbers of people, and with giving people numbers.

From the Red Guard, Graham makes a huge jump to 'the lentil pot of my moral broth'. The connection, of course, is food, but where he was afraid of being eaten before, here he seems to be doing the cooking. And why lentils, which hardly seem the right diet for the Chinese? The answer is to be found in the story of Jacob and Esau in the Bible. Graham, who was himself an elder brother, is identifying with Esau, the elder brother of Jacob, who 'came out red' from the womb (Genesis 25.25). (This is another connection to the Red Guard.) Esau was tricked out of his birthright by his younger brother Jacob in exchange for a 'red pottage [...] of lentiles' (another occurrence of the colour red). The story ends: 'thus

Esau despised his birthright' (Genesis 25.29–34). In Graham's version, it is he, the elder brother, who is the cook, for he cannot blame his brother for tricking him out of his birthright. The mess of pottage of the biblical story has become a 'moral broth', soup and brother at the same time. He worries that his own cooking (or writing) activities constitute the despising of his birthright. His prescription for this anxiety is, as always, to carry on as before, constructing poetic objects ('make me make') and, at the same time, a new identity ('make me make me'). This identity will be defined not by any living community but by the community of language; it will be a thing of words rather than flesh and blood, not Sydney Graham but Syntax Gram.

This brief account of one element of Graham's extraordinary unofficial corpus presents us with some difficult questions. What are publishers, critics and readers to make of this mass of unpublished material? Should it be appropriated for textuality, like the poems in Skelton's collection of manuscript pieces, *Aimed at Nobody*? To do so is to impose a finality upon it that it does not possess. Perhaps in leaving it in its present state Graham has come as close as it is possible to come to what Roland Barthes called the 'writerly' text,[42] since it would be necessary in effect to make a text of it for oneself, to finish its writing, before one could satisfactorily read it. In challenging readers to this task, Graham is also challenging the commodification of literature in which he so uneasily acquiesced in the late published poems.

At the same time, there is something tragic about the clusters, as there is about his career as a whole. Like all his work, they are an attempt to achieve the impossible, to combine the absolute control of a writer putting down words for his own amusement with the absolute love of a perfect son and servant of the community. Automatic writing is apparently a means of submitting oneself to a force beyond one's own will, and Graham, as we have seen, regarded this force not as an unconscious part of his psyche but as a transcendent community; he believed that he was giving up control to his 'fluxy mother', language. But his treatment of it was hardly that of a subordinate: he coined new words, distorted and parodied established phrases and rearranged conventional syntax. The effects may sometimes approximate to the flux of spoken communication to which he had sought to find a written equivalent from the period of *The Nightfishing* and *The White Threshold* onward, but this flux is achieved at the cost of a greater isolation than that of any published text. Far from putting the results of these experiments at the service of the community, he refrained from introducing them into the public arena where control would be shared by his readers. He wanted to keep his mother to himself. To read the clusters, then, is to gain a glimpse of the private verbal playground of a remarkable writer – but it was a playground in which he could never be entirely happy or free from guilt.

Notes

1 Peter Bürger, *Theory of the Avant-Garde*, trans. Michael Shaw (Manchester: Manchester University Press, 1984), p. 47. See Lopez, *PWSG*, pp. 154–161, for a bibliography of Graham's unpublished writing. I consider another important section of it, the manuscripts relating to an unfinished poem titled 'A Dream of Crete', in 'Where the People Are: Language and Community in the Poetry of W.S. Graham' (unpublished PhD thesis, University of Southampton, 1998), pp. 181–91 (hereafter, Francis, *WPA*).

2 In the Special Collections Department, University of Victoria, British Columbia, Canada. References to these manuscripts will appear in the text as 'Clusters' followed by the date. Because of the general eccentricity of the clusters, I shall refrain from confirming unusual phrases with the word 'sic'.

3 Letters to Ruth Hilton, 21 March 1967 and 22 March 1967, *Nightfisherman*, pp. 209–11.

4 André Breton, 'Manifesto of Surrealism', in *Manifestoes of Surrealism*, trans. Richard Seaver and Helen R. Lane (Ann Arbor: University of Chicago Press, 1972), pp. 3–47 (22–23). Emphasis original.

5 Breton, 'Manifesto of Surrealism', p. 26.

6 Breton, 'Manifesto of Surrealism', pp. 29–30.

7 Breton, 'Manifesto of Surrealism', p. 24, and note.

8 Breton, 'Manifesto of Surrealism', p. 30.

9 Breton, 'Manifesto of Surrealism', p. 24. Emphasis original.

10 Breton, 'Manifesto of Surrealism', p. 21.

11 J. Gratton, 'Runaway: Textual Dynamics in the Poetry of André Breton', in Ian Higgins (ed.), *Surrealism and Language: Seven Essays* (Edinburgh: Scottish Academic Press, 1986), pp. 30–45 (31). Emphasis original.

12 Lopez, *PWSG*, pp. 61–74; Francis, *WPA*, pp. 132–33.

13 W.S. Graham, *2ND Poems* (London: Nicholson and Watson, 1945), pp. 21–22; *CP*, pp. 209–12.

14 See Rosalie Murphy (ed.), *Contemporary Poets of the English Language* (Chicago: St James Press, 1970), p. 436.

15 'Notes on a Notebook' (in the collection of the Humanities Research Center, University of Texas at Austin).

16 Letter to Edwin Morgan, undated, *Nightfisherman*, pp. 118–23 (123).

17 Anna Balakian, *Surrealism: The Road to the Absolute* (Chicago: University of Chicago Press, 1986), pp. 146–47.

18   See Jacqueline Chénieux-Gendron, 'Toward a New Definition of Automatism: *L'Immaculée Conception'*, *Dada Surrealism*, 17 (1988), pp. 74–90 (76–80). Earlier, Breton had condemned Soupault's use of titles as an 'error' ('Manifesto of Surrealism', p. 24).

19   See Lopez, *PWSG*, p. 6.

20   Michael Riffaterre, *Semiotics of Poetry* (Bloomington: Indiana University Press, 1978), pp. 12, 139.

21   Alternatively, since four and two make six (the missing number from the date), he may be trying a mathematical game as opposed to his more usual verbal ones.

22   Murphy (ed.), *Contemporary Poets of the English Language*, p. 436.

23   For example, Lopez, *PWSG*, p. 90; Damian Grant, 'Walls of Glass: The Poetry of W.S. Graham', in Peter Jones and Michael Schmidt (eds), *British Poetry Since 1970: A Critical Survey* (Manchester: Carcanet, 1980), pp. 22–38 (28); Tom Leonard, 'Journeys', *ER75*, pp. 83–87 (83).

24   See Samuel Beckett, *The Unnamable*, in *The Beckett Trilogy: Molloy, Malone Dies, The Unnamable* (London: Picador, 1979), p. 268.

25   See also *AN*, p. 24.

26   Sigmund Freud, *Jokes and their Relation to the Unconscious*, trans. James Strachey, ed. James Strachey and Angela Richards (Penguin Freud Library, 6; Harmondsworth: Penguin, 1976), p. 67; *The Psychopathology of Everyday Life*, trans. Alan Tyson, ed. James Strachey, Angela Richards and Alan Tyson (Penguin Freud Library, 5; Harmondsworth: Penguin, 1975), pp. 94–183.

27   On the portmanteau and paronomasia in Carroll, see Jean-Jacques Lecercle, *Philosophy of Nonsense: The Intuitions of Victorian Nonsense Literature* (London: Routledge, 1994), pp. 44–48, 65–67. On the portmanteau in Joyce, see Derek Attridge, 'Unpacking the Portmanteau, or Who's Afraid of Finnegans Wake', in Jonathan Culler (ed.), *On Puns: The Foundation of Letters* (Oxford: Basil Blackwell, 1988), pp. 140–55.

28   Compare Carroll's composite insects, the 'Rocking-horse-fly', 'Snap-dragon-fly' and 'Bread-and-butter-fly'. Lewis Carroll, *Through the Looking-Glass and What Alice Found There* (London: Macmillan, 1971), pp. 51–53.

29   See also *Nightfisherman*, p. 210.

30   Maurice Blanchot, *The Space of Literature*, trans. Ann Smock (Lincoln, NE: University of Nebraska Press, 1982), p. 179.

31   Francis, *WPA*, pp. 66–70.

32   Cf. Jacques Derrida, *Of Grammatology*, trans. Gayatri Chakravorty Spivak (Baltimore: Johns Hopkins University Press, 1976), p. 12; Francis, *WPA*, pp. 66–70.

33   See Lopez, *PWSG*, pp. 93–94; Robert Graves, *The White Goddess: A Historical Grammar of Poetic Myth* (London: Faber and Faber, 1952), p. 24.

34   See Ferdinand de Saussure, *Course in General Linguistics*, ed. Charles Bally and Albert Sechehaye, with the collaboration of Albert Riedlinger, trans. Roy Harris (London: Duckworth, 1983), pp. 13–14 (where *langue* is translated as 'language' and *parole* as 'speech').

35   'Notes on a Poetry of Release', reprinted in *Nightfisherman*, pp. 379–83 (380).

36   Saussure, *Course in General Linguistics*, p. 118.

37   See Derrida, *Of Grammatology*, p. 151.

38 See also Lopez, *PWSG*, pp. 81–82.

39 Sigmund Freud, *Analysis of a Phobia in a Five-Year-Old Boy*, in *Case Histories 1: 'Dora' and 'Little Hans'*, trans. Alix and James Strachey, ed. Angela Richards, Penguin Freud Library, VIII (Harmondsworth: Penguin, 1977), pp. 167–305 (291).

40 *Nightfisherman*, p. 379.

41 See Francis, *WPA*, pp. 181–91.

42 See Roland Barthes, *S/Z*, trans. Richard Miller (London: Jonathan Cape, 1975), p. 4.

From **To My Wife at Midnight**

Are you to say goodnight
And turn away under
The blanket of your delight?

Are you to let me go
Alone to sleep beside you
Into the drifting snow?

Where we each reach,
Sleeping alone together,
Nobody can touch.

Is the cat's window open?
Shall I turn into your back?
And what is to happen?

What is to happen to us
And what is to happen to each
Of us asleep in our places?

[...]

Are you asleep I say
Into the back of your neck
For you not to hear me.

Are you asleep? I hear
Your heart under the pillow
Saying my dear my dear

My dear for all it's worth.
Where is the dun's moor
Which began your breath?

7

Dependence in the Poetry of W.S. Graham

PETER ROBINSON

I

Reviewing *The Nightfishing* in 1956, James Dickey wrote that W.S. Graham was 'the most individual and important young poet now writing in English'.[1] Graham was then 38 years old. His poetry, and his literary life, would seem to have been expressions of independence. In a review of *The White Threshold* from 1950, Edwin Morgan saw Graham as remaining 'undistracted and unwooed', while Calvin Bedient in 1974 assumed that '[his] cultivated eccentricity argues the right to stand alone'.[2] But independence had its price. Others have seen Graham's poetry, at least up to *The Nightfishing* (1955), as only too dependent on the voice of Dylan Thomas. Kenneth Allott, on the basis of that volume, grudgingly accepted that 'W.S. Graham is probably a poet, although one who cherishes some bad poetic habits and is excessively literary'.[3] Edward Lucie-Smith was not much warmer, putting Graham's independence, which he implies is mere isolation, down to unfortunate coincidences of publishing.[4] He makes Graham's reputation painfully dependent on the tides of literary fashion. So when Morgan wrote of Graham's 'undeviating and dangerous single-mindedness', was it challengingly 'dangerous' for the reader, or damagingly thus for the poet and his poetry's reception?[5]

The solitude of independence can be bracing, but also chilly. Damian Grant describes Graham as 'concerned with putting into words those sudden desolations and happiness that descend on us uninvited there where we each are within our lonely rooms never really entered by anybody else and from which we never emerge'.[6] For Graham, life appears an imposed independence, from which release may be sought in poetry. His brief manifesto, published in 1946, is called 'Notes on a Poetry of Release'. In this aloneness and isolation of the self, Graham's poetry finds an irreducible condition, but the actions of his poems, recognizing and speaking from that solitude, shape communicating messages that are emblems of aloneness, potentially relieved. This project continually comes up against questions of dependence and independence – questions that Graham's chosen way of life also highlighted.

If independence has its price, for Graham, who dedicated himself singlemindedly to his poetry, it was one that others would also have to pay, not least Nessie Dunsmuir, his wife. Here is one dependence in independence, and Graham's letters exemplify it in detail. Writing to Sven Berlin on 12 March 1949, he reported that '[t]hings are at their worst ever financially and it will be a fight to keep out of a job of some kind', adding later in the letter that '[a]fter this I write to London to try to borrow £10 to pay the back rent here' (*Nightfisherman*, p. 87). Things never got much better, though they were mitigated by several supporters, such as the painters John Minton, Roger Hilton and Bryan Wynter, by Harold Pinter and the poet Robin Skelton, who bought manuscripts on a regular basis. On his 1974 reading tour of Canada, Graham offended his supporter, with temporarily difficult results, as is made clear in a letter to Bill and Gail Featherston:

> I think I've fucked myself with Robin and he has stopped the money. (Say nothing to Robin. He will probably tell you.) I think all along the line I was compelled to be 'agin' and I couldn't help it. Bill, I've written him and said that I would like to do our MALAHAT and I hope his anger doesn't extend to stopping that. Now, Bill, do not broach the money subject with Robin. I mean the £25 a month he has been paying me for the last year for MSS and all the notebooks. I must have been daft, Ness says. Why didn't I just keep my trap shut. OK OK OK
>
> (*Nightfisherman*, pp. 269–70)

Here, a person who *is* fiercely independent, but whose chosen course has forced him inevitably to depend upon patrons and friends, has experienced embarrassing ambivalences and conflicts, which may well have emerged on his Canadian tour. Graham's letters are frequently exercises in managing the shame of having to cadge and maintaining the self-esteem that is simultaneously being attacked by the need to borrow.

In a letter that begins by informing Skelton of the death of the poet's friend, Bryan Wynter, and which admits to being drunk in the morning, Graham concludes with a characteristic attempt to express a connective feeling and to reserve an autonomous toughness:

> Rob, I go to the funeral on Saturday. Who shall I be? Shall I put on the intense face or the concealing face or the interesting face? Did I like him? Did I love him? Were you in Canada when I was there? Give me a hug across the sea.

> Sylvia, give me a wee kiss. I am not really sentimental. I am as hard as
> Greenock shipbuilding nails.
>
> *(Nightfisherman*, p. 288)

The role-playing in this, messy as it is, can be assumed from the series of
questions about the kind of face he will wear at Wynter's funeral. Yet
more vulnerably exposed, in a 27 June 1972 letter from Cornwall to his
wife in Scotland, Graham wrote: 'I miss you more than I can tell you. To
be without you here is some experience of something. It is not that I am a
weak man. I have my strong side somewhere if only I could find it'
(*Nightfisherman*, p. 111). What makes this more convincingly self-descriptive
is that it contrasts 'weak' and 'strong' qualities of the self, rather than
'sentimental' and 'hard' aspects of a social performance. While the poet's
dependent vulnerability may be revealed in the letter to his wife, it is
frequently coped with by travesty and denial in his correspondence with
others.

Graham's idiom for addressing interlocutors in the poems, his first-
name terms, his 'my boy' and 'my dear', is similarly touched with a gauche
instability – an instability that stands in self-critical relation to both his
recorded social behaviour and his epistolary style.[7] One of the most
dramatic instances of a stylistic instability, its oscillation between a
piercingly overdone tenderness and a cold-faced denial, is in a letter of 15
April 1973 to the Duncans:

> Here I am. Alone in this place and I write to you across the night shires of
> England. Do I like you both because I am alone awake in my night
> surrounded house? I dont know. You might be something. Who knows? At
> least I make you to myself something now. Tall shy Ronnie. Compact, easy to
> love, Henriette. My dears, here I am sitting at my great creative typewriter
> typing my life away for some reason. Dont be so daft. I am only trying to
> speak 'from one aloneness to another.'
>   I have a tenor singing the best aria from Turandot and it is turning my
> brain to slush. So sweet, so good. That is all right. Hold me in your four arms,
> you two. Come my dearest dears. Enough. Finis.

Vertically up the margin beside this passage, Graham wrote: 'Do not read
this letter as a softness. I am as hard as fucking nails.'[8] Yet there is a
softness, a weakness, a vulnerability, both within the letter itself and in
Graham's felt need to annotate it with the cliché 'hard as nails', plus the
expletive as an intensifier.

Graham's letters suggest that there are weaker and stronger conditions
of dependence. The weaker exists where bodily life is compelled by

reliance upon something – drink, for example – whose effect on the desiring body when received can be largely predicted. There is a causal relationship between the stimulant and its effects. The word's second meaning in the *OED* is: 'the relation of having existence conditioned by the existence of something else'. A baby has such a dependence on its mother's body; it is in '[the] condition of being a dependant', which is the *OED*'s third meaning and extends to 'subjection' or 'subordination'. A prisoner is in an enforced dependence on his guards. If the word is used to express relations between autonomous adults in society, dependence will involve greater risk, for the effects of others upon whom we depend are less predictable than mother's milk, a prisoner's food or a drinker's bottle. Whether or not the provision of these needs can be relied on is another matter. 'You can depend on me' also implies that the undependability of others is ever-present and must be fended off by an assurance that a promise, for example, will be kept.

That life repeatedly involves depending and being dependent on others implies that the word can describe relations where the effect or character of that upon which we depend is uncertain. The *OED*'s fifth meaning takes this condition of dependence within uncertainty to an extreme limit: 'the condition of resting in faith or expectation (upon something)' and it then cites Jowett: 'Living [...] in dependence on the will of God'. The ways of God are not revealed to us and cannot be presumed upon even by the most faithful of the faithful. This fifth sense is crucial to Graham's poetry, for that lonely room 'never really entered by anybody else and from which we never emerge' leaves relations with other people dependent on hope, trust, and varying degrees of a necessarily risk-laden confidence. Graham's letters exemplify on almost every page an acute awareness of the dangers involved in the expression of relationship.[9]

Three principal and related areas of dependence can be seen in Graham's work: dependence upon words; dependence upon an inter-locutor; and dependence upon a reader. Yet with his poetry the direction of dependence may equally be reversed: language dependent upon its users; listeners dependent upon what they are in the process of hearing; readers dependent upon the poet. Dependence in his poetry is strong for two reasons: because it does not rely upon knowing or assuming the nature or effects of that on which it depends; and because, since the direction of dependence can be reversed, the interdependence of both presupposes not the subjection or subordination of the *OED*'s third meaning, but an equality of trust and reliance upon each other in uncertainty.

Graham's work also explores, however, a ranging awareness of weak dependences: there are poems that include childhood and parental relations, several that inhabit or refer to prisons and asylums, and many that touch on drinking.[10] His poetry seeks the creation of a strong dependence out of those weak relationships. Graham's explorations of mutual dependence subsume his 'right to stand alone' into a poetic context strengthened by the acknowledgement of a primary human need for relationship. Relationship is all the more necessary and bracing for Graham because it occurs in poems attentive to the chill conditions that isolate us from each other. In maturity, weak dependences may be indications of damage or unmitigated vulnerability; Graham's poems work to transform the weak into the strong.

II

Such a project is complex for a poet particularly because the poet's dependence on the sound of words can appear irretrievably 'weak'. In Tennyson's lines from *The Princess*, 'The moan of doves in immemorial elms, / And murmuring of innumerable bees,'[11] readers are to imagine the bees humming and to cherish the skill with which the poet has collocated 'immemorial', 'murmuring' and 'innumerable'. These words have nothing in themselves to do with bees, and it is this gratuitousness in the sound patterns of poems that can be thought demeaning. In his 'Conversation about Dante' (1933–34), Osip Mandelstam describes the sound of *Inferno* 32 as having a 'deliberately shameless, intentionally infantile orchestration'.[12] It includes the line: 'né da lingua che chiami mamma e babbo' ('nor for a tongue that cries mamma and papa').[13] Mandelstam thinks the canto imitates the sound of a baby calling without shame – it appearing shameful for a grown man to make sounds like 'chiami mamma'. Rather than bees, Tennyson's lines might echo 'seventeen-months-old Christine', as reported in Dorothy Burlingham and Anna Freud's *Young Children in Wartime* (1942), 'who said: "Mum, mum, mum, mum, mum" [...] continually in a deep voice for at least three days'.[14] The extent of a poet's dependence on the sound of words (and it is this aspect that, to differing degrees, marks the poet out from all other writers) may express a preserved residuum of feeling related to the complete dependence of a baby on a mother for food and well-being. Poets are fed by the nature of their mother tongue.

The revulsion that some readers experience from Dylan Thomas's music may be explained by the poet's dependence on the sounds of words: Thomas's poetry can be felt to reveal a weak subjection to verbal music, a helplessness that relies on auditory power alone to restore the bliss of a satisfied infant. The more the poem appears to coordinate sounds for their own sake, at the expense or in excess of purposeful conceptual speech, the worse embarrassment may become.

José Ortega y Gasset has contrasted the pleasure of being drunk with that of winning in a sweepstake, to illustrate his point that '[an] aesthetic pleasure must be a seeing pleasure'. Ortega notes: 'The drunken man's happiness is blind. Like everything in the world it has a cause, the alcohol; but it has no motive. A man who has won a sweepstake is happy, too, but in a different manner; he is happy "about" something.'[15] Graham's poem 'Press Button to Hold Desired Symbol' from *Malcolm Mooney's Land* (1970) links drinking, gambling and writing poetry, and inquires which of them may produce the greatest 'seeing pleasure'.

The poem describes Garfield Strick playing the fruit machine in his pub, the King William the Fourth in Madron, Cornwall:

King William the Fourth's electric One
Armed Bandit rolls its eyes to Heaven.
Churchtown Madron's Garfield Strick
Stands at the moment less than even[.]

The following stanzas encourage him to keep on trying although he's losing, and although while the pictures of fruit expensively whirl his 'wife is stirring jam at home'. Graham's quatrains rhyme on second and fourth lines, and the 'chances of rhyme', as Charles Tomlinson has called them, are brought into analogous relation to the chances of the machine paying up.[16] The poem sketches a sense of Strick's dependence on these wheels of fortune with its references to 'the worship of his eye', 'the orchard of magic seed', and the 'oracle' that 'rolls / Its eyes too fast for him to read'. The poem ends with the flush of drinkers in the pub being surprised by Strick's flush of success:

King William the Fourth pays out
With a line of clattering oranges.
Garfield turns. His glass shatters
Its shape in our astonished gaze.

In the high air on thin sticks
The blanched rags in the wind blow.

The brass cylinder turns round
Saying I know I know I know.
(*CP*, p. 168)

Unlike the drink in the glass, whose alcohol has its cause and effect relation through brain chemistry, the flush of the gambler's success has a relation to skill, as is underlined by Graham's imperative title: 'Press Button to Hold Desired Symbol'. Thus, the gambler's winning can be a seeing pleasure, despite not being able to read the fruit because it spins too fast, because the luck of the payout is interwoven with Strick's best efforts at judgement and the speed of hand that the fruit machine player develops. Graham's 'Press Button to Hold Desired Symbol' draws attention to the element of luck and chance in its composition by aligning the paying out of the fruit machine with the poem's coming out – as if the knowledge of the brass cylinder was what had made the final stanza felicitously close with a row, not of oranges, but of 'I know'.

Why did Graham choose to have the winning 'line' a row of oranges, rather than plums or bells? It's much easier to rhyme on 'plums' and 'bells' than it is on 'oranges'. The difficulty of finding rhymes in English is sometimes illustrated in the handbooks by citing the notion that there is no full rhyme in the language for the word 'orange'[17] and Graham's closing rhyme in that penultimate quatrain ('oranges / gaze') is not much more than an assonance. The relationships between freedom and constraint in creative choice (and between cause and effect in produced aesthetic effects) are much more open to opportunity, unpredictability, invention and the like. Consequently, the flush of success when a poem comes right is that much more 'seeing' than is the case in gambling. The number of elements that have been brought into concord, and significant discord, by human skill is incalculably greater. There is, as it were, so much more to see in the seeing pleasure.

Even with the so-called 'chances of rhyme', the fact that concepts and ideas are associated by homophonic associations is not, at the level of a poet's creative life, a matter of chance at all. As Wittgenstein observed: 'It is an accident that "last" rhymes with "fast". But it is a lucky accident, & you can discover this lucky accident.'[18] Similarly, it is, for a serious poet in French, perhaps an unlucky accident that 'amour' rhymes so well with 'toujours', or, looked at as opportunity rather than constraint, a lucky accident that in English there are so few full rhymes for 'love'. Yet such relations of sound and sense are not matters of luck, but judgement. Wittgenstein's word in the original German for 'lucky' is, in fact, 'glücklich', which could be translated more felicitously as 'happy': a 'happy accident'. The happiness or luck involved here depends on the poet's having a vast repertoire of competences in the relationships offered by the sounds and meanings of words. Thus, dependence of the poet on the medium, words, is a mutual dependence, for the words are entirely dependent on the medium of the poet for finding their happiest and most memorable auditory and semantic combinations.

III

The complexities of interdependence in the field of composition are matched by those in the field of reading and its aesthetic pleasures. The experience of discussing a poem's auditory components, and attributing meaning to them, suggests that the fluidity of pronunciation, accent, stress, pitch and tone makes it dangerous for poet and critic alike to depend too confidently on how the poem will sound in another's ear, or on what responses this hearing may or may not prompt. Michael Schmidt has noticed that '[f]rom an early attitude of complete trust in words [Graham] grew more cautious with them, introducing discipline and distance between them'.[19] Later work contains numerous poems that explore the poet's dependence on words, which assume that words are not to be relied on like so many units of alcohol. Part 8 of 'Approaches to How They Behave' from *Malcolm Mooney's Land* begins: 'And what are you supposed to say / I asked a new word but it kept mum' (*CP*, p. 172). Dependence on words which live independently of the writer is an irreducible difficulty and condition of writing poetry.

The temptation to retreat from this fact is referred to in 'Notes on a Poetry of Release', where, reminding himself of Mallarmé's advice to the painter and amateur sonneteer Edgar Degas ('Mais, Degas, ce n'est point avec des idées que l'on fait des vers [...] *C'est avec des mots*'), Graham states: 'The most difficult thing for me to remember is that a poem is made of words and not of the expanding heart, the overflowing soul, or the sensitive observer. A poem is made of words' (*Nightfisherman*, pp. 379–80).[20] Damian Grant wrote that the poet's early work shows 'Graham drunk with words'. Similarly, Schmidt describes early Graham as 'word-drunk' and 'in the thrall of Dylan Thomas'.[21] With these descriptions, Graham is likened to a prisoner and a drinker, going to words as to a bottle of whisky and to Thomas's poetry as to a plate of food pushed under a door, weakly dependent on them.

'Explanation of a Map' in *2ND Poems* (1945) shows some of the difficulties in this respect produced by Graham's early work:

> My word
> Knows mister and missus, measure and live feature,
> So fume and jet of the floor and all its towns
> Wording the world awake and all its suns.
>
> (*CP*, pp. 29–30)

Graham was trained as an engineer and many of his poems have the separateness of made objects. Yet it is the construction of these lines from 'Explanation of a Map' that causes dissatisfaction. A large claim is voiced in 'My word / Knows' and it is not substantiated by the analogical sound effects standing in for the substance of the world, as in 'mister and missus, measure and live feature'; the alliteration and internal part-rhyme feel like words snatched at and settled for. Not 'Wording the world awake', they lull to enchant with a gesture at wholeness: 'and all its towns', 'and all its suns'.

The much-reiterated comparison between Graham and Dylan Thomas is partly mistaken. Thomas's word music is frequently occasioned by a well-signalled, if vague, theme: innocence, mortality, the continuum of nature and human life. 'Poem in October' enthrals with simple words and cadences:

> These were the woods the river and sea
> > Where a boy
> > In the listening
> Summertime of the dead whispered the truth of his joy
> To the trees and the stones and the fish in the tide.[22]

The last line of anapaests demonstrates a simple dependence on rhythmic predictability. Graham tends not to give readers the purchase of a general thematic concern, and neither do separate objects become so easily part of a rhythmic surge.[23]

'Here next the Chair I was when Winter Went', for instance, from *Cage without Grievance* (1942), touches the standard themes of love and death:

> So still going out in the morning of ash and air
> My shovel swings. My tongue is a sick device.
> Fear evening my boot says. The chair sees iceward
> In the bitter hour so visible to death.
>
> (*CP*, p. 19)

Graham's best mature work has a similarly discrete movement in short
sentences between particulars, as here from 'My shovel' to 'My tongue',
'my boot' and 'The chair'. These lines depend far less than 'Poem in
October' on overt sound effects to give form; the things are not bound up
into an incantatory unity that would rob them of their separate existences.
The 'device' / 'iceward' rhyme of a final and a penultimate syllable, for
example, hints that every act of speech moves the speaker nearer to the
grave. The poet speaks and walks towards the end of the day, the disappearance of light, a cold darkness in which death can still see to snatch
at him. The movement of the poem announces a thread of being: quiet,
undemonstrative, and with plenty of space for thought to live between the
sentences, as between the words, allowing the reader's mind into a process
of pondering, moving on and returning. This is one value in a poem's
resistance to ready thematic absorption, as Graham wrote in 'Notes on a
Poetry of Release': 'The meaning of a poem is itself, not less a comma. But
then to each man it comes into new life. It is brought to life by the reader
and takes part in the reader's change. Even the poet as a man who searches
continually is a new searcher with his direction changing at every step'
(*Nightfisherman*, p. 382). For there to be 'change at every step' recognized
and performed in a poem, there must be memory of previous states, and a
memory for the sounds of words that have come before.

It is this desire to change as he goes that distinguishes Graham's
rhythms from those of Dylan Thomas. Thomas's lines are rhythmically
deft and flexible, but also firmly determined, as in the close of 'Fern
Hill':

> Oh as I was young and easy in the mercy of his means,
>   Time held me green and dying
> Though I sang in my chains like the sea.[24]

Security is again found in a line of anapaests. Their chant is firmfooted.
Graham's rhythm moves with a lighter, exploratory tread. Here is the first
sentence of 'Since All My Steps Taken', the opening poem of *The White
Threshold* (1949):

> Since all my steps taken
> Are audience of my last
> With hobnail on Ben Narnain
> Or mind on the word's crest
> I'll walk the kyleside shingle
> With scarcely a hark back

To the step dying from my heel
Or the creak of the rucksack.
(*CP*, p. 47; *WT*, p. 9)

The poet's steps, Bedient notes, 'listen to themselves', and he adds: 'even
as the venturer resolves not to hark back, he yet does, perhaps must'.[25] The
poem moves to touch on 'All journey, since the first / Step from my father
and mother', and depends upon its auditory process. It is attending to its
own past. Yet in the lightness of Graham's rhythmic tread there is a
dependence that is neither shameful nor demeaning, because each note
walks apart as it is sounded together with the others. The eight lines of the
first sentence are delicately rhymed: taken / Narnain, last / crest, shingle /
heel, hark back / rucksack. The extent to which a reader harks back is
carefully modulated, though increasingly heard, as the rhymes culminate
in the slightly askew stresses on 'hark back and 'rucksack'.

A speaking, not a chanting voice in these lines lets the stresses fall
irregularly, though the poem is sure-footed enough. Graham said of his
rhythm:

> Although I love the ever-present metronome in verse, I am greedy for my
> rhythmic say. The gesture of speech often exists, moving seemingly counter to
> the abstract structure it is in. The three-accent line, not specially common in
> the body of English poetry, even a kind of straitjacket, interested me enough
> for me to keep to it for a bit and try to ring the changes within.[26]

The measure of 'Since All My Steps Taken' is the iambic trimeter, the
'three-accent line'. In shorter measures the placing of individual syllables
becomes even more crucial to rhythmic poise, and Schmidt has noticed
Graham's use of monosyllables, 'which have an isolated verbal integrity
for him'.[27] In the second line of this poem ('Are audience of my last'),
should the stress fall on the final syllable of 'audience' or on 'of' or 'my'?
This is Graham's 'gesture of speech' and only two stresses are clearly
determined, those on 'last' and the first syllable of 'audience'. In the first
line ('Since all my steps taken'), the word 'taken' wrong-foots the final,
expected iamb, becoming a trochee. The rhythm derives not so much
from an 'abstract structure' with words 'moving seemingly counter', not a
sensed underlying pattern with variations, but from a ranging voice
which, for the guidance of the reader, refers to a pattern whenever there
might appear to be none: thus, after 'taken' the iambic returns at the
beginning of the next line, is lost again, and resumes with 'my last'. The
reader cannot depend upon Graham's most characteristic rhythms as

upon a metronome. His rhythms depend to that extent upon trust. Through its rhythmic vicissitudes the poem hears voices 'walking towards that other'; harking back and hoping forward animates its form with a living process – 'the elation of being alive in the language'.[28]

IV

Graham's development into the moving poet of the later collections depended upon his courage in articulating 'the elation of being alive' and 'of being alive in the language'; in other words, his power to express the dependencies of life within the relative autonomy of his completed poems, as here in four lines from 'Letter II', published in *The Nightfishing*:

> Tonight in sadly need
> Of you I move inhuman
> Across this space of dread
> And silence in my mind.
>   (*CP*, p. 111)

James Dickey saw that '[t]here are all kinds of violence to syntax, like "tonight in sadly need," but you feel you do not need to forgive these, since many of the poet's best effects depend directly upon such wrenchings'.[29] Yet if that line 'tonight in sadly need' depends upon the peculiarity of the adverb of manner placed as if it were an adjective, the words themselves signify a dependence that is sad, and unfortunate, and a pity. It's as if to be in need of someone were itself a sorry state, or again: 'To show you need something from another person destroys any chance of receiving it.' Does the condition of need in 'Letter II' render the speaker 'inhuman'? Or is it because this is a poem speaking? Or does the speaker feel inhuman because of the evident isolation from which he seeks release?

The poem calls upon the addressed figure to come into the poem by responding, but no words return:

> O offer some way tonight
> To make your love take place
> In every word. Reply.

A few lines later, other imperatives ring with an unrelieved isolation:

>   Break
> Break me out of this night,

This silence where you are not,
Nor any within earshot.
Break break me from this high
Helmet of idiocy.

Graham's first enjambement and his penultimate line respond to a
prompt from Tennyson's desolating poem of human isolation and time's
passing, 'Break, Break, Break' . In the second part of 'Malcolm Mooney's
Land', he similarly harks back to the same poet's lyric from *The Princess*,
'The splendour falls on castle walls / And snowy summits old in story'
with 'the new ice falls from canvas walls' (*CP*, p. 143).[30] In the lines above,
his rhyme of 'are not' and 'earshot' sounds a hollow echoing note, as does
'high' and 'idiocy'. These words imply a sharp dissatisfaction on the part
of the writer with his orientation towards other people through his poems.
The urgent calling upon another, who is later revealed as a love and muse,
suggests a need for renewal that depends upon the at least tacit existence of
an interlocutor.

The original distinction I made was between a weak, subservient dependence on a known and craved-for stimulus, and the strong dependence
upon something that involves a 'condition of resting in faith or expectation'.
In 'About an Interlocutor' (1913), Mandelstam argues that addressing
living interlocutors, the poet's friends and relations as it might be, 'takes
the wings off the verse, deprives it of air, of flight. The air of a poem is the
unexpected. Addressing someone known, we can only say what is known.'[31]
Yet even those to whom we are closest remain distinctly unknowable. Just
as we cannot know the future, so we can never guarantee how the other
person will behave; as a result, speaking, a projection into the future,
necessarily involves a risk that, while it can be reduced through familiarity,
cannot be absolutely removed. This element of risk keeps the air and life
in a poem. Graham's lyrics to his wife Nessie Dunsmuir would be cases to
counter Mandelstam's idea.

In a letter dated 11 October 1950, Graham wrote from the Ortho Ward
of the Royal Cornwall Infirmary:

> All Art is the result of trying to say to an other one *exactly* what you mean.
> Because we are all each so different from each other inside (different even from
> good friends we think we are extremely sympathetic to), one of the things we
> try again and again is to establish communication. What a stuffy pompous
> lecture. FINIS.[32]

Again Graham's point is hedged about by come-off-it second thoughts.
Despite such flurries of guardedness, his mature and later poems – located

'within our lonely rooms never really entered by anybody else and from which we never emerge' – ever more directly come to express the need to achieve relationship within conditions that assume that other people remain 'all each so different from each other inside'. Other people's differences and their being unknowable increase with Graham's consciousness of identity's fluidity. His poems do not presume upon the existence or nature of the person addressed, or, if they do, they acknowledge that presumption as a danger in dependence, a dependence that in Graham's poems more usually rests upon the insecurities of hope and expectation.

A tone to invoke an interlocutor appeared early. 'No, Listen, for This I Tell' from *Cage Without Grievance* doesn't let on who is being addressed. Yet since this poem is addressed neither to friends nor relations, it hardly tests Mandelstam's proposition; and the uncertainty of addressee allows the poem its distinct 'air of […] the unexpected'. Advance is marked in *The White Threshold* by the poems to inscribed interlocutors, the concluding 'Three Letters'. They are addressed respectively to Graham's brother, his father, and his mother. All three are dedicated to the memory of his mother. Many of Graham's interlocutors are the recent dead. They sustain a separation between speaker and addressee that creates a dependence within and through inevitable isolation. In these poems and in Graham's later elegies for Peter Lanyon and Bryan Wynter, 'The Thermal Stair' and 'Dear Bryan Wynter', Graham's work has inhabited and explored the isolation of the voice within its own realm. Its aloneness sounds in the fictive question forms of 'Dear Bryan Wynter' ('Do you want anything? / Where shall I send something?'). These are not rhetorical questions because answers are not presumed in their structure, tone or context, and they are not functional questions because they could not conceivably be answered. Yet how distinctly they invoke the interlocutor's present absence, expressing a need that is answered to only by the calling itself, only by the still poem speaking.

These recognitions in Graham's later work appear in the deepening solitude of his love poems for Nessie Dunsmuir. The first of these, 'Except Nessie Dunsmuir' from *2ND Poems*, is not addressed to her:

Call what the earth is quiet on her equal face
That has a mouth of flowers for the naked grave
Sucking my thumb and the mill of my pinched words
In the dumb snecked room chiming dead in my ear.
Now time sooner than love grows up so high
Is now my warfare wife locked round with making.

(*CP*, p. 43)

The second-person address would be crucial to Graham's development, for the experimental confidence of these lines banishes from the poem's texture much of the feeling for a context, or circumstance, which it strains to voice. 'Is now my warfare wife locked round with making' may imply some trouble and strife for a woman married to a poet, but the assurance of 'making' turns 'warfare' and 'locked round' into instances of its own inspirational force and self-importance. There is reflexivity in 'locked round with making', for while the phrase may describe the domestic context of a poet's wife, it also describes the woman in the poem itself. Yet 'her equal face' and 'a mouth of flowers' appear to issue from need.

The second-person address of 'I Leave This at Your Ear' from *Malcolm Mooney's Land* creates a notional space in which the poet's wife rests, and, because in a lyric poem the 'you' addressed cannot usually answer, this supposed place is also a landscape that the poet cannot enter. The lyric voice of a second-person address calls into life another unheard voice that it can never be; Graham's poems of this kind, like his questions that do not presume or imply an answer, depend not on describing or prescribing what the addressee should be like, but on finding her inviolable and inscrutable:

> I leave this at your ear for when you wake,
> A creature in its abstract cage asleep.
> Your dreams blindfold you by the light they make.
>
> The owl called from the naked-women tree
> As I came down by the Kyle farm to hear
> Your house silent by the speaking sea.
>
> I have come late but I have come before
> Later with slaked steps from stone to stone
> To hope to find you listening for the door.
>
> I stand in the ticking room. My dear, I take
> A moth kiss from your breath. The shore gulls cry.
> I leave this at your ear for when you wake.
>
> (*CP*, p. 157)

The second line, 'A creature in its abstract cage asleep', relates ambiguously to two possible antecedents: it could refer to 'you', who then are 'A creature'; or it could refer to 'this', the poem. Forming a self-contained object with its enclosing rhymes on first and third lines, its repetition of first and last lines, the poem attributes wholeness to the sleeping wife. There is neglect in Graham's apologetic 'I have come late but I have come before / Later with slaked steps': the word 'slaked' might hint at drinking into the small hours on an earlier occasion, while in this instance the poet may only have neglected her because he has been devoting himself to his art, producing the poem that he now leaves at her ear. 'To hope to find you listening for the door', he writes, a man resting in faith or expectation, dependent upon a known but unknowable other person.

Collected Poems 1942–1977 closes with 'To My Wife at Midnight', another second-person address, thriving on a child-like, but not a childish, questioning of silence:

> Where we each reach,
> Sleeping alone together,
> Nobody can touch.
>
> Is the cat's window open?
> Shall I turn into your back?
> And what is to happen?
>
> What is to happen to us
> And what is to happen to each
> Of us asleep in our places?
>   (*CP*, p. 261)

Once again the enclosing rhymes of the three-line stanza (reach / touch, open / happen) separate the figures in the poem and give them wholeness. The price for this integrity is isolation. To be alive is to be alone, yet the poet's words depend upon being brought to life in readers. So long as they live within others, they make the bed in which the poet and his wife lie singularly together and inseparably apart.

V

W.S. Graham's winning tone in 'Dear Bryan Wynter' or 'To My Wife at Midnight' is a hard-won simplicity. Does this quality of directness achieved by calling upon an intimate but isolate interlocutor carry as far as the unknown reader? Can the poet's voice also invite the reader into a form of interdependent relationship? Schmidt did not see it that way when he wrote: 'Graham feels a strange hostility towards the reader, the "you" he addresses; he watches us warily, at the same time watching himself'.[33] *Aimed at Nobody*, the title given to the posthumous 'Poems from Note-books' volume, sounds, in isolation, an aggressively uncommercial note.

The poet's widow used a joke to mitigate the chosen title in her preface: 'the work of the notebooks survived his rigorous judgment and *Aimed at Nobody* affords an opportunity for "somebody" (or "nobody!") to encounter it' (*AN*, p. vii). The poet's anonymous reader is indeed like a child's Mr Nobody, but in the context of the 'Proem' from which the phrase was borrowed, Graham's words are making an issue of the 'aimed' rather more than the 'nobody', because he too qualifies its chillingly apparent indifference to readers:

> It is aimed at nobody at all.
>
> It is now left just as an object by me
> to be encountered by somebody else.
>   (*AN*, p. xi)

Aiming poems at specific people risks straitjacketing their aesthetic trajectories, and, as we have seen, Graham's sense of another's unknowability saves his addressed poems from a presuming to know that would diminish them. Being by definition unknown, the anonymous reader offers a more severe danger to the poet presupposing an audience and its nature. Here, the poem's dependence on a reader is set within a necessary unknowing, a necessarily bracing independence.

Yet Graham's tone is frequently more quizzical and entertained than hostile or blankly matter-of-fact, as in these two stanzas from 'Untidy Dreadful Table' in *Implements in their Places*:

> I sit here late and I hammer myself
> On to the other side of the paper.
> There I jump through all surprises.
> The reader and I are making faces.
>
> I am not complaining. Some of the faces
> I see are interesting indeed.
> Take your own, for example, a fine
> Grimace of vessels over the bone.
>   (*CP*, p. 198)

And in the fifth part of 'A Private Poem to Norman Macleod', what Schmidt calls the 'grandeur and humility' of isolation can be heard in Graham's changing tone:

> Remember the title. A PRIVATE
> POEM TO NORMAN MACLEOD.
> But this, my boy, is the poem

You paid me five pounds for.
The idea of me making
Those words fly together
In seemingly a private
Letter is just me choosing
An attitude to make a poem.
                (*CP*, p. 221)

The grandeur lies in the datedly upper-class idiom, 'my boy'; the humility in the childlike 'just me'. Graham is watching himself: this is neither a truly private poem which happens to have been published, nor is it aimed at a known readership. Graham brings the poem nearer to whoever reads it by speaking for a few sentences at the magazine editor who wrote inviting a contribution. Within a possible context of weak dependence, the 'five pounds', the poem gains strength from the candour with which Graham speaks to himself as to a possible listener or reader in 'Remember the title' and 'The idea of me making / Those words fly together'.

The letter of 15 April 1973 to the Duncans I commented on earlier, its oscillation between a piercingly overdone tenderness and a cold-faced denial, is not so much a tryout for the mode of the poems as a careering parody of it – a point indicated by the allusion to his own poetry of trial communications from isolation. The tonal weaknesses in the letter are wrapped up with the attempt to hold the projected natures of the interlocutors in the style: 'Tall shy Ronnie. Compact, easy to love, Henriette. My dears […]'. Graham's 'my boy' in 'But this, my boy, is the poem / You paid me five pounds for' does not fail the poem's precarious tonal balance, because no intimacy of address is being claimed. The 'my boy' expresses an edgy distance, an 'uneasiness', not a seeing eye to eye. By contrast with the 'my dearest dears' of the letter, the 'My dear' of 'My dear, I take / A moth kiss from your breath' in 'I leave this at your ear for when you wake' has identified a tender familiarity strengthened by his wife's not hearing what the poet has written until she wakes and inhabits the 'creature in its abstract cage' herself. Comparing Graham's verse addressed to interlocutors with his expressively idiosyncratic letters reveals just how much creative control of both pitch and tone the poems winningly demonstrate.

'Notes on a Poetry of Release' is much concerned with the role of the reader. 'The poem is itself dumb,' Graham writes, 'but has the power of release. Its purpose is that it can be used by the reader to find something out about himself'. He goes on: 'The poem is not a handing out of the same packet to everyone, as it is not a thrown-down heap of words for us to choose the bonniest. The poem is the replying chord to the reader. It is the reader's involuntary reply' (*Nightfisherman*, p. 381). What these last two, themselves rather inscrutable, sentences suggest is that the poem is composed as a reply to an imaginary reader. This is the case when the imaginary reader is a single interlocutor. 'I called today, Peter, and you were away', which opens 'The Thermal Stair' (*CP*, p. 154), rises upon the air of however many previous exchanges between the two men, one of whom is now truly an imaginary reader because dead. This 'replying chord to the reader' might indicate that the poem creates its ideal reader, but Graham's '[the] poem is not a handing out of the same packet to everyone' suggests rather that it is aimed at our actual, incomprehensible variousnesses – rather than a never-to-be-encountered ideal type.

Interpreting Graham's poems is not a free-for-all. 'I leave you this space / To use as your own', writes the poet in the fortieth part of 'Implements in their Places', but adds 'I think you will find / That using it is more / Impossible than making it'. The outer reaches of the not possible are stretched for here in 'more / impossible', but Graham nevertheless boldly goes for the final frontier: 'Here is the space now' and instructs the reader to 'Write an Implement in it'. There follow four lines that would require ingenuity in being read aloud:

    YOU.........................
    YOU.........................
    YOU.........................
    YOU.........................
                (*CP*, p. 246)

Graham ends the section with 'Try. Try. No offence meant', acknowledging the awkward fact that readers can't use the space as their own, and that the poet's urging them to do so is playing with a taboo in the conventions for relations between writers and readers. Yet the potential offence in Graham's behaviour lies only in his making evident on the page an impossibility that goes to the heart of the fact that responding to poems has little to do with filling in the blanks on a form. What's more, responding to them in the time-honoured fashion requires the inhabiting of certain conventions. Section 40 of 'Implements in their Places' is a hollow taunt to the reader. The poet may 'leave' us 'this space / To use as [our] own' but the gaps remain part of Graham's poem, impossible for us to use. The reader depends on the poet to fill up his own lines, and

Graham confesses that he has been playing low tricks when he concludes the section: 'Try. Try. No offence meant'. Consequently, when the poet wrote in 1946 that '[the] poem is the replying chord to the reader. It is the reader's involuntary reply' he may have meant that, reading a poem, we are not free to decide what words are used, the uttered words are involuntary in that sense, and yet, we are free to put down the book. Each person reads and intonates the poem with natural variousnesses inviolably intact; every reply will have its legitimate differences. As Graham also wrote in 'Notes on a Poetry of Release': 'Each word is touched by and filled with the activity of each speaker' (*Nightfisherman*, p. 380).

Each Graham poem depends on readers for vitality and significance. Yet readers in turn depend on the poem itself, which is their involuntary reply. They are invited to use it to find out something about themselves, for the poem, as Graham said, 'is brought to life by the reader and takes part in the reader's change'. The reader is in a position to do this because Graham has, by not defining or prescribing who they are or should be, left them with the chance to achieve what he requests for himself in the second part of 'What is the Language Using Us for?':

> I want to be able to speak
> And sing and make my soul occur
>
> In front of the best and be respected
> For that and even be understood
> By the ones I like who are dead.
>
> I would like to speak in front
> Of myself with all ears alive
> And find out what it is I want.
>
> (*CP*, pp. 192–93)

My arguing for a strong dependence on the language, on interlocutors and on readers in Graham's poetry has depended upon a listening reader. Both of us have been dependent upon the strength with which the poet followed out a direction outlined in 'Notes on a Poetry of Release' and which, in the body of his work, he fulfilled: 'It is a good direction to believe that this language which is so scored and impressed by the commotion of all of us since its birth can be arranged to in its turn impress significantly for the benefit of each individual. Let us endure the sudden affection of the language' (*Nightfisherman*, p. 383). To 'endure the sudden affection of the language': the pleasure of unexpectedly receiving warmth is characteristically tempered by its being sensed as an imposition upon us.

This, finally, is the ambivalence towards dependence which, over more than forty years, vivified the poetry that Graham 'left just as an object' and which here has been 'encountered by somebody else'.

Notes

1 James Dickey, *Babel to Byzantium: Poets and Poetry Now* (New York: Farrar, Straus, 1968), p. 45.

2 Edwin Morgan, cited by Damian Grant, 'Walls of Glass: The Poetry of W.S. Graham', in Michael Schmidt and Peter Jones (eds), *British Poetry since 1970* (Manchester: Carcanet, 1980), p. 22; Calvin Bedient, *Eight Contemporary Poets* (Oxford: Oxford University Press, 1974), p. 166.

3 Kenneth Allott, *The Penguin Book of Contemporary Verse* (Harmondsworth: Penguin, 2nd edn, 1962), p. 309.

4 Edward Lucie-Smith, *British Poetry since 1945* (Harmondsworth: Penguin, 1970), p. 103. The argument that Graham's reputation suffered at the hands of the Movement has been discussed in Lopez, *PWSG*, pp. 12–19 and Andrew Crozier, 'Thrills and Frills', in Alan Sinfield (ed.), *Society and Literature 1945–1970* (Brighton: Harvester, 2nd edn, 1983), pp. 199–33.

5 Morgan, cited in Grant, 'Walls of Glass', p. 22.

6 Grant, 'Walls of Glass', p. 28.

7 See Julian MacLaren-Ross, *Memoirs of the Forties* (1965), cited in Lopez, *PWSG*, p. 4.

8 R. Grogan (ed.), ' "Dear Pen Pal in the Distance": A Selection of W.S. Graham's Letters', *PN Review*, 73 (1990), p. 16. This letter does not appear in *The Night-fisherman*.

9 In a notebook of 1949, Graham wrote: 'To show you need something from another person destroys any chance of receiving it. People love him who does not need love' ('From a 1949 Notebook', *ER75*, p. 36). The first sentence acknowledges a need and gives advice about self-esteem and its relation to receiving what you need. The second suggests why many love a God who does not need their love. In the second sentence, Graham is making 'need' into a sign of weak dependence. A strong dependence is implied in his first sentence.

10 See 'To Alexander Graham', 'Clusters Travelling Out', 'Letter III', *CP*, pp. 113–15, 184–88, 215–16.

11 Alfred, Lord Tennyson, *The Poems of Tennyson*, ed. C. Ricks (London: Longman, 2nd edn, 1987), II, p. 288.

12 Osip Mandelstam, *Selected Essays*, trans. S. Monas (Austin, TX: University of Texas Press, 1977), p. 34.

13 Dante, *Inferno*, 32, l. 9. The translation is my own.

14 Cited by Adrian Stokes in the Preface to *Inside Out*; see Adrian Stokes, *The Critical Writings*, ed. L. Gowing (London: Thames and Hudson, 1978), II, p. 141.

15 José Ortega y Gasset, *The Dehumanization of Art and Other Writings on Art and Culture* (Garden City, NY: Doubleday Anchor, 1956), p. 25.

16 Charles Tomlinson, 'The Chances of Rhyme', in *Collected Poems* (Oxford: Oxford

University Press, 1985), pp. 194–95.

17 Graham rhymes 'orange' with 'courage' at the close of 'The Visit', *UP*, p. 17.

18 Ludwig Wittgenstein, *Culture and Value*, ed. G.H. von Wright et al. (Oxford: Blackwell, rev. edn, 1998), p. 98e.

19 Michael Schmidt, *An Introduction to 50 British Poets* (Manchester: Carcanet, 1979), p. 299.

20 Hugh MacDiarmid may be recalled here too, stating in his *Lucky Poet* (1943) that the act of poetry was 'not an idea gradually shaping itself in words, but deriving entirely from words' (quoted in Douglas Dunn [ed.], *The Faber Book of Twentieth-Century Scottish Poetry* [London and Boston: Faber and Faber, 1992], p. xxi).

21 Grant, 'Walls of Glass', p. 23; Schmidt, *50 British Poets*, p. 298. In the 1949 notebook, Graham enters beside the heading 'words' a close paraphrase of T.S. Eliot's remarks on allusiveness in his essay 'The Music of Poetry' (in *On Poetry and Poets* [London: Faber and Faber, 1957], pp. 32–33). The previous entry in the notebook quotes the essay directly. The critical self-consciousness, restraint and control implied in Eliot's remarks helped shape Graham's development.

22 Dylan Thomas, *Collected Poems 1934–1952* (London: J.M. Dent, 1952), p. 96.

23 Graham listed his major themes in J. Vinson and D.L. Kirkpatrick (eds), *Contemporary Poets* (London and New York: St Martin's Press, 1979), p. 575, but these give little away about the character of particular poems.

24 Thomas, *Collected Poems*, p. 151.

25 Bedient, *Eight Contemporary Poets*, p. 164.

26 Vinson and Kirkpatrick (eds), *Contemporary Poets*, p. 575.

27 Schmidt, *50 British Poets*, p. 299.

28 Graham's phrase for one of his principal themes, in Vinson and Kirkpatrick (eds), *Contemporary Poets*, p. 575.

29 Dickey, *Babel to Byzantium*, p. 42.

30 See *Poems of Tennyson*, II, p. 231.

31 Mandelstam, *Selected Essays*, p. 59.

32 Cited in *ER75*, p. 5; not in *Nightfisherman*. Graham was in hospital after falling off a roof and breaking his leg.

33 Schmidt, *50 British Poets*, p. 302.

From **Dear Bryan Wynter**

This is only a note
To say how sorry I am
You died. You will realise
What a position it puts
Me in. I couldn't really
Have died for you if so
I were inclined. The carn
Foxglove here on the wall
Outside your first house
Leans with me standing
In the Zennor wind.

Anyhow how are things?
Are you still somewhere
With your long legs
And twitching smile under
Your blue hat walking
Across a place? Or am
I greedy to make you up
Again out of memory?
Are you there at all?
I would like to think
You were all right
And not worried about
Monica and the children
And not unhappy or bored.

8

Achieve Further through Elegy

FIONA GREEN

When Edwin Morgan was called up to do military service in 1940 he destroyed most of his correspondence, including all but one letter from W.S. Graham. The sole survivor was a crumpled page that Morgan salvaged for his essay 'A Poet's Letters'. Edwin Morgan chose to begin the tribute to his friend with this early letter because 'it show[ed] two things which were always important to Graham: the reading aloud of poetry and the influence of music.'[1] That small remnant of correspondence is a fitting point of entry for my essay too because of the differing notes on which it begins and ends. Graham starts his letter in robust voice: 'Dear Morgan, It is indeed myself, Graham'. There is a hint of urgency to this signing on, as though Graham worried that he might not get to the end of his letter, the conventional place for signing off; and as it happened, he didn't, or didn't quite. The remains of that same message greet the reader who embarks on the nightfisherman's *Selected Letters*, and in that embodiment the note to Morgan ends like this: '... I feel I am disintegra ... [fragment of a torn page dated by E.M.]'.[2] With 'disintegra ...' Graham very nearly finishes himself off. His untimely end, and the coincidence between his own ellipsis and the editorial bracket that follows it, may have been accidental, but it would be nice to imagine that the letter had anticipated and resigned itself to the fragmentary end it was to meet in the hands of its recipient. In this epistolary version of himself gra(ham) really did disintegrate.

W.S. Graham knew the risk he took every time he committed himself to paper. The conscript sent out to cross the 'abstract scene / stretching between' poet and reader or letter writer and recipient is dispatched on a perilous mission and lives a precarious existence.[3] Knowing that he survives only at the whim of the medium that carries him, Graham resists his dissolution as often as he submits to it. His poem 'No, Listen, for This I Tell' begins with a plea for unmediated contact, but, as though slipping between the faultlines of its own script, that same poem ends in the giddy liberation of failure: 'We fall down darkness in a line of words' (*CP*, pp. 23–24). Likewise in his letters Graham often sounds like the caller who fears that the phone line has gone dead, and emphatically checks that someone is 'still there'. These contrary moods – lively self-assertion and helpless vertigo – persistently alternate in Graham's work. Buoyantly pitching up – 'it is indeed myself, Graham' – and just as often 'lost in foxes of falling down', the nightfisherman casts his perplexed and perplexing lines.[4]

Graham was dogged (and frequently foxed) by the knowledge that to 'fall down darkness in a line of words' was his writerly fate. His letters and poems are wise to the fragility of selfhood, keeping a wary vigil on the losses that come in the wake of writing. In these respects his work might seem to anticipate those theoretical discourses that are habituated to the absence on which writing is founded, and according to which the writer enters into his own death immediately he puts pen to paper. But to proceed too hastily along that familiar line of thought and to decide along with it that the human subject is well overdue for burial would be to miss on the way the best part of this discriminating and recalcitrant poet. Because Graham knew the difference between the writer's figurative demise (dying on paper) and 'going down the man-hole' (dying for real). Even though he liked to play on the canny resemblance between these two kinds of dying, his understanding of the difference between them equipped him for the kind of work that is the subject of this essay: that is, the art of losing whose poetic mode is elegy. Peter Sacks maintains that the elegist's task is to find in language not just loss itself but some compensatory mechanism whereby losses may be restored: 'the elegy [...] gives us the chance to view man in tension with, rather than inertly constituted by, the language that so conditions him'.[5] It is to that tension that Graham's poems and his letters are most alive.

Graham's poems and letters speak across to each other in several ways, one of which is simply that words sometimes travel between them. He often tried out drafts of his poems on his correspondents, and he would also tease out the meanings of epistolary phrases in the poetry, in which environment their strangeness would suddenly revive. One example of this is when his announcement 'it is myself', much used in the letters, turns up in 'The Nightfishing'. In the context of that poem the perky phrase acquires a certain gravity, awakening us to our peculiar habit of presenting ourselves by merging first and third persons: 'It is myself. / So he who died is announced. This mingling element / Gives up myself (*CP*,

p. 101). This is one of many instances in Graham's oeuvre when dying and writing do coincide, but it is as well to notice here that 'gives up' does not imply submission to the linguistic medium: the mingling element of written language offers up even as it threatens to drown the poet's crafty self. And although Graham is well versed in two arts – elegiac and epistolary – whose very existence testifies to absence, that does not inure him to loss: 'Speaking to you and not / Knowing if you are there / Is not too difficult', he writes to Bryan Wynter (*CP*, p. 255). But 'speaking to you and not' is no less hard for his having got used to it.

The writing of elegy enables as well as records the poet's work of mourning, and it is within psychoanalytic accounts of that process that theorists of elegy have most frequently framed their investigations.[6] Freud's 'Mourning and Melancholia' is much visited in these accounts, and though, as David Shaw warns us, we should be wary of assuming that good therapy necessarily makes good art (strong mourners are not always strong poets),[7] Freud's essay does offer a model of the grieving mind that transfers productively into the workings of poetic language. According to Freud, the mourner gradually withdraws his libidinal attachments from the object he has lost, and 'bit by bit' reattaches them elsewhere.[8] The elegist may find that exchange mechanism in the substitutive tropes available in the work of his predecessors, and as he draws on established literary stock he enters into a further set of transactions, inserting himself into a line of poetic inheritance. Although, unlike his modernist forebears, Graham infrequently works through direct quotation or allusion, the ghosts of literary predecessors lurk within squinting distance of his poetry, so that literary debts accrue in even the sparest of his styles. Most in his element when he is most at sea, Graham follows in the wake of elegists who have lamented 'the washed-away dead' (*CP*, p. 35). Hopkins, a persistent presence in Graham's early work, is heard especially in his 'Many Without Elegy', which sounds the depths and surfaces of *The Wreck of the Deutschland*; and there is another elegy for the drowned, Milton's 'Lycidas', that teaches Graham more generally about the ups and downs of elegiac economies.

As well as establishing a figurative balance sheet of losses and gains in his poetry, Graham was also beset by financial difficulties of a more literal kind. He was much indebted to the friends whose generosity kept him afloat until 1974, when he was awarded a civil list pension – 'which means', he said, '£500 a year till I go down the man-hole' (L 275). His correspondence is punctuated with requests for funds and thanks for those received. He wrote one such letter to John Minton in 1944. It begins, 'Cornwall winday and night 13 10 44 and the house rocks like a boat bobbing on the graves of night dear Johnny' (*Nightfisherman*, p. 26). It is a habit of Graham's to include the epistolary preliminaries (the sender's location, the date, the recipient's name) in the body of the text rather than banishing them to the sidelines. In this way 'dear Johnny' is carefully housed within the opening sentence, and the mode of address reinvested with an intimacy that most upper-case 'Dear's are denied. Brought in as it were from the outside, 'dear Johnny' is protected from the stormy weather of the wider world. It turns out that Graham's letter was a stand-in for one that had not been so safely kept:

> I wrote a letter but it's lost and with the wind but maybe someone's posted it and it's got you. I am careless but the wind is a bit furious and you know it is not hard to lose a letter some times. It said thanks for wired money and then got a bit shy about the middle and said so sorry to have to ask you Johnny and then finished with a grand flourish about getting away from here for a while and glad when fare comes. If I can remember it said those things.

This is more careful than it might seem. Graham makes up for the lost letter by making it up out of memory, and in doing so creates a small margin whereby he can distance himself from what he is asking. If his first letter had 'got a bit shy about the middle' its successor was shyer still about what it had to ask, Graham speaking by proxy of its imperson – '*it* said [...] so sorry'. And that substitutive move travels further, through to the flourish about 'getting away from here'. The one that really got away was the original letter; the fare Graham asks for will allow him to make a similar departure.

These playful substitutions make way to something more grave. 'It is not hard to lose a letter some times', Graham says, meaning both that it is not difficult and that it is no great loss. But accidental misplacement measures uneasily against a harder loss: in the postings of 1944 it was not only letters that went missing. Graham goes on,

> And I am sorry about your brother and you must feel so helpless about it. Today ten shillings came thanks. With Nessie here it's less lonely but time for me to be away for a while. Poor Nessie is so sad and worrying about Frank. I'm sad about it too and wish he and I had been more together. I hope he turns up.

Richard Minton was killed in September 1944, and Nessie Dunsmuir's friend Frank (Frantisek Koranda) had been reported missing in action

(*Nightfisherman*, p. 24 n. 4). The abrupt changes of direction and scale in Graham's letter – from the helplessness of bereavement to a matter of ten shillings – might seem a bit careless; yet there is discretion here also, in the small discrimination between an expression of apology ('it said sorry to have to ask') and one of condolence ('I am sorry about your brother'). As the lost letter may have been found, perhaps franked, and delivered of its loneliness ('maybe someone's posted it and it's got you') so perhaps Frank will also turn up; but the wartime environment makes these equivalences seem precariously balanced. The weather does not help: 'Here great gales have gone on with high white waves on the sea and the wind like a flying wall. You could be knocked down if you didn't hold on to safety somewhere. All the leaves are off and lots of growing things broken and hanging.' As the pages of his letter were 'with the wind', so 'all the leaves are off', and here I think Graham begins to put together the various losses his letter has counted in passing, and to submit them to the formal code of the elegist. Those 'growing things broken and hanging' perform in a minor key the substitutive tropes of pastoral elegy. When his friend's premature death forced Milton to 'shatter [...] leaves before the mellow-ing year' he held on to the safety of a traditional token even as he broke it apart.[9] To suggest that Graham's leaves, his 'growing things broken and hanging' are likewise figurative is not to imply they weren't also real; rather that living for most of his life at the 'very end then of land' (*CP*, p. 77), and exposed there to violent changes in the weather, Graham was well acquainted with the natural world's powers of destruction and renewal, and provided with ample resources that might be cashed into the exchange mechanisms of pastoral elegy.

The poems in Graham's first volume, *Cage Without Grievance* (1942), dress themselves in 'pastoral and camouflage of wars'.[10] When Edwin Morgan received his copy, it seemed to him that Graham had chosen to take refuge in an abstract landscape too far removed from the reality of global conflict: 'I read it when I was in the Forces, in Egypt. I was disappointed by the collection, and wrote to say so. It may be that my feeling that the contents were escapist was unfairly sharpened by a consciousness of my own position in the middle of the desert campaign'.[11] One can see why, from that position, Morgan might have found some-thing escapist in the lush verbiage of lines such as 'Who longingly for violetcells prospect the meads' (*CP*, p. 15), or, as he put it in a phrase that Graham seems to have taken to heart, thought them 'unreal, without meaning, severed from true and naked emotion'.[12] Graham did not enlist his poetry conspicuously in the service of contemporary events, nor address it to a reading public who could be 'a bit certain they [were] not being hoaxed (for here is something we can understand)'. He knew that the experiential difference between himself and Morgan caused misunderstanding, that his explanations could not 'touch the other side of the territory where you simply find my poetry shy of true thought' (*Nightfisherman*, p. 14). Nevertheless he did muster a defence of his own side in his reply to Morgan, distinguishing his chosen vehicle from the kind of 'nice rivetted up wagon' that would have offloaded a more marketable message for the reading public: 'the poets set up fishops to sell fish to the people who want fish and they all call the fish poetry and the fishmongers they call poets. And poetry is not fish but another stuff entirely. People want always to do with the stuff they can weigh, the mapped part where things always fall down and never fall up into Heaven' (*Nightfisherman*, p. 15). Graham falls down often in his letters, or falls apart and pulls himself back together. But the thought that he wanted his poems to fall *up* is especially pertinent to one kind of elegy. The consolation offered by elegies for the drowned (of which 'Lycidas' is the paradigm) is the promise that what goes down will at last come up.

In his letter to John Minton, Graham brought into proximity two distinct kinds of loss: the mislaying of a letter and the death of a brother. To mistake one of these for the other would be more than a bit careless. The bereaved are unlikely to be consoled by the thought that the dead might turn up. But when someone drowns, misplacement and bereavement do coincide: the drowned are doubly lost – temporarily misplaced as well as permanently absent. Only when the elegist has located the body and brought it home to a recognizable landscape (in Milton's case, to the landscape of pastoral) can the funeral rites be conducted. Poetic ritual is but 'false surmise' (l. 153) while the body is adrift. So Lycidas is prone to the whethers that keep Milton's grammar suspended:

> Whether beyond the stormy Hebrides
> Where thou perhaps under the whelming tide
> Visit'st the bottom of this mounstrous world;
> Or whether thou to our moist vows denied,
> Sleep'st by the fable of Bellerus old,
>
> (ll. 156–60)

Graham's wartime poem for 'the washed-away dead' is 'Many Without Elegy' (*CP*, p. 35), a title that, buoyed by its internal rhyme, floats free of his characteristically troublesome syntax. To follow the drift of that title is to expect a poem dedicated to the Many whom death has undone, but whose position has yet to be mapped within the coordinates of poetic convention. Yet when Graham's poem begins again, repeating its title in the first line, 'Many without elegy' takes an unexpected direction:

Many Without Elegy

Many without elegy interpret a famous heart
Held with a searoped saviour to direct
The land. This morning moves aside
Sucking disaster and my bread
On the hooped fields of Eden's mountain
Over the crews of wrecked seagrain.

There they employ me.

Once 'Many' is roped in as the subject of 'interpret', its referent shifts. The Manys that preside over the poem and structure it, beginning alternate stanzas, no longer refer to the unmourned dead, but to a lively community of workers who 'interpret', 'dig', 'project', labouring to fathom loss 'without elegy'. The last line I have quoted seems to know where it is: 'There they employ me' takes a sense of place as given, yet were we to ask of the first stanza exactly *where* Graham is employed we would find ourselves at a loss. Whereas 'held with a searoped saviour' promises secure anchorage, the syntax presents a surplus of internal connections (does 'held' attach itself to 'Many' or to 'famous heart'?); and if 'to direct / the land' points towards a well-governed environment, the syntactic difficulty is compounded by a problem of reference: is the saviour a *genius loci* presiding over the landscape, or does 'land' identify him as an earthly director of the nation? On this kind of inspection, the syntactic rigging of the stanza harbours meaning to itself, keeping reference somewhere in the offing.

If Graham's poem gives too little and too much in the way of syntactic steerage and referential guidance, we might do better to get our bearings from its literary affiliations. 'The hooped fields of Eden's Mountain' might, like Milton's Satan, have in prospect a rural mound, its summit rounded by 'a circling row / Of goodliest trees',[13] from which lofty place, 'over the crews of wrecked seagrain' plunges into a compression of Hopkins's startling question in *The Wreck of the Deutschland*: 'is the ship-wrack then a harvest, / does tempest carry the grain for thee?'[14] It is the compound 'seagrain' that finds many kin in Hopkins, and Graham's 'held with a searoped saviour' has also taken direction from the fourth section of *The Wreck*:

I steady as water in a well, to a poise, to a pane,
But roped with, always, all the way down from the tall
    Fells or flanks of the voel, a vein
Of the gospel proffer, a pressure, a principle, Christ's gift.

Hopkins's aural gifts – his running in these lines all the way down from
'well' through 'always / all / tall / fells' – proffer much to Graham's early
poetry, and in 'Many Without Elegy' he takes soundings like these from
The Wreck, washing them through the end of the second stanza:

There they employ me. I rise to the weed that harps
More shipmark to capsizing, more to lament
Under the whitewashed quenched skerries
The washed-away dead. Hullo you mercies
Morning drowns tail and all the bells
Bubble up rigging as the saint falls

The 'I' here is variously employed: rising as if from underwater, it finds
itself entangled at the surface, vested in the weeds of mourning. At the
same time, just beneath 'rise to the weed' lies the cliché 'rise to the task', as
though the poem's taskmasters were those elegists for the drowned in
whose wake Graham writes. To follow that lineage is to harp on an old
theme, and 'harp' can be transitive too: to harp something is to bring it
out, often from below and especially from the dead.[15] But instead of
bringing the dead to the surface, the stanza tips over, capsizing into a
lamentation top-heavy with sound effects. In 'hullo' we hear the bottom
of the ship uppermost, and as bubbles of sound rise up the rigging, sense
drowns into a muted hull-ell-ou-lia. From this Hopkins-like sea-romp,
the last line, 'Bubble up rigging as the saint falls', tips over to invert the
controlled reciprocity that lifted Lycidas: 'sunk low, but mounted high'
(l. 172). Along the way, 'Many' has multiplied ('More / more / morning')
so that rather than raise a singular body, Graham's capsized craft visits the
bottom of the monstrous world, producing yet more to lament.

'Many Without Elegy' moves up to and down from the weedy surface.
It also moves laterally, as in 'This morning moves aside'. That sideways
motion is glimpsed again in the third stanza:

Many dig deeper in joy and are shored with
A profit clasped in a furious swan-necked prow
To sail against spout of this monumental loss
That jibles with no great nobility its cause.
That I can gather, this parched offering
Of a dry hut out of wrong weeping.

'Jibles' catches the eye and ear by its strangeness. One snag is over pronun-ciation – whether it would rhyme with quibbles or Bibles. The proximity of 'jibles' to 'nobility' gives the short *i* the benefit of that doubt, and though 'jibles' is a stranger to the *OED*, Scots dialect has something close to it: 'to jibble' is 'to spill (a liquid) by agitating its container'.[16] Agitating somewhere between gibber and babble, jible sounds like a trivial thing to do in the face of monumental loss. The poem's nautical lexicon also wants us to preserve 'jib', the small sail which, swung from one side of the craft to the other, steers a course against the prevailing wind. 'Jibles', then, gathers both the spillage of 'spout' and 'wrong weeping', and the means to sail against them. In this small way the poem refuses to range its equipment on one side or the other of an argument about the proper way to mourn, but tacks in and out of the various directions of elegy.

While steering a tactical course between and around these procedures, 'Many Without Elegy' accumulates a weight of negatives (as in '*no* great *no*bility') and these are thrown into relief when, in the final stanza, the crowded syllables suddenly thin out:

> [...] No I'll inherit
> No keening in my mountainhead or sea
> Nor fret for few who die before I do.

Caught between religious consolation and 'the outworn theme' of reason purged of faith, Matthew Arnold exclaimed, 'the nobleness of grief is gone – / Ah, leave us not the fret alone!'[17] Having done with spouted grief 'with no great nobility its cause', Graham leaves us not a lonesome fret, but a sharp dismissal of the debts the poem has accrued, and a decision to give up the whole thing as a bad business. 'Many' reduces to 'few', giving the last line a pivot around which to balance itself, so that in the end Graham's poem closes not with a commemoration of the dead, but with a line that commends *itself* to memory.

In among the tangled cordage of 'Many Without Elegy' hang these lines:

> Gone to no end but each man's own.
> So far they are, creation's whole memory
> Now never fears their death or day.

'Gone to no end' begins to string out the line of a solitary life, running the hope of its not finishing in parallel with a doubt over purpose: departed yet not finished, or died for no good cause? The caesural 'but' undoes that snag, turning the line to face its dead end in 'each man's own'. Next to this, 'So far they are' steps back to gain a broader perspective on loss: 'creation's whole memory' opens onto the grand vantage of geological time which holds each singular death or day in its preserving scope. The longer view of 'creation's whole memory' recalls the stanza towards which the whole of *In Memoriam* moves:

> That God, which ever lives and loves,
>   One God, one law, one element,
>   And one far-off divine event,
> To which the whole creation moves.[18]

The weary way of Tennyson's grieving did not finish at the end of his poem. Instead, as it moved towards that 'one far-off divine event' the closing stanza held its resolution in distant prospect.[19] Graham's memorable last line ('Nor fret for few who die before I do') sounds like a decision to set things aside rather than see them through. Closer to Tennyson's postponing hope are the opening lines of his last stanza: 'Here as the morning moves my eyes achieve / Further through elegy', where the unpunctuated syntax leaves 'my eyes' open to behave as both object and subject – 'the morning moves my eyes' giving out as 'my eyes achieve' takes over. Graham remembered those curious lines in a letter to Bill Montgomerie, where he quoted them to exemplify an aspect of his poetic technique: '[in] "my eyes achieve further through elegy" [...] the word "achieve" does its dictionary meaning and also suggests the word "move"' (*Nightfisherman*, p. 21). Were it to do its dictionary meaning properly, 'achieve' would carry a sense of finality. But 'achieve *further*' lets completion slip a little so that 'move', readily available nearby ('the morning moves'), sidles in. And given the usual doings of eyes, there is yet one more tempting substitution: we surely want to read 'my eyes *see* further through elegy'. These several alternatives – 'my eyes achieve / move / see further through elegy' – shift around one another, as though in the suspended animation of the restless drowned, so that the spliced line reels in a network of definitions: a set of conventions whereby to move others, the elegy also offers a process through which the mourner himself can move, making further progress towards the end of grief. In the end Graham's achievement was not to do *without* elegy, but to see *further through* it: he would manage in later years to see what it was up to, and at the same time to discover in it a lens that brought personal loss into sharp focus. But he had to go through some other business before he could get things straight.

It is often complained that the poems in *Cage Without Grievance* and

2ND Poems are disobligingly cryptic. Bits of loveliness bob to the surface, tempting us to reach down and catch them. But when, having grasped each one, we stop to fret over its senses – much as I have been doing – the poetic whole from which the fragment arose will tend to disintegrate for want of attention. This readerly myopia is something from which Graham himself suffered. When he heard that Norah Montgomerie was working on an illustration for his 'Many Without Elegy' he wrote to her: 'I will [...] be interested in it as a remark of some objectivity on the poem. You know how one's work can be too close and one stands on the paw of the Sphynx and finds it impossible to see the shape of it in any way significant. So he has to climb down off the paw and walk fifteen years away till he sees it across an expanse of wilderness' (*Nightfisherman*, p. 30).

In the mid-1940s Graham rose to the task he set himself here, that of getting some distance on his poetic objects. By seeing further he might see them whole. He was reluctant to let his poems go until they had settled into independent shape and were ready to live a released life on their own. Those that refused to mature were written off, as he explained to David Wright: 'sometimes I find a poem when finished never sets, never breaks apart from me and becomes a separate organic. Then it's scrapped. I'm moving towards what I call "a poetry of release." In LISTEN. PUT ON MORNING. I feel I'm coming near it' (*Nightfisherman*, p. 46). It is often tempting to insert a 'u' into Graham's mornings – and in the case of the title he mentions here, more than usually so, since the poetic project he describes finds an analogue in the process of separation and release that is part of the mourner's work. The poems including 'Listen. Put on Morning' that were to become Graham's third book, *The White Threshold*, may not invest in funerary dress, but poised at the threshold between the living and the dead they do mark the stage in the elegiac process when a choice has to be made between looking back and moving forward, between remembering and forgetting, between holding on and letting go. In the making of these poems, as in the process of mourning, distance is crucial to the achievement of completion and severance.

The publication of *The White Threshold* in 1949 conferred on Graham 'the snob stamp of Faber' (*Nightfisherman*, p. 76), Eliot's seal of approval bringing him to the centre of the literary establishment, though he still lived at the very end of land, on the Cornish shoreline that gave his book its title. We might wonder what it was in *The White Threshold* that attracted Eliot's attention. Although on that question no documentary evidence has yet come to light, it is worth conjecturing that Eliot recognized in Graham's work something akin to his own.[20] Local coincidences suggest that Graham was reading *Four Quartets* while he was writing the poems for *The White Threshold*: his 'Older stranger by stranger' (*CP*, p. 81), for example, is reminiscent of Eliot's 'As we grow older / The world becomes stranger, the pattern more complicated / Of dead and living',[21] and like Eliot he displaces the military idiom of a world at war onto a skirmish with linguistic equipment: his 'Silence alone / Answers clean out raiding my speaking fields' musters something of Eliot's 'raid on the inarticulate / With shabby equipment always deteriorating'.[22] But we need not infer a direct line of influence for the connection between Eliot's book and Graham's to matter. My suggestion is that Eliot saw in Graham something he recognized, because both poets, working through a pattern of dead and living, seem to have been setting their affairs in order, and both did so against the background of war and in the uneasy period between wars.

While Graham was writing these poems he was also at work on his essay 'Notes on a Poetry of Release'.[23] This project likewise involved the shaping of 'a separate organic', a labour that Graham worked at with Eliot in the background. He writes, 'the labourer going home in the dusk shouts his goodnight across the road and History has a new score on its track. The shape is changed a little' (*Nightfisherman*, p. 379). Imagining history thus, as a permanent yet mutable structure which accommodates and is altered by each individual utterance, Graham adds his own score to an essay published in the aftermath of war, Eliot's 'Tradition and the Individual Talent'. The smallness of each adjustment in Graham's scheme ('the shape is changed a little') corresponds with Eliot's conception of the process whereby the new work of art gains access to the 'simultaneous order' of tradition: with the entry of each new work, says Eliot, 'the *whole* existing order must be, if ever so slightly, altered'.[24] Graham notices these slight adjustments at various degrees of magnitude, from the large scale of history to the small measure of the poetic line. In each case the meaning of each part depends on its relation to the organic whole, so that much as in Eliot's tradition 'the relations, proportions, values of each work of art towards the whole are readjusted', for Graham 'the meaning of a word in a poem is never more than its position' (*Nightfisherman*, p. 382).

In the essay that does not entitle itself to the final word on its subject, but merely 'Notes on', Graham takes up his Eliot-like thought that with every new score on its track the shape of history 'is changed a little' and reimagines it in the measure of the poem: 'though do I move along words in a poem when, after all, as I am at the last word and look back I find the first word changed and a new word there, for it is part of the whole poem and its particular life depends on the rest of the poem' (*Nightfisherman*, p. 382). The stumbled syntax of this sentence – in which 'when, after all, as I am at the last word' is not the last word – haltingly performs its meaning, which entails playing off against one another two senses of 'last', on one side 'final' and on the other 'most recent'. This double sense of 'last' crops up in the first poem of *The White Threshold*:

Since All My Steps Taken

Since all my steps taken
Are audience of my last
With hobnail on Ben Narnain
Or mind on the word's crest
I'll walk the kyleside shingle
With scarcely a hark back
To the step dying from my heel
Or the creak of the rucksack.
                              (*CP*, p. 47)

Graham marches into his book with sparer verbal equipment and renewed purpose. He keeps his eyes front, but still, his newly filled rhymes insist that the ear hark back from 'the creak of the rucksack' to 'scarcely a hark back'. His sprightly step carries the baggage of memory – the Kyleside of childhood – but carries it lightly. Just as each most recent step will itself be changed by those that take its place, so, according to his essay, 'history continually arrives as differently as our most recent minute on earth' (*Nightfisherman*, p. 379). The curious thing is that this stepping away never quite reaches a point of departure; despite its resolute forward march, 'Since All My Steps Taken' comes full circle, finding its end in its beginning.

Whereas for as long as we live our last word, like the step dying from the walker's heel, is only the most recent, the last words of the dying are made to bear a heavier burden, having the ultimate say on the pattern of a finished life. This is the truism to which Lawrence Lipking appeals when he says that for the ageing poet, 'above all a book is needed [...] last works, like last words, have a special aura of authenticity'.[25] *Four Quartets* looks to Lipking like one such book. Even so, within it Eliot hesitated around the thought that the accumulated experience of age should have the final say. Thus, 'East Coker':

> There is, it seems to us,
> At best, only a limited value
> In the knowledge derived from experience.
> The knowledge imposes a pattern, and falsifies,
> For the pattern is new in every moment
> And every moment is a new and shocking
> Valuation of all we have been.
>
> (ll. 81–87)

The modifying clauses ('there is, it seems to us, / At best, only…') hedge limits on the thought expressed here, while the insistent 'and's ('and falsifies [...] / And every moment') accrete unease: along such paratactic lines there could always be one more 'and' to supersede the last, and so to reshuffle the pattern that the sentence has most recently set. Still, Lipking might be right that *Four Quartets* was the outcome of the ageing poet's preoccupation with 'the logic of the whole',[26] that Eliot looks in retrospect to have been setting his affairs in order. Thirty years his junior, in 1944 W.S. Graham considered himself unready for a collected works, but the volume he was working towards was governed by an organizing structure comparable to Eliot's.[27] Whereas *Four Quartets* was 'to set a crown upon [a] lifetime's effort', in *The White Threshold* Graham found himself 'locked into furious outcome of *half* [his] life'.[28] His book did not emerge from the experience of a lifetime, and he was hardly middle aged (or as he would sharply put it, 'muddle-edged' [*Nightfisherman*, p. 281]), but he had begun to experience those things – the death of a parent, for example – that nudged him towards the generational front line, sending him back to childhood and forward to imagining what it might be like to go it alone.

The tendency of the poems in *The White Threshold* to face both ways means that they rarely leave their most recent words behind, nor step decisively into a last word. In 'My Final Bread', for example, the 'Final' of the title is undone by the perpetual comings and goings floated in the body of the poem: 'Part sailored by my own likeness part maintaining / My continual farewell. I am continual arrival' (*WT*, p. 13). These continual arrivals and farewells, like Eliot's mimicry of aged hesitations, give rise to a peculiar feeling of stasis. That the making of 'a separate organic' might bring the poetry to a standstill militates against the 'poetry of release' that Graham was looking for. This is, it seems to me, a difficulty he inherited from Eliot. Eliot's tradition is conservative in the sense that it changes only gradually, and in that it tends not to let things go: as he wrote of the changing mind of Europe, 'this change is a development which abandons nothing *en route*'.[29] For the elegist, things are not exactly abandoned *en route*, but the lost object (be it a person or a habit of writing) must at some stage be left behind. Because the poetry of *The White Threshold* is organized along organicist lines, Graham finds it hard to let anything go, and sometimes, instead of reaching the end, he gets stuck in the melancholic middle.

Four Quartets accumulates the gravity of last words, but it is also a poem of the middle. Released as a whole in the midst of conflict, it had been composed partly between wars:

> So here I am, in the middle way, having had twenty years –
> Twenty years largely wasted, the years of *l'entre deux guerres* –
> ('East Coker', ll. 172–73)

Graham's book eventually came out in 1949, but it had been written in wartime (1944–1946), and, as far as Graham was concerned, also between wars. In the shapely frame of retrospect 1945 marks a definitive end point, but for Graham as for many of his contemporaries the armistice seemed merely a hiatus, war's aftermath having the uneasy feeling of an interlude '*entre deux guerres*'. He was sceptical about the peace and kept away from the public celebrations: 'everywhere within flagpole distance is a union jack but we stay here quietly in our surrounded field. [...] It is an ominous peace but conceals the germs of something worse than before' (*Nightfisherman*, pp. 44–45). If in wartime his 'arkvan' had seemed a pastoral retreat, in the ominous peace of war's aftermath his 'surrounded field' sounds like territory under siege.

An article of 1944 by Alex Comfort had predicted the discomforts of the post-war climate: 'we know perfectly well what is coming, and we dread the end of the paroxysm more than the paroxysm itself'.[30] Graham read the piece after the armistice, and was moved to write an unusually politicized letter to its author: 'I find it difficult to talk to people about me not being on the side of this present freedom which is being fought for and yet of course not with fascism. The words now, "Democracy" and "Fascism" seem to have become completely soluble in each other and unite into one mistaken Progress' (*Nightfisherman*, p. 54). Graham found it difficult to take sides, and his retreat from the forces of history (progressive or otherwise) resulted sometimes in a siege mentality that offered no way forward and no way out. This happens in 'Definition of My House':

> Halfway victim to the many, halfway victorious
> Orator of infant earth's all nations all nature's

His halls and heights, weathers and contraries;
My arms my walls fend off, my vaned roof ferries
the fire-armed day.
[...]
It's no room lost for less than the whole advance
Into all sides. Dwelling there shelter's innocence
Halfway keeps off my own, halfway keeps once
And changing all, my work and what it fountains.

(*WT*, p. 50)

There is some flailing about in this, as though the poem were haplessly at war with itself. 'It's not room lost for less than the whole advance / Into all sides' has it all ways at once, and finding no way out of the claustrophobic space the poem has built around him, Graham retreats further into his work, into lines whose internal modulations produce only more of the same. The half measures in 'Definition of My House' might have drawn on an editorial statement in *Life and Letters*: 'The Prime Minister promises a lessening of austerity. But he does it by promising "Half-way back to Pre-War Standards this Year." The first two words are a mistake; half-way still implies division, reduction, rather than multiplication and increase, and "back" is not a forward-looking word. [...] We are in a half-way house of the ages, using science but not controlling it, and our minds reflect this condition.'[31] This describes very well the half-way house to which Graham is confined. He was no doubt acquainted with the issue of *Life and Letters* in which the editorial appeared, since it also contained some poems of his; in one of these, 'Lying in Corn', he accurately pinpointed the position of betweenness that was the outcome of his internalized war:

Fought-over by word and word
This day between my heart and brain lies down
Locked into furious outcome of half my life.[32]

Like his poems, Graham's letters of the post-war years have the edgy feel of someone 'locked in'. He wrote to Minton, 'it gets that I'm almost ready to start h[itch] hiking just away from Cornwall, the direction being just "away" not "to"' (*Nightfisherman*, p. 39). He did eventually get away when in 1948 he was invited to go on a lecturing trip to the USA. It was from the distance of New York that he wrote the last words of *The White Threshold*, 'Three Letters' addressed to his brother, father and mother. At the end of a volume that had set out 'All journey, since the first / Step from my father and mother / Towards the word's crest' (*CP*, p. 47), these letters achieve the kind of release he had been looking for. He said of

'Three Letters': 'there's a great distance between the man who wrote them and the man who wrote the rest [of *The White Threshold*]' (*Nightfisherman*, p. 98). That distance was not only geographical; it was also formal and elegiac. Distance is sometimes alarming for the letter writer: in epistolary space the beast of misreading is apt to prowl. But spatial and temporal removal ally themselves to the cause of the elegist. The dead must be set apart before they can be seen in their proper relation. In 1948 Graham needed room to manoeuvre; his past needed room to lie down.

In the first section of 'The White Threshold', the internally patterned stanzas threaten to 'well over', until each is shored back into shape by the single-line breakwaters, in variations of 'I walk towards you and you may not walk away' (*CP*, p. 77). The poetry's tidal push and pull seems time-less (alternate stanzas begin 'always'), internalized change working against temporal advance. The timeless also reigns over the temporal in Eliot's tradition: only in a space devoid of chronology can 'the past [...] be altered by the present as much as the present is directed by the past'.[33] By contrast to these simultaneous exchanges between past and present, or between incoming and outgoing tides, 'Three Letters' proceeds in simple three-foot lines step by step to the point of walking away. There is still recourse to memory, all three letters lying under the parenthesis '(*In memory of my mother*)', but they seem to know where they are going from the outset:

To My Brother

Alastair approach this thirty
Lines with a homing memory.
Each step speaks out the springtime.
Our Clydeside merges home.

The morning rises up.
The sun's enamoured step
Crosses the ancient firth.
Your breath crosses my breath.

Graham had had a spring in his step since 'Since All My Steps Taken'. Here each step treads a stair in his brother's name. Looking homeward brings parallel fraternal journeys together, rather than merging present and past. The sun's (and sons') enamoured steps rise up, casting light across the firth, an inlet which makes way to an outlet:

The firth makes light of us
Exchanged on those waters

Between Gareloch and Greenock
Wearing woodshell and rowlock.

The exchange between childhood and adulthood does not end in
deadlock: instead the cross between Gareloch and Greenock makes 'rowlock', a fulcrum against which to push forward. Light dawns at the end of
this poem ('These words make light of us'), and it does not come out of
heavy weather.

The second letter, for Graham's father, is also about changing and
exchange, as in the chiasmus of these lines:

As alike as a *memory early*
Of "The Bonny *Earl o' Moray*"
Fiddled in our high kitchen
Over the sleeping town.
                    (emphasis added)

That formal exchange is reciprocal, and as though dancing to the ballad
played overhead, the change-rounds turn towards moving away:

A fraction's wink and I
And my death change round softly.
My birth and I so softly
Change round the outward journey.

In the letter to his brother, the light of the rising sun had fallen across the
firth; with his father, falling light falls across:

This night this word falling

Across the kindling skies
Takes over over our bodies

As the last words released to his brother made serious light of fraternal
embrace, here his word makes a gentle generational takeover, 'kindling
skies' keeping kinship alive.

The poem for his mother completes the journey of 'Three Letters'. In
The White Threshold Graham loses his footing sometimes in clusters of
adverbs, as in 'Three Poems of Drowning': 'locked into under / The grave
mounded sea kept under with stone' (*CP*, p. 72), or in 'The White
Threshold': 'Drowned under behind my brow so ever' (*CP*, p. 77). Writing
to his mother he is careful to see exactly where 'under' might lock her:

Under (not ground but the mind's)
Thunder you rest on memory's

> Daily aloneness as rest
> My steps to a great past.

His parent is not locked underground, as in fact the parenthesis does not properly lock its contents (it should end after 'but'). Leaving that aside, 'Under / Thunder' does sound like the return of heavy weather; but again he moves further away:

> In words I change them further
> Away from the parent fire.
> Look. Into life or out?
> What son did you inherit?

The ins and outs of the third line here remember '*Locked into* furious *out*come of half my *life*', and the fourth asks whether inheritance can go both ways between mother and son. But, as though weary of the endless back and forth, Graham looks for a stopping place:

> Sometimes like loneliness
> Memory's crowds increase.
> Suddenly some man I am
> So finds himself endless stream
>
> Of stepping away from his
> Last home, I crave my ease
> Stopped for a second dead
> Out of the speaking flood.

Craving ease from endlessness, 'suddenly' and 'stopped for a second dead' wrest the temporal out of the timeless. Loss must be inserted into a chronology if it is to be left behind, and that these poems lie under a date (Spring 1948) as well as an epitaph is testimony to their craving the ease of the timely. The poem knows that in 'these thirty lines' there is only a little further to go. Since the beginning of the book, in 'Since All My Steps Taken' Graham had been listening for something: 'Day long I've listened for, / Like the cry of a rare bird / Blown into life in the ear, / The speech to the dead horde'. At the end of 'Three Letters' that speech is blown into life again, but the restless manoeuvring is done:

> Under (not ground but the words)
> You rest with speaking hordes.

There's a great distance between the man who crossed *The White Threshold* and the man who made *Implements in their Places* (1977). I want to turn finally to the last poem in that volume, 'Dear Bryan Wynter' (*CP*, p. 255), the most artless and at the same time most knowing of Graham's poems. In the poetic spectrum of his oeuvre, from the encrypted apparatus of the 1940s to the plain speaking style of the 1970s, 'Dear Bryan Wynter' comes at the transparent end. Its pane is so clear, in fact, that readers are likely to find, as Graham did when he re-read the poem at some distance from its immediate occasion, that it simply 'loosen[s] a tear from the eye' (*Nightfisherman*, p. 331). Even if that immediate response is the proper one, telling us to probe no further and making exegesis seem an impertinence, the epistolary frame of 'Dear Bryan Wynter' does ask us to see through it to the correspondence that has been at work throughout: that is between the elegy and the letter.

It is a convention in letters of condolence for the writer to find himself at a loss for something to say, and so to resort to convention. Commonplaces are the stock in trade of this genre, the most familiar of which is the writer's apologizing for having no more to say than 'I'm so sorry'. If pained by the inadequacy of formulaic sympathies, the writer had better not dwell too long on the difficult time he is having composing his message, lest he claim for himself a portion of the suffering that belongs to its recipient. When we send our condolences we do not suffer with the bereaved, and epistolary distance properly measures the difference between our own difficulty and that of the person we want to comfort. Better to send something (anything), even an offer of help when there is no help to be offered, in the hope that the mere existence of the letter will matter. 'This is only a note / To say how sorry I am' acknowledges the distance between what the poet writes and what he might say had he the words. The turn of the line that follows, 'To say how sorry I am / You died' turns that apologetic convention full in the face of loss. Graham could have softened the shock by giving us more pause: had he written 'how sorry I am / *That* you died', the ghostly anapaests lurking in the first two lines might have had time to steady themselves. Instead, 'You died' carries a double stress that is not easy to bear.

When Bryan Wynter died, Sydney Graham's first response had been to write a letter to another friend, Robin Skelton:

> It is morning, Robin, and I am very drunk.
> Bryan Wynter died last night. Whether you knew him or not does not matter. I could have got drunk for any simple reason. He happened to be a man who was very near me in my life for about 30 years. I can't believe it. This is not a letter to tell you that somebody has died. You don't know him any

how. But here I am up in the early Madron morning drunk as a hand-cart or any adjective you may choose wanting to tell you that he will never come into the house again tapping at the back window. I can't believe it. But here we are, Robin, still going through our lives as we respectively do. Are you there? Is your dog there? I make your dog a symbol.

(*Nightfisherman*, p. 287)

The coincidences between this letter and 'Dear Bryan Wynter' are readily apparent: 'not a letter to tell you somebody has died' turns into 'only a note / To say how sorry I am / You died'; 'I make your dog a symbol' does not travel far to the related species in 'I know I make a symbol / Of the foxglove on the wall'. Beyond those developments, this letter tells us something more about 'Dear Bryan Wynter', if only by contrast, and it has to do with Graham's perfect control of tone. Arthur Hallam complained to Emily Tennyson about 'how little a letter gives one': 'it contains no looks, no tones – that is the great, deplorable, alas irremediable loss'.[34] That we have to *ascribe* tone to letters (we have to write voice into silent script) testifies to the irrecoverable nature of speech. But poetry does sometimes give signals about how it ought to be voiced. It would have been easy in a poem that deals in clichés ('how sorry I am'; 'How are things?'; 'I would be obliged if...') for Graham to have raised his tonal eyebrows at the formulae he quotes. He does not do that. More sober than the letter to Skelton, the poem does have room for some jokes, but chooses not to poke fun at the phrases that avail themselves at this difficult time. Graham does not berate his words for their inadequacy, and whereas in the letter to Skelton he apologizes for his habitual apologizing ('this is the last of my being sorry'), the poem makes no apology for saying only 'how sorry' he is.

From the outset the idiom and syntax lean toward the formal: 'I couldn't really / Have died for you if so / I were inclined'. As it turns out, he is somewhat inclined:

> [...] The carn
> Foxglove here on the wall
> Outside your first house
> Leans with me standing
> In the Zennor wind

Now that the gusty moment of disbelief in the letter to Skelton has blown over, he leans in his poem on what small props the language and landscape can offer him. Just when the balance of 'Dear Bryan Wynter' might have tipped over into nostalgia, familiar phrases give secure ground on which to stand upright:

Anyhow how are things?
Are you still somewhere
With your long legs
And twitching smile under
Your blue hat walking
Across a place?

In the letter to Skelton, the weary thought that things go on 'anyhow' alerts him to the worry that they might not: 'But here we are Robin, still going through our lives as we respectively do. Are you there? Is your dog there?' and much as in Auden's line, 'the dogs go on with their doggy life', in the face of catastrophe the dogged indifference of daily habit is a source of strange comfort as well as pain.[35] In a letter of condolence, 'Anyhow, how are things' would certainly have been out of place; but it is perfectly placed here in its imagining that life *does* go on: 'Are you still somewhere' is less desperate than Graham's 'Are you there?' in the letter to Skelton. In the poem it is not a phatic checking on a dead line, but brings both the rest of 'still' and a lively cartoon that makes up the force of a whole personality from the memory of gesture.

As Graham resorts to familiar epistolary phrases in this poem, he also holds on to some remnant of elegiac convention. Wynter's 'twitching smile' and 'blue hat' resurrect the closing frame of 'Lycidas' ('At last he rose, and *twitched* his mantle *blue*' [l. 192]). Though Graham is not, even at the end of the poem, 'just ready to start out' for fresh woods, he does rise to them in the middle:

I am up. I've washed
The front of my face
And here I stand looking
Out over the top
Half of my bedroom window.
There almost as far
As I can see I see
St Buryan's church tower.
An inch to the left, behind
That dark rise of woods,
Is where you used to lurk.

The landscape inclines with him, from 'tower' through 'rise' and on upward to the stars whose light falls across 'Housman's star / Lit fences'. Almost as far as Graham can see we see that punning habit that might catch a glimpse of Bryan buried in 'Buryan'. But he is not there – he is not quite confined to that cryptic little plot. That is because Graham *can* see further through elegy. He does so by passing beyond wordplay, or rather catching what lurks beside and behind it. An inch to the left, he can see the wood for the verbal trees, and through it to the lurking figure beyond.

He wrote to Skelton, 'Rob, I go to the funeral on Saturday. Who shall I be? Shall I put on the intense face or the concealing face or the interesting face?' Which face is he wearing in 'I've washed / The front of my face'? The tone in these lines is hard to describe. The voice, like the face, is scrubbed clean of too mournful an expression, but its speaker is not exactly putting on a front. His voice is not quite flat, but we can surely trust it: it has no side. This is the position Wynter's dying puts him in: up front, on tiptoe, but carefully not over the top. The mood of the letter to Skelton was less cautious – 'here I am up in the early Madron morning drunk as a hand-cart'; and a measure of this poem's sobriety is its careful positioning, especially of 'here' and 'there'. 'Speaking to you and not / Knowing if you are *there*' gets a response when the poem begins again: in 'This is only a note / To say I am *aware* / You are not *here*'. 'Aware' carries the spectral rhyme of 'there' to stage a meeting across the line-break with 'here'. Perhaps the heres and theres could change places (perhaps he could have died for him).

The poem, like the letter to Skelton, has much to say about knowing ('and not / Knowing') and if the tone is knowing, it is calmly self-aware rather than twitchingly self-conscious. What Graham knows comes out fully at the end of his poem, and it has been prepared for from the start. The long 'o's in 'Only a note' shrink first into recurrent 'and not's:

> I would like to think
> You were all right
> *And not* worried about
> Monica and the children
> *And not* unhappy or bored.
>
> 2
> Speaking to you *and not*
> Knowing if you are there
> *Is not* too difficult
>   (emphasis added)

But whereas in 'Many Without Elegy' he had withdrawn at last into negatives, here he does not tie himself irrevocably to nots. 'Only a note' finally recovers its long 'o's, releasing them into what he and Wynter know best:

I know I make a symbol
Of the foxglove on the wall.
It is because it knows you.

The letter to Skelton also draws to a close with some Os: 'I am not really sentimental. I am as hard as Greenock shipbuilding nails. O O O. I have fallen here on the floor. Can you lift me up. WOW that's a good ending'. It would have been a good elegiac ending if he had fallen and someone had lifted him up. But this is not the end. There is a postscript: 'PS I read this letter now and decided that, in spite of what it reveals, I should let it go to you'. Although the letter writer does not yet know it, letting go is the proper end of grief. To achieve that release, the mourner must knowingly put his trust in a substitute for what he has lost. A floral symbol plucked from the landscape is the best known of elegiac tropes, and Graham makes no apology for drawing on that convention. It is, of course, rather less conventional for a letter of condolence to go from the bereaved to the dead; but in that misdirection Graham's epistolary elegy finds its target. This is the finest elegy Graham wrote, and one of his finest poems. In its perfect control it is ungovernably sad.

The editors of *The Nightfisherman* suggest that Graham's poem 'The Constructed Space', 'read again after the poet's death [...] takes on some of the qualities of an elegy' (*Nightfisherman*, p. 377). The last lines of that poem certainly have that quality: 'Yet here I am / More truly now this abstract act become' (*CP*, p. 153). But if part of Graham is there in the constructed space of artful abstraction, there are some other lines beginning 'here I am' that have qualities for which he should also be remembered. When in 1984 he was too unwell to attend a gathering in his honour, he wrote something for the friend who was to take his place. It was a poem addressed to his audience in the guise of a letter, itself enclosed in a letter to his stand-in. Through all those writerly frames, his voice comes through:

Dear Pamela,
'Here I am, standing in front of you and W S Graham has given me the introduction and he says – just read this, nothing less and nothing more.'

'Dear Audience, listening to poetry
being put into sound, especially words
in an unexpected sequence, is not
necessarily an unhappy thing.
You will be all right. If I have
made these poems

well, some of you should get
something. I send you my regards
from the end of the peninsula'
        (*Nightfisherman*, p. 374)

Graham commits himself to writing and entrusts his words to a substitute,
but his familiar voice does not disintegrate. Reading his letter even at this
distance from its immediate occasion, I think Graham is still there in
person. It is indeed himself – nothing more and nothing less.

Notes

1   Edwin Morgan, 'W.S. Graham: A Poet's Letters', *ER75*, pp. 39–47 (39).
2   *Nightfisherman*, p. 12.
3   W.S. Graham, 'The Constructed Space', *CP*, p. 152.
4   Graham wrote 'I'm lost in foxes of falling down' in a 1944 letter to John Minton
    (*Nightfisherman*, p. 20); the phrase comes up again in 'The Lost Other' (*CP*, p. 64).
5   Peter Sacks, *The English Elegy: Studies in the Genre from Spenser to Yeats* (Baltimore:
    Johns Hopkins University Press, 1985), p. xiii.
6   Sacks's *The English Elegy* remains the most convincing of these accounts; see
    especially chapter 1, 'Interpreting the Genre: The Elegy and the Work of Mourning'.
    In his *Poetry of Mourning: The Modern Elegy from Hardy to Heaney* (Chicago:
    University of Chicago Press, 1994), Jahan Ramazani argues that twentieth-century
    elegists, sceptical of works of mourning in which human loss is turned to aesthetic
    gain, tend instead towards the melancholic side of grief: W. David Shaw, in *Elegy and
    Paradox: Testing the Conventions* (Baltimore: Johns Hopkins University Press, 1994),
    tests the convention of invoking Freud as well as the conventions of elegy.
7   See Shaw, *Elegy and Paradox*, chapter 6: 'Does Good Therapy Make Good Art?'
8   Sigmund Freud, 'Mourning and Melancholia' (1917), trans. James Strachey, in
    Metapsychology, ed. Angela Richards (Penguin Freud Library, 11; London: Penguin,
    1984), pp. 251–68 (253).
9   John Milton, 'Lycidas' (1637), in *Complete Shorter Poems*, ed. John Carey (London:
    Longman, 1971), pp. 232–54, l. 5. Further references to 'Lycidas' are to this edition,
    cited by line number.
10 W.S. Graham, '1st Letter', in *Cage Without Grievance* (Glasgow: Parton Press, 1942),
    p. 12.
11 Morgan, 'A Poet's Letters', p. 39.
12 I quote Morgan's letter from the one Graham sent in reply to his (*Nightfisherman*, p.
    14).
13 John Milton, *Paradise Lost* (1667), ed. Alistair Fowler (London: Longman, 1968),
    Book IV, ll. 146–47.
14 Gerard Manley Hopkins, *The Wreck of The Deutschland* (1875), in *Gerard Manley
    Hopkins*, ed. Catherine Phillips (Oxford: Oxford University Press, 1986), pp. 110–21,
    Section 31.

15 *OED*: Harp. v. trans. 8: 'he'd harpit a fish out o' saut water'.

16 Mairi Robinson (ed.), *The Concise Scots Dictionary* (Aberdeen: Aberdeen University Press, 1985).

17 Matthew Arnold, 'Stanzas from the Grande Chartreuse' (1885), in *Matthew Arnold*, ed. Miriam Allott and Robert H. Super (Oxford: Oxford University Press, 1986), pp. 159–65, ll. 107–108.

18 Alfred, Lord Tennyson, *In Memoriam A. H. H.* (1850), in *The Poems of Tennyson*, ed. Christopher Ricks (London: Longman, 2nd edn, 1987), III, p. 459.

19 Peter Sacks puts it well: 'the end [of *In Memoriam*] is a postponement [...] one tends to collapse upon the final word rather than advance according to its meaning' (*The English Elegy*, p. 201).

20 Tony Lopez has found 'no record of the relationship on Eliot's side, according to the Faber archive'. Lopez sees 'much in common' between *Four Quartets* and *The Nightfishing*: 'T.S. Eliot and W.S. Graham', *Scottish Literary Journal*, 19.1 (1992), pp. 35–46 (37).

21 T.S. Eliot, 'East Coker' (1940), in *Four Quartets* (London: Faber and Faber, 1944), p. 27, ll. 189–91.

22 W.S. Graham, 'Lying in Corn', *WT*, p. 12; Eliot, 'East Coker', ll. 179–80.

23 The essay was first published in *Poetry Scotland*, 3 (1946); it is reprinted in the appendix to *The Nightfisherman*. Further references are to page numbers in this reprint.

24 T.S. Eliot, 'Tradition and the Individual Talent', *The Egoist*, 6.4 (September 1919), pp. 54–55 (55).

25 Lawrence Lipking, *The Life of the Poet: Beginning and Ending Poetic Careers* (Chicago: University of Chicago Press, 1981), p. 67.

26 Lipking, *Life of the Poet*, p. 65.

27 He wrote to John Minton, 'Some firm wrote me asking if I would consider doing a collected works of WS Graham. Of course No' (*Nightfisherman*, p. 57).

28 T.S. Eliot, 'Little Gidding' (1942), in *Four Quartets*, p. 44, l. 130; Graham, 'Lying in Corn', my emphasis.

29 Eliot, 'Tradition', p. 55.

30 Alex Comfort 'October, 1944', *Now*, 4 (1944), pp. 44–48 (44).

31 Editorial, *Life and Letters*, 48.103 (March 1946), pp. 153–55 (154).

32 *Life and Letters*, 48.103 (March 1946), p. 208. This issue of *Life and Letters* also included 'Shian Bay', 'The Voyages of Alfred Wallace', and Nessie Dunsmuir's 'Raith Pit'.

33 Eliot, 'Tradition', p. 55.

34 Letter of 7 April 1832, quoted in Eric Griffiths, *The Printed Voice of Victorian Poetry* (Oxford: Clarendon Press, 1989), p. 101.

35 W.H. Auden, 'Musée des Beaux Arts' (1938), in *The English Auden: Poems, Essays and Dramatic Writings 1927–1939*, ed. Edward Mendelson (London: Faber and Faber, 1977), p. 237. I am indebted to Jenny Woodman for bringing this line to my attention.

Letter X – My dear so many times

My dear so many times
My dear, more than this is
Is nothing to the high
Silences unhailed
That surge around us all
Ways wearing us away.
It is easily said
You lie somewhere there
Elegantly under
Unrehearsed possibilities
Of language turning and
Turning with the slow
Drift of the stellar stoure.
Yet I turn a little
Towards where you may be
My dear, seeing the started
Poem grow bolder out
Of the corner of my eye.
And this becomes almost
A place where those two
We loved as once stand
On either side of language
To watch. And so even
That is something if nothing
More than making from
The behaviour of silence
Maybe the slow gathering
Way at night over
The unhailed water held
Still for a moment within
These words becoming
Our obstacle in common.

9

Graham and the Numinous: 'The 'Centre Aloneness' and the 'Unhailed Water'

HESTER JONES

W.S. Graham's poem 'The Constructed Space' in *Malcolm Mooney's Land* has become something of a landmark for readers of his poetry. Here Graham, despite his frequent refusals to offer easy interpretations of or explanations for his writing, seems to be providing a remarkably concise enactment of what so often happens, or nearly happens, in it. In line with much of his other work, what happens in 'The Constructed Space' has to do with the limits of speech, with the attempt to approach the other that is hoped to exist beyond the limits of the self, and with the discovery of the 'true' self in this act of transcendence.

The poem opens with the word 'Meanwhile' and ends in the present: the self discovered in the act of writing is 'More truly now this abstract act become'. It begins, therefore, in a transitory, fleeting time, and the immediate present of its ending, 'now', is the poem's closest approach to the infinite and the timeless. Although past, present and future are included in the poem (and correspond loosely to its three stanzas), as a whole it has something of a *carpe diem* quality to it in the sense that memory and anticipation of the end serve to intensify the poem's movement towards its ultimate 'now'.

The last line's confidence follows, however, both moments of apparent authority, when the speaker says, for instance, 'It is like that, remember', and absolute negations of such authority, when Graham drastically confesses complete uncertainty:

> Or maybe, surely, of course we never know
> What we have said, what lonely meanings are read
> Into the space we make.

> (*CP*, pp. 152–53)

Structurally and thematically this proves to be a turning point in the poem, and such 'turns' have an epiphanic quality in Graham's writing. Here, and, I shall suggest, at many points in his work, an echo of T.S.

Eliot's *Four Quartets* can be heard, particularly of 'East Coker', and Graham uses the echo to convey the sense that his searches for communication with another and for personal authenticity carry a spiritual resonance, that his poetry is following a mystical path.

Eliot, of course, explores the experience of mysticism's negative way in contemporary terms. '[L]et the dark come upon you', he urges, 'Which shall be the darkness of God'. And he goes on:

> when an underground train, in the tube, stops too long between stations
> And the conversation rises and slowly fades into silence
> And you see behind every face the mental emptiness deepen[.]'

In what follows, I shall argue that Graham goes a stage further than Eliot and sets out to 'construct' a space between 'stations', a space between what is remembered and known. In that space, insight and relation may occur. Between the 'I' and the 'you' of the poem Graham creates a space that involves both 'we' and the becoming of the poem – a becoming that may release and recreate both 'I' and 'you'. In other words, Graham approaches the transcendent not only through the negation of the contemporary and the human but also within both of these and especially through relationship, through 'the space we make'.²

These concerns come together in a particularly concise way in 'The Constructed Space', so I shall spend a little more time considering the poem before showing how similar preoccupations emerge elsewhere in Graham's work. 'The Constructed Space' begins by seeming to anticipate the reader's yearning for meaning, for matter:

> Meanwhile surely there must be something to say,
> Maybe not suitable but at least happy
> In a sense here between us two whoever
> We are. Anyhow here we are and never
> Before have we two faced each other who face
> Each other now across this abstract scene
> Stretching between us.
>
> (*CP*, p. 152)

This opening is both masterfully accomplished in the public mode Graham acknowledges and just as surely Graham's own, idiosyncratic and wayward voice. The words tug between flux and achieved moment ('Meanwhile […] say'), between forceful assertion and shaky uncertainty ('surely there must'), and above all, between the safe, yet subjective world of the self and the established, yet uncongenial world of poetic form and readership. The poet-speaker is an innocent in exile, stepping like Milton's Adam with his reader Eve for company out into an unfamiliarly hostile world.[3]

Yet this moment, this 'Meanwhile', we are told, is 'happy / In a sense'. What sense does Graham mean? The cadence is again surreptitiously Eliotian: in 'The Dry Salvages', Eliot writes of 'the moments of happiness [...] the sudden illumination'.[4] This, I think, is the direction Graham moves in when he uses the same adjective in its surprising location: 'maybe not suitable but at least happy / In a sense here between us two whoever / We are'. He is writing here of contact, of human interaction, as a mystical 'achievement', worked towards, as he writes, 'against subjective odds' and within the 'public place' of the poem. The moment of illumination is desacralized, stripped of the Eliotian shimmer of religious feeling and language, but, against the odds, Graham's verse retains some of the penumbra of numinous encounter.[5]

Human friendship, as manifested in the form of the letter, whether prose or verse, lies perhaps at the centre of this project. Graham, though, often finds the negative way to run through the chimeras of 'what I mean' and each person's 'subjective odds'. The prison of the self and the chasm of the world both make true, interactive contact almost an impossibility. He shows his alertness to this danger when, for instance, the scene is said to be 'Stretching between us'. His present participle leaves room (as the past would not) for the possibility that no contact is actually made between 'us'; that the 'space' of the poem stretches to reach either poet or reader and falls short of both. Such a giddy loss of bearings is one of Graham's great strengths. Here and elsewhere he makes us free-fall through the space between the poet and the reader.

In the lines, Graham also dramatizes social ineptitude with a gruff impatience at such constraint. One expects a 'scene', still more an abstract scene, to stretch grandly 'before' and even away from the viewer and not to be held 'between' two such. 'Stretch' in this tense and limited context becomes as narrow a room as a fallen world: an image of expansive freedom is reduced to one of embattled threat. The scene, like the child in the story of Solomon's judgement, is threatened with being torn apart by rivals in love.[6] There is no promise of cooperative endeavour, of a shared work through which, as Alexander Pope puts it in the 'Epistle to Jervas', 'each from each contract new strength and light'.[7] Rather, friendship threatens to be broken on the rack of art. Alternatively, the scene can be seen to resemble the beast in Graham's 'The Beast in the Space' that 'thumps its tail / On silence on the other side', both fawning and nerving itself to pounce or bite (*CP*, p. 147). In Graham, that is, a stretch may herald a leap. Although therefore the space is a connection, the suggestion remains that it is a tensile, temporary one, one that may, like elastic or a rubber band, spring out of grasp at any moment.

Linguistically, the stretch is mirrored by sound: that of 'scene' picked up in 'between' and echoed more subtly in 'we' and 'happy' and initiated in the first word of the poem, 'Meanwhile'. In temporal terms, 'Meanwhile' gives only the promise of transitoriness, admitting that this moment is just a substitute for something else, more substantial and significant. Likewise, the poem's energy starts with a burst and then flags. Its iambic line tends to begin with a trochaic reversal, an initial confidence ('Maybe not suitable but at least happy') and ends with a wavering weak syllable, particularly around the central lines of each stanza. This tendency is overcome when the poem reasserts itself and the 'saying', '*becomes*' (my emphasis). The saying assumes, in other words, an identity and with that identity the truth is partly lost.

The poem follows a sequence, then, from early confidence to doubt to a more insistent authority, which is seen, lastly, as itself an obstacle to telling the truth. The sequence of feeling is characteristic of Graham more widely and registers his sense that the process of writing is self-defeating. But there are also movements within the poem that suggest a happier outcome, often via the repetition of particular, simple words. I have mentioned 'across', which in the first stanza is used antagonistically, to denote blockage between I and you, between poet and reader, present and past self. Such deadness and obstruction is perhaps embodied in the limping, near-perfectly regular iambic feet. The feet move but the voice stands still.

In the last stanza, however, 'across' falls not mid-line but at the end of the second line and denotes transition and communication rather than obstruction:

> I [...] construct this space
> So that somehow something may move across
> The caught habits of language to you and me.
> (*CP*, p. 153)

The impatient and imperative 'must' of the first stanza has shifted to the more tentative and prayer-like 'may', and the ineffable process of communication is honestly acknowledged in the incantatory 'So that somehow something may move across / The caught habits of language to you and me'.

While the argument of the first verse moves downward in expectation ('Maybe not suitable but at least happy'), the third advances: 'I say this silence or, better, construct this space', and the 'space' is unconfined by punctuation or syntax so that it may retain 'something' of the original character of I and you that is lost in the more formal 'public place'. Similarly, the first line of the poem is determined by public, social standards and vocabularies: an external 'code' and expectation of communication is invoked and then, in the middle verse, replaced, superseded by 'some intention risen up out of nothing'. The waste land of the 'beginning' is resurrected by the hidden life of meaning. When 'something' occurs the second time it is not just a substitute for nothing, as at first, but rather a unique, fresh, original utterance emerging out of the unknowable depths of the self.

The line distantly remembers the spirit of God that moves upon the face of the deep before the Creation begins. It also recalls lines from the poem's first stanza: 'here we are and never / Before have we two faced each other who face / Each other now'. These in turn recall a famous passage in St Paul's First Letter to the Corinthians, 'For now we see through a glass, darkly; but then face to face', which was important to Graham throughout his career.[8] In 'The Constructed Space', Graham unbalances the Pauline image of mutuality with a phrase that gives back a broken image of itself: 'faced each other who face / Each other now'.[9] In place of confrontation he gives us temporal succession; while the biblical trajectory looks from the darkness and uncertainty of the present, 'now', to the surety and clarity of the future, 'then', Graham's future is dark and his past solitary. Only the present contains the possibility of 'home'.

The 'times', then, are key to this 'home'. Graham writes:

> And times are hastening yet, disguise is mortal.
> The times continually disclose our home.
>   (*CP*, p. 153)

'Times' is a word both dismissive in connotation, suggestive of treacherous fashionableness, and also containing in germ the sum of many individual moments, each of infinite value and meaning in its own right. Times both 'disguise' and 'disclose', conceal and reveal. They are like the 'face' of God, representing divine fulness and also hinting at the fulness that is not perceived but can only be inferred. What we see is 'only a face', a momentary phenomenon, yet the word 'face' in its tradition and history also carries the expectation of revelation and fulfilment.

A conventional morality might remind us that mortality is simply a disguise, hiding our spiritual being. Graham to some extent agrees with this: the phenomenal world passes and will reveal a higher truth when its disguise vanishes. Yet this vanishing, as the second of the two lines suggests, happens within 'The times'. Our true 'home' is disclosed within the experience, rapid and ungainly, that forms our lives. Our home is at hand or, as Graham puts it more jovially in 'Clusters Travelling Out', 'at my elbow' (*CP*, p. 187), like a familiar spirit offering steadying inspiration.

Graham's powerful and moving tribute to the painter Peter Lanyon, 'The Thermal Stair', also in *Malcolm Mooney's Land*, continues this response to the numinous quality of earthly things, the sacredness of the mortal world that is our home. In the poem, Graham addresses his friend, Peter, as if speaking to St Peter, the rock of the church, the emblem of steadiness: 'Give me your hand, Peter, / To steady me on the word'. Peter, the fisherman, lends a gritty strength and reminder of the poet's own maritime beginnings: but also, irrevocably, it connects him to denial and absence because, in all the Passion narratives, St Peter deserted Jesus.[10] Graham says, 'I called today, Peter, and you were away'. Moreover, as in the Bible, the poem contains three denials, the third most distanced and authoritative: 'Lanyon, why is it you're earlier away?' But this absence, this failure of companionship and acknowledgement, is seen too as an opportunity for the word itself, the 'best' of the man, to be made known:

> You said once in the Engine
> House below Morvah
> That words make their world
> In the same way as the painter's
> Mark surprises him
> Into seeing new.
>
> (*CP*, p. 155)

Lanyon's death leaves space for Lanyon's word to stand, but throws the grieving friend into a reactive unsteadiness, a sense, perhaps, of his own work as closer to the 'chuck of jaws' than the forceful industry of the 'early beam / Engine'.

Elegy encourages invidious comparisons, but as the speaker invokes Lanyon it is to remind himself of the futility of such comparisons:

You said "Here is the sea
Made by alfred wallis
Or any poet or painter's
Eye it encountered. [...]
We all make it again."
                    (*CP*, pp. 155–56)

Each of us 'makes it' in our own particular way and consequently to some extent in our own image. It is Lanyon's voice saying this in the poem and his words are remade by the poem. It is as if he is allowing Graham to use his self for Graham's own ends; that, like the sea, of which he is now a part, he has become a kind of universal possession to be turned and remade by whoever looks on him. Peter, the rock, lends reassurance and encouragement: he exists, in this sense, through and by means of the space left by the poet's own unsteady self-confidence. He lives to offer affirmation of the speaker's talent.

As the poem muses over the connection between art and sacrificial suffering, echoes of Auden's 'Musée des Beaux Arts' may be heard. Graham's poem has for its dedication 'for the Painter Peter Lanyon killed in a gliding accident 1964'. Auden's poem explores the dogged indifference of the world to 'the dreadful martyrdom', the 'important failure', of Icarus as he plunges from the sky into the sea.[11] Events of worldly significance rub shoulders with petty mundanity; the grand and the bathetic alternate. The equivalent to Auden's point in Graham's poem can be found in the speaker's clashing impulses. He recreates the tone of easy camaraderie of drinking companions ('Peter, we'll sit and drink / And go in the sea's roar') and also uneasily tries to rise to the height of his now dead friend: 'Find me a thermal to speak and soar to you from'. Gliding's superb effortlessness confronts Graham's boisterous bonhomie; Lanyon's paintings encounter 'Italy [hanging] on a wall' in an advert.[12]

Consequently, Graham's tribute touchingly lacks the weight it might have invoked: it isn't clear to what extent the surrounding world elevates Lanyon's achievements by contrast. The poster is equivalent, instead, to the 'expensive delicate ship' in Auden's poem which 'sailed calmly on' despite the catastrophe it witnesses – oblivious of, or deliberately indifferent to, the human suffering involved. Including the poster implies, too, the presence in Graham himself of a life that goes on, of other interests, unelevated, prosaic desires and hostilities. Moreover, like Icarus, Lanyon has crashed. He kept himself going only for a time and this makes his gliding part of a human world. It may even be one source of his attraction for the poet. Lanyon's 'uneasiness', his failure to enjoy for long the superhuman (or merely privileged) life of the world-renowned artist, offers Graham a welcome correlative for his own endeavours.[13] These uneasy, self-suspecting feelings mean that friendship and betrayal seem inextricably connected in the poet's mind. The attempt at loyalty and devotion appears doomed to failure, particularly when the friends are both artists.

Yet, in Lanyon's absence, the speaker imagines friendship and reminds himself: 'Climb here where the hand / Will not grasp on air' (*CP*, p. 156). It is a wonderful pair of lines, evoking the jolting shock of loss, the kindly reassurance packaging in its negative a sort of aerial comfort. Graham stretches at, grasps out for, the rock of companionship and holds only air. And yet, he writes, the artist

> steers his life to maim

> Himself somehow for the job. His job is Love
> Imagined into words or paint to make
> An object that will stand and will not move.
> (*CP*, p. 155)

With Lanyon gone, the speaker dignifies his calling, seeing it as a divine, perhaps Christ-like mission. In Milton's 'Lycidas' the death of King makes way for Milton's sense of poetry as a divine vocation: here, too, art becomes a work of 'Love', elevated by his friend's participation in it. Furthermore, these lines lend the poem's title a particular significance. 'The Thermal Stair' refers to the thermals, the rising columns of hot air, which the glider relies on for its flight. In this way, it connotes both passive acceptance of a given movement and also the willed, committed effort of a purgatorial ascent to spiritual enlightenment and purification.

At work, then, in 'The Thermal Stair' and less explicitly in 'The Constructed Space' is a religious or quasi-religious vocabulary, frame of reference and sensibility. The question of Graham's religious allegiances or interests has been raised in one or two places and, it seems to me, remains unresolved. Tony Lopez has commented on some of this but reaches rather mixed conclusions. In *The Poetry of W.S. Graham* he acknowledges that in 'The Nightfishing' '[the] Christian imagery is a steady feature of the poem' (Lopez, *PWSG*, p. 72) and explains that this 'sets the fishing-trip in the Christian tradition of a voyage home, passing through the cares and temptations of the world to reach heaven and union with God'. Lopez also states that 'the survival of religious feeling in secular and specifically elemental experience is one of the main characteristics of Graham's early and mid career', leading up to and including 'The Nightfishing' (Lopez, *PWSG*, p. 24). Lopez concludes, though, that the allusion to such imagery amounts to a 'reserved intimation of seriousness, rather than a statement of faith. "Grace", "light" and "dead" become, in the context of this poem, words which have a glamour cast back on them from a religious meaning that can no longer be confidently managed.' He adds that he doubts whether a statement of faith could be made from the position of the dispersed self that speaks from Graham's poems. However, the 'place' of the poem is, Lopez concedes, 'sacred', set apart from normal life, and Christian language is used to signal this specialness.[14]

In a 1981 interview with Lopez, Graham seemed to confirm this conclusion in describing himself as not a religious poet (see Lopez, *PWSG*, pp. 23, 135n). However, elsewhere Graham sounds less decisive. He remarks, in a letter about the imminent marriage of his friends Ronnie and Henriette Duncan: 'I write better when I don't have anything to say or reply to anything. Anyhow. Who should I ever get my forces together to reply to but GOD. Am I going a bit too far?'[15] The back-pedalling is characteristic, and so is the essence, if such there is, of what Graham is saying: that he does not write to say anything, or is hampered if aware of such an objective. The letter also suggests a connection in his mind between his reluctance to give poetry a 'take-away-able' message and his feeling that poems are addressed to God. Moreover, Graham says 'to reply to' God, and the verb immediately suggests epistolary poems, which are often written as replies to previous, usually imaginary, letters from the person addressed.

Graham's 'Notes on a Poetry of Release' is similarly caught up in declaring that his poetry is 'about' nothing and that it is, in some sense, a speaking to God. Graham writes:

> It is no help to think of the purpose as being to 'transfuse recollected emotion' or to 'report significantly' or indeed to think of it as a putting-across of anything. The poem itself is dumb but has the power of release. Its purpose is that it can be used by the reader to find out something about himself [...] The poem is not a handing out of the same packet to everyone, as it is not a thrown-down heap of words for us to choose the bonniest.
>
> (*Nightfisherman*, p. 381)

These words are a recapitulation of an earlier, often-quoted section of the 'Notes', which begins, 'The most difficult thing for me to remember is that a poem is made of words and not the expanding heart, the overflowing soul, or the sensitive observer'. They develop the earlier passage by stressing a positive element: the poem 'is not a handing out of the same packet' but it 'can be used by the reader to find out something about himself'.

The second section of the 'Notes' extends the idea of the poet as not so much telling the truth as provoking in the reader better self-understanding. Graham presents the poet as the descendant of Blake, endeavouring '[to] bisect the angle between God and Man and find the earliest distance between head and heart. [...] To bring about the reader's Involuntary Belief', delighting in the truth and holiness of life, while standing himself at a remove from that life. In part he is amidst that spilling life, taking 'notes' or 'book[ing] the phrases of drinking and affection', as he calls it, in the swell and swill of experience. As he 'books the phrases' the poet makes them memorable, but he also arrests and even punishes them for their transgressions. He serves thus as a kind of referee or arbitrator, keeping the peace through the 'swift metaphors of the moment', but also preserving them for later scrutiny, 'booking' them for another moment, in both his own and his reader's attention.

It is no accident, therefore, that the 'Notes' end with a version of a section from the book of Job (ch. 28), verses that seem to pay tribute to 'man's' limitless achievements, the scores he makes on the created world:

> Man setteth an end to darkness,
> And searcheth out to the furthest bound
> The stones of thick darkness and of the shadow of death.
> He breaketh open a shaft away from where men sojourn [...]
>   (*Nightfisherman*, p. 383)

Graham's extract seems to close unambiguously, but he has earlier said, with equal certainty, that 'the meaning of a word is never more than its position'. This extract's meaning is given further depth by its original position. In the Bible, the verses go on to counter the opening celebration of man's gifts by asking: 'where is the place of understanding? Man knoweth not the price thereof; neither is it found in the land of the living [...] Whence then cometh wisdom? And where is the place of understanding? [...] God understandeth the way thereof and he knoweth the place thereof' (Job 28.12-23). Graham's omission of these later verses is telling, but ambiguously so. Perhaps the poem becomes itself the prototype of divine wisdom, the closest to God in a world now without God. Or perhaps Graham's silence reveals an illustration of what he earlier suggests: that 'the poet does not write what he knows but what he does not know'. It is for the reader to offer the 'reply' to this unfinished quotation; and, as suggested in the quoted letter, sometimes, at least, the imagined reader is God.

Having said this, Graham also at many points takes pains to repeat that the words on the page are 'all we have'; they are our only access to ultimate meaning. Earlier in 'Notes', as if sensing this tension within himself between words and that which goes beyond words, he writes: 'It is easy to mistake a poem for a different thing with a different function and to be sad when it does not put out what it is not. In the end then are those still words on the paper and arranged half-victim to the physical outside, half-victim to my Morality's origins, out of this dying and bearing language' (*Nightfisherman*, pp. 379–80). The second sentence declares an 'end' ('are those still words') but the structure works against such closure, tugging the words apart between art and accident. They 'are', and are also 'arranged'. Perhaps most of all, the 'expanding heart' easily cramps the words, not least because the words may often appear recalcitrant, unprepossessing and in need of support from the reader. Yet reluctance in language is a quality Graham seems both to admire and to envy. Take the unwieldy phrase 'does not put out what it is not', for example. The emphasis here falls on the reader's pre-emptive expectations of the poem, which distort and obscure its 'real being'. The verb 'put out' suggests, perhaps, plant-like tendrils that guide the reader to its 'root' or essence of meaning. Alternatively, though, the phrase could carry a more antagonistic colouring, so as to suggest that we look to poetry to gratify our instincts for vindication against what 'puts us out', to fulfil vicariously our desires for conquest over what we 'are not'. But the poem does not actively refute or destroy its 'other': it is just itself, immune to such desires for the eradication of alterity.

This account of the poem as simply itself – 'those still words on the paper' that just 'are' – might, on the other hand, also bear a more positive reading, closer to Keats's idea of negative capability. The poem could be said potentially to respond to and accommodate the 'other' through its silent being. This aspect of the passage is essentially unclosed and indefinite. Nonetheless, Graham's location of both infinite autonomy and infinite accommodation of the 'other', of 'what it is not', imbues the poetic word with transcendent power.

Several times in the 'Notes', this shift from a competitive to a coexisting movement may be observed in Graham's language. Take his use of the word 'score', for instance, which includes senses of achievement and affliction. Graham writes 'Time and again I am scored by the others' and 'History has a new score on its track'; he repeats in the 'Notes' a passage which serves as a refrain: 'It is a good direction to believe that this language which is so scored and impressed by the commotion of all of us since its birth can be arranged to in its turn impress significantly for the good of each individual. Let us endure the sudden affection of the language' (*Nightfisherman*, p. 380). Language here is personified. Like the biblical Word of God, it has been born and has passively suffered, as if on the cross, the 'commotion of all of us'. The cadence here might lead the reader to expect the word 'sins', but the word 'commotion', often used also in Graham's letters, suggests instead the chaotic disorders of history. '[I]n its turn' turns such disorder, surprisingly, into benefit from the shifts and alterations of meaning within poetry. But this benefit, Graham implies, may also scar or score us, and demand our submission to its 'affection', its effect, on us.

Here once more we see Graham's characteristic marriage of under-statement and shock-tactics: affection seems too mild a word, and 'endure' too extreme. But the collocation transforms our understanding of the kind of love that this might be. The speaker steps down from his individual position in the service of this 'affection': he loses his own agency as he speaks of language's loss of freedom in its 'affection' for the world. This loss, however, Graham hopes, may lead to a kind of triumph, to an indelible mark on history that comes out of 'impressing' readers, includ-ing potentially Graham himself. Once more, then, the word is seen to be both immediate, familiar, unprepossessing, yet also beyond and above our grasp.

As I have mentioned, Tony Lopez seeks to replace any emphasis on a religious concern with one on the 'interaction of man and world' (Lopez, *PWSG*, p. 74). Lopez is perhaps here identifying Graham's humanist tendencies, and in doing so perceiving his efforts to differentiate himself from the differently mystical timbres of his predecessors Thomas and Hopkins and, more significantly, those of his patron and colleague, T.S. Eliot. The pervasive influence of Eliot does need to be shrugged off, and 'interaction' certainly becomes Graham's preoccupying concern. I would suggest, however, that such negotiations within the world become for Graham the potential locus for experience of the transcendent, even if that transcendence manifests itself through the shifting, fragile, unstable medium of the epistolary address.

Secondly, I want to question whether it is appropriate to dismiss so easily Graham's use of this religiously inflected language, when language is for Graham so central and constitutes in his mind the very poem itself. Furthermore, a letter to Edwin Morgan, written in April 1949, confirms Graham's abiding concern with spiritual exploration, expressed quite conventionally in a language of belief:

> The sea in The White Threshold is a changing symbol. It is variously – the Continual Arrival from 'otherness' – the element through which we all move and with the urge to really contact and share with the other 'inner sea' of other people and break the centre aloneness. Yet the centre aloneness is the greatest joy and gift from Him. If sharing it were easy it would be nothing. – the mingling, always moving, spontaneous morality of the 'heart' as opposed to the outside constructions of order because we are a world and live together. – and the sea with no exactness but with nonetheless intensity and positivity – moving mingling with a storm 1000's of miles away having effects and movements at our door – Edwin, I really love being on the sea. There I have feeling of freedom and cleanness and being part of a great energy which has nothing to do with any morality and is completely unhuman.
>
> (*Nightfisherman*, pp. 92–93)

Graham goes on to downplay the importance of editors to his poetry and asserts that art will impact on the reader or not, irrespective of editors:

> It either unites with us to our advantage or doesn't unite with us at all. By 'to our advantage' I mean to our enlargement of spirit. So, more and more, I realise the aloneness is a joy to live in and talk there to the most marvellous listener which is within my imagination and the limitations of that listener are the limitations of my poetry. [...] But O the few who will really get the subtle heartbreaking gestures of speech woven and positioned so exactly in a poem – a very very few. And the striving to communicate the merest wink of torment or sudden drench of sweetness is as though one were talking to God.
>
> (*Nightfisherman*, p. 94)[16]

Much here is essential to Graham's way of thinking. There is the edgy concern to clarify what one might think could be left to the reader's imagination: the sense, for instance, that the sea operates variously, as a 'changing symbol'. When in poetry does it not, one might wonder. Also, more interestingly, Graham asserts that the white threshold in his poem is a stable symbol of a dynamic action, the movement from the alien, the 'other' as Graham calls it, to the self, which is also other and alien. Many of Graham's phrases as he explores this area have a preacherly ring to them. Graham's unpredictable but recurrent resorting to prophetic, homiletic diction might be read as an almost fraudulent heightening. It might be seen as an escape clause, perhaps, a reliance on the robes of authority when on sticky ground. It can be dismissed as a vestige of Dylan Thomas's influence. Nonetheless, in a writer for the most part so resolutely given to a disarming lack of interest in public morality, the tone is strikingly didactic and deserves pausing over.[17] It suggests, I would say, two things: firstly, the impact of John Donne on Graham at this period and later; and, secondly, Graham's sense that communication with others (and with the other that is oneself) is very like a religious experience.

Graham had been reading Donne's sermons a few years earlier in 1945 (see *Nightfisherman*, p. 50) as well as writing in 1946 to William Montgomerie, 'good to hear from you and the lovely copy of Donne' (*Nightfisherman*, p. 67). Donne's rhetoric may, I think, be felt as a presence at various points in Graham's work. There is not scope here to be extensive, but two points of contact should perhaps be mentioned. Both are concerned with the essence of communication: love's limited effects on the individual's 'centre aloneness'. In the famous poem 'The Ecstasy', Donne writes:

> When love, with one another so
> > Interinanimates two souls,
> That abler soul, which thence doth flow,
> > Defects of loneliness controls.

Many of Graham's epistolary poems, I think, dramatize this interaction, and lament the loss of such an 'abler soul'. The earlier verse in the poem that has described the lovers' timeless union runs:

> And whilst our souls negotiate there,
> > We like sepulchral statues lay;
> All day, the same our postures were,
> > And we said nothing, all the day.[18]

In its combination of serenely ironic humour and grave scepticism, the poem has some qualities in common with Graham's Letter III (first published in *The Nightfishing*), which is something like a love poem. Donne uses the tetrameter quatrain to endorse the expressions of mutual 'interinanimation'. Graham, though, uses his familiar and balder three-stress line to bring the assurances of harmony into fuller question:

> We shall lie held here
> In the moving hull of Love
> Face to face making
> The perfect couple perfect.

So, under every eye,
Who shall we perish to?
Here it's endlessly us
Face to face across
The nine-waved and the berry-
Stained kiss of the moved sea.
And not one word we merge in
Here shall we unmarvel
From its true home.

(*CP*, p. 114)

Donne's 'lay / All day, the same our postures were' and Graham's
wonderfully laconic and simple 'Here it's endlessly us' both partly mock,
partly encapsulate the spiritual, non-timely essence of love; and both
writers see this experience as going beyond words: 'and we said nothing,
all the day', 'And not one word we merge in'. Both, though, imagine
being immortalized in this moment, and look in on themselves from the
future with a kind of equanimity. Graham says 'We shall lie held here / In
this moving hull of Love', 'Move here. We'll choose inshore, / But that's
not their concern'. Donne, in the final verse of his poem, declares:

And if some lover, such as we,
    Have heard this dialogue of one,
Let him still mark us, he shall see
    Small change, when we'are to bodies gone.[19]

Particularly at this point in the late 1940s when Donne was, thanks to
Eliot, a mainstream figure, Graham invokes him when pursuing his own
'dialogue of one'.

Donne's sermon 'Mundus Mare' may also have a bearing on Graham,
in particular on his use of the metaphor of the sea. Donne is more
aphoristic than Graham is in his letter to Edwin Morgan when he writes:
'the world is a Sea, but especially it is a Sea in this respect, that the Sea is
no place of habitation, but a passage to our habitations'.[20] More importantly, though, the difference and similarity between Donne and Graham
illustrate how intensely Graham looks at what happens when one person
speaks to another.

Graham's didactic phrase in that letter was 'the element through which
we all move', but he unsettles this island of comfort with the phrase 'and
with the urge to really contact and share with the other "inner sea" of
other people and break the centre aloneness'. As Graham talks about
isolation, he is quite lucid; as he broaches the gesture of contact the syntax

quavers and fractures. The word 'other' reassures the reader of individual identity each time it is used; but that reassurance also generates the violent and contradictory image that ends the sentence, 'break the centre aloneness'.

We have already imagined that aloneness as being like a sea, amorphous, elusive, vacillating; counterfeiting sometimes, perhaps, as the shifting element of language does, on which we walk at our peril. But if it is indeed amorphous it cannot, at least, be 'broken'; and it may not have a centre. The words struggle to establish certainties and the struggle seems to lead to a frustrated violence, working through the emphatic gestures towards contact, expressed by the two phrases: 'and with the urge' and 'really contact and share'. Naturally, we might expect the image of contact and sharing to form the climax to this sentence, but Graham goes beyond the comforting objective of sharing to end with the possibly sexualized image of rupture and offcentring.

The following sentence is in cadence even more homiletic than the previous one, and apparently without irony: 'Yet the centre aloneness is the greatest joy and gift from Him. If sharing it were easy it would be nothing.' The last clause, 'it would be nothing', savagely breaks the centre of imagined ease, or absence of difficulty: for such absence devalues the endeavour. The first sentence implies that 'the centre is too precious to share'. Instead, we are given this ambivalent, challengingly opaque, almost Blakean aphorism: that difficulty enhances the value of the effort of sharing, and also, sharing has to remain a challenge, since too much familiarity breeds contempt.

It is now in the passage as if this centre aloneness is a pearl, hard to share and hard to break; there's a strident disparity between this and the sea metaphors in service previously. But it's clear too that the two movements are not necessarily contradictory in Graham's understanding. When he returned to the theme in a letter to Alan Clodd, ten years later, he is saying much the same but less metaphorically and more schematically:

Whatever intelligence made us (He, She, It) made us so beautifully and so well knit with the paradoxical hunger –

1 – To be one, in one's identity and indestructible in anything or anyone else. To have been given one's own unique gesture of consciousness.

2 – To always want to share the aloneness, to share what happens in one's own lonely room, to wonder how alike or unlike one is from someone else. So we have these two things, not necessarily contraries. The responsibility of

aloneness without which life would be nothing and the hunger for love, to be recognised as what we *think* we are and loved for that.

(*Nightfisherman*, p. 142)

These movements are re-enacted, as often, in the structure of Graham's response to his correspondent's enquiries about his poem 'The Night-fishing'. He explains very exactly:

> I wanted to write about the sea and make it a grey green sea, not a chocolate box sea. I wanted to speak about the boat maintained on its strange element and sailing out, dividing the water with its bow and keel, lifting up by the water rushing in underneath [...] although I wanted to write about the sea it was not the sea only as an objective adventure (if there is such a thing) but as experience surrounding a deeper problem, which everybody is concerned with.
>
> I mean the essential isolation of man and the difficulty of communication. To speak much about what I have tried to say in THE NIGHTFISHING and discuss those ideas which are, you might say, take-away-able would be to curtail what the poem says to you and that, after all, is maybe greater or less than I had in mind but is certainly not the same and it is certainly unique.

(*Nightfisherman*, p. 144)

This becomes choppy, and then increasingly defensive. The poem is realistic, not a fantasy of the sea; still, it is not merely realistic, it is allegorical; but not merely allegorical, it is more than that and to say what that 'more' was would be to express the ineffable. Graham's tone enacts and illustrates his point: the difficulty of communication. Equally though, the hunger to explain, to make himself be understood, though not 'taken away', not taken for less than he is – this impulse too is not sold short.

The point is repeated in later letters. To Bryan Winter (19 November 1958) Graham writes that 'we should not expect poetry (even although it is an object of words which we might use every day) to hand us out a little nutshell truth which we have pleasure in agreeing with'.[21] Similarly, in a longer and later letter to Norman Macleod in which Graham works through 'The Nightfishing' in the wake of preparing a reading of it for the radio, he quotes from the third section of the poem what he sees as the 'message' statement, hedging it '(and please take note of the inverted commas there)'. The paragraph ends, 'The objective world constructed round the vision (allow that word) like the kernel round a nut' (*Nightfisherman*, p. 172). Again, Graham tries to prevent the reader from extracting an 'easy' meaning apart from the subjective vision of the whole poem, but in doing so he must at some point concede a 'centre' and an outside. His second parenthesis displays the discomfort this generates. His reversal of the familiar, with the nut preceding the kernel, goes some but not all the way to allaying this unease.

He is not disputing the category of the 'objective'. Rather, by displacing it and reducing the emphasis on quantifiable 'meaning', he redresses the balance between material and spiritual values. The tone in which this area is treated is often edgy and wary, as if Graham is reluctantly responding to the needs of his limited readership. But there is also a tone of mystical wonder at the inherent value of such 'vision'.[22]

The sixth section of 'The Nightfishing' is, indeed, both the most accessible in terms of meaning and experience, and also, as Graham wrote in the letter to Macleod, the most mysterious: 'There is hardly a thing I know about this "bit" of poetry. There it is, in some ways more to do with me than all parts of my poem. [...] This section, more than any other section in The Nightfishing seems, for me, to stand alone and almost exist as a poem on its own. It has a quality which, since then, I have not been able to repeat' (*Nightfisherman*, p. 174). He quotes the lines: 'Thus, shed into the industrious grave / Ever of my life, you serve the love / Whose motive we are energies of'. He comments in particular on the 'of' that closes the line and relates this placing to 'some kind of lyrical statement which is also formal and even abstract'.

The quality of writing in this final section is particularly well sustained, and it is also one of the most Eliotian passages in Graham's writing. It recalls the first section of 'East Coker', where 'you lean against a bank while a van passes', and also the last which writes of the 'time for the evening under lamplight / (The evening with the photograph album)'. Notes of 'Burnt Norton' can be heard too; Graham is recreating a kind of 'moment in the rose garden', a moment of calling. In Eliot's poem:

> The bird called, in response to
> The unheard music hidden in the shrubbery,
> And the unseen eyebeam crossed, for the roses
> Had the look of flowers that are looked at. [...]
> Go, said the bird, for the leaves were full of children,
> Hidden excitedly, containing laughter[23]

Eliot's moment passes, it disappears within time. But Graham works the mystical 'calling' or naming into the fabric of this section . He is first 'leaned at rest in lamplight with / The offered moth and heard breath'. The word 'with' here, unlike Eliot's line where lamplight closes off the sense, prepares the self to connect with the world of voices. While Eliot's experience is closer to a haunting, Graham's is 'endured' in the moment. He does not 'follow' but he is 'as at hushed called by the owl'. With this sanction he assumes full agency where before he was merely 'leaned at rest':

I leaned and with a kind word gently
Struck the held air like a doorway
Bled open to meet another's eye.
(*CP*, p. 105)

In form this resembles the phrase quoted earlier about the need to 'break the centre aloneness'. The gesture of contact is abrupt and invasive, the moment where the typewriter key impacts, shattering the night-time silence. The verse quoted above, ending 'energies of', similarly opens up syntactically the idea of connection with the world through 'love'; a love that the ritualized 'shedding' of blood and tears through communication makes possible. The earlier self of the 'recent madman' is 'shed' too into the memory, his ghost laid to rest, perhaps. 'For there you'll labour less lonely', Graham assures himself. Through writing the aloneness of the self is both cherished and alleviated.

Many of Graham's poems express the shock of otherness, the potential for constant estrangement from the unfamiliar that is the other. Progressively throughout his career, they creatively confront this shock. By presenting a self that is a sea, an eternally fluid centre of being, Graham finds a way in which he can approach that strange 'encountered face' ('The Nightfishing', *CP*, p. 102). The metaphor he consistently resorts to when describing this encounter is that of walking on the water.

Tony Lopez usefully compares Graham's early poem 'The Lost Other' with Hopkins's *The Wreck of the Deutschland* and identifies similarities of diction between the two, without saying a great deal more than this (Lopez, *PWSG*, pp. 48–50). Hopkins's poem places at its centre a vision in which Christ walks on the water to save a nun and take her to heaven. The last section of 'The Nightfishing', like many moments in Graham's writing, uses a similar metaphor to express a miraculous 'salvation': 'Very gently the keel / Walks its waters again. / The sea awakes its fires'. The 'Seven Letters' that follow 'The Nightfishing' (in both the original volume and *Collected Poems*) similarly make use of the image. In Letter I, for example, Graham writes 'I / Hack steps on the water', and in Letter II, 'I walk the dead water / Burning language towards / You where you lie in the dark / Ascension of all words' (*CP*, pp. 106, 109, 111).

One might say that rather than being exactly letters, these poems are prayers to an absent listener, a God who, like Job's God, has left the prophet abandoned in the darkness. Letter II continues:

Yet where? Where do you lie
Lost to my cry and hidden
Away from the world's downfall? [...]
Take heed. Reply. Here
I am driven burning on
This loneliest element. Break
Break me out of this night,
This silence where you are not,

                    (*CP*, p. 111)

Both Hopkins and Graham invoke the biblical accounts of the call of St
Peter, who ran to meet Christ across the water; then, as the storm rose,
Peter lost confidence and started to drown. This episode is shortly followed
by Peter's affirmation of Jesus as Christ.[24] A reciprocal process of affirmation and self-discovery is described, in which the miraculous walking on
the water is crucial. Graham's poetry focuses so often on this incident
because he sees the process of communicating with another person as
being similarly miraculous, elemental and self-affirming. Communication
stretches between us, thwarted by the storms of self-doubt and what he
calls 'my ego house'. And, like a miracle, 'Communication is', as he says in
his 'Private Poem to Norman Macleod', 'always / On the edge of ridiculous' (*CP*, pp. 219, 221).

In 1958, Graham published a poem in the magazine *Encounter*, 'Letter
X – My dear so many times', which he never collected. In it, he writes in a
manner close to that of the earlier verse letters. It is my last example of
how Graham's epistolary writing responds to and conveys this religious
sense of communication, that reaching another person is an everyday
event (not chocolate-boxy at all), and at the same time miraculous.

My dear so many times
My dear, more than this is
Is nothing to the high
Silences unhailed
That surge around us all
Ways wearing us away.[25]

'Seven Letters', published in *The Nightfishing* in 1955, ends naturally enough
with Letter VII. Letter X seems an arbitrary number, perhaps a secret one
(like 'Station X'). I wonder too whether the letter is a pun on 'times' and
on the kiss with which letters sometimes close. 'My dear' is a different
'dear' each time, and yet each invocation is as nothing to the vast 'unhailed'
silences. 'Unhailed' is a striking word and in a sense the centre of the poem.

While the silence is unbroached, it is also both 'unheld' and unsanctified: 'The unhailed water [is] held / Still for a moment'. As the speaker begins to write in 'The Nightfishing' he strikes 'the held air'. He catches the moment, the gesture between the alone self and the other. The silence is a part of the indifferent world, which in 'Letter X' is 'Turning with the slow / Drift of the stellar stour'. Despite the world's mere drift, however, the poem persists: 'Yet I turn a little / Towards where you may be / My dear'. 'And so', Graham tentatively claims in the poem's closing lines:

> even
> That is something if nothing
> More than making from
> The behaviour of silence
> Maybe the slow gathering
> Way at night over
> The unhailed water held
> Still for a moment within
> These words becoming
> Our obstacle in common.

The uncertain, faltering movement here (where the progress of the poem is achieved around many of the line endings such as 'nothing / More', 'held / still' and so on), modestly and inexorably assumes a transcendental force for good, 'These words becoming / Our obstacle in common'. Address is offered as a secular hallowing, a making holy of the unregenerate wastes of experience.

Graham, typically, suspects such claims:

> It is easily said
> You lie somewhere there
> Elegantly under
> Unrehearsed possibilities
> Of language

In a sense, this is a kind of retaliation to the suggestion that in 'hailing' the other, the silence, in walking on the water of separateness, the difference can be contained, annulled or 'held'. For to say 'you lie' contains of course the intimation of deceit, of false claims of purchase on the inarticulate. 'You' lie nowhere, except in the 'turns', the revolutions and elusive transformations of language.

Despite the evidence of time's decay and language's duplicity, the speaker declares, 'Yet I turn a little / Towards where you may be'. There is the potential of such encounter at one hand, and the 'started / Poem' at the other. And at this moment of bifocal vision, at (as it were) the point of intersection between the worlds of human and transcendent creation, something happens:

And this becomes almost
A place where those two
We loved as once stand
On either side of language
To watch.

For the first time in the poem, movement stops and time 'stands' still: the line is arrested, nearly stalled, on 'stand'. The 'you' expected, in the convenient phrasings of language, to 'lie under' the text is (through the poet's tentative 'turn / Towards where you may be'), made to stand over it like a tutelary spirit. The 'you' is offered a kind of resurrection through poetic 'conversion'. Similarly, we expect to read 'as one', yet read 'as once'. The one moment in time is included in the moment of personal meeting and union, so that not only two people, but two disparate moments in time, past and present, 'almost' concur. And with this moment, with the temporal and transcendent realms in equipoise, the moment of encounter between 'we', the 'I' and the 'you' of the poem is made possible. It is acknowledged to be at least 'something' which the subsequent making of the poem works to hold and recreate.

Turns may be just drift and bring forth only wreckage; but the actively managed 'turn' towards 'where you may be' can make something from that 'unhailed water'. This something is 'almost / A place'; the poem is not quite a substantial locality; more, as Graham puts it elsewhere, a constructed 'space', with freedom to 'grow bolder' when not looked at too directly. The poem seeks to intimate and release both reader's and writer's 'Involuntary Belief'. Graham falters here at seeing 'face to face', but darkly, 'out of the corner of my eye', he yields abundant harvests.

Notes

1 T.S. Eliot, 'East Coker', in *Collected Poems: 1909–1962* (London: Faber and Faber, 1963), p. 200.
2 Graham, *CP*, pp. 152–53.
3 See the close of Milton's *Paradise Lost*: 'The world was all before them, where to choose / Their place of rest, and Providence their guide; / They, hand in hand, with wand'ring steps and slow, / Through Eden took their solitary way' (Book XII, ll. 646–49).

4 T.S. Eliot, 'The Dry Salvages', in *Collected Poems*, p. 208.

5 'The Constructed Space' echoes 'East Coker' too, where Eliot describes the struggle to 'learn to use words': 'Because one has only learnt to get the better of words / For the thing one no longer has to say, or the way in which / One is no longer disposed to say it' ('East Coker', pp. 202–203). Graham puts it more succinctly and also with less resignation in the second stanza: 'And even then we know what we are saying / Only when it is said and fixed and dead' (*CP*, p. 152). As often in Graham's writing, punitive repetition flogs the line to death, but in doing so it challenges us to see new sayings, new turns of meaning, in its retrospective glances.

6 See 1 Kings 3.16-28.

7 Alexander Pope, 'Epistle to Mr. Jervas With Dryden's Translation of Fresnoy's Art of Painting', in *Poetical Works*, ed. Herbert Davis (Oxford and New York: Oxford University Press, 1966), p. 631, l. 16.

8 See Genesis 1.1 and 1 Corinthians 13.12.

9 Compare this with Graham's 'Letter III': 'We'll drink / Ourselves here face to face / A one for the road across / More than these words', and 'We shall lie held here / In the moving hull of Love / Face to face making / The perfect couple perfect' (*CP*, pp. 113, 114).

10 Peter's denial is narrated in all four Gospels; see Matthew 26.69-75; Mark 14.66-72; Luke 22.54-62; John 18.25-27.

11 W.H. Auden, 'Musée des Beaux Arts' (1938), in *The English Auden: Poems, Essays and Dramatic Writings 1927–1939*, ed. Edward Mendelson (London: Faber and Faber, 1977), p. 237.

12 *CP*, pp. 154, 156. Gliding suggests an ease with the light breezes of social intercourse, which Graham himself notably lacked. By contrast, Graham's friendship with Lanyon seems cemented by its impoliteness, its jokey and high-flown disparagement of the world of banal cultural discourse symbolized by the woman on the poster with the drink. She, 'In some polite place' (*CP*, p. 156), apes the heights of art gracefully achieved by Lanyon.

13 Such semi-famous figures are often subjects of epistolary verse: Graham's predecessor in the genre, Alexander Pope, likewise looks to contemporaries such as the painter Jervas, whose gifts may complement but not overshadow his own.

14 See also Edwin Morgan's discussion of religious language in 'The Nightfishing', Chapter 10 below, and Tony Lopez's account of 'The Nightfishing' as 'post-Homeric and post-Christian – loaded with Christian meanings but also located within ordinary work experience' (see p. 38 above). In the second clause, I would want only to change 'but also' to 'and also'.

15 ' "Dear Pen Pal in the Distance": A Selection of W.S. Graham's Letters', ed. R. Grogan, *PN Review* 73 (1990), p. 16. It is striking that this letter was not selected for *The Nightfisherman*, although others in Grogan's selection were reprinted there.

16 Compare 'Hilton Abstract', 'Hell with this and hell with that […] We either touch or do not touch' (*CP*, p. 169).

17 The 'Notes on a Poetry of Release' tones down its prophetic claims. A poem 'can be used', Graham says, as if almost mocking the role of the poet as prophet. The key paragraph, written twice in the 'Notes', begins modestly 'It is a good direction to believe'. When his language is in danger of becoming grandiloquent and authoritative,

Graham mitigates his claim with a tentative phrasing, as in the diminutive title, 'Notes on …' (*Nightfisherman*, pp. 380, 381, 383).

18 John Donne, 'The Ecstasy', ll. 17–20, 41–44, in *The Complete English Poems*, ed. A.J. Smith (Harmondsworth: Penguin, 1971), pp. 54, 55.

19 Donne, 'The Ecstasy', ll. 73–76, p. 56.

20 John Donne, 'Mundus Mare', in *Donne's Sermons: Selected Passages*, ed. L. Pearsall Smith (Oxford: Clarendon Press, 1919), p. 73.

21 *Nightfisherman*, p. 163. The sentence comes from a notebook Graham sent to Wynter.

22 The metaphor of the kernel recalls Julian of Norwich, who saw God and the whole universe within a walnut.

23 Eliot, 'East Coker', I and V; 'Burnt Norton', I, in *Collected Poems*, pp. 190, 196, 203.

24 This sequence occurs in the Gospels of Matthew and John, though Peter walks on the water with Jesus only in Matthew's version of the story. See Matthew 14.22-33 and 16.16 and John 6.16-21 and 67-69.

25 W.S. Graham, 'Letter X – My dear so many times', *Encounter*, 10.1 (January 1958), p. 42. All subsequent quotations from the text are from here.

From **Johann Joachim Quantz's Five Lessons**

The Last Lesson

Dear Karl, this morning is our last lesson.
I have been given the opportunity to
Live in a certain person's house and tutor
Him and his daughters on the traverse flute.
Karl, you will be all right. In those recent
Lessons my heart lifted to your playing.

I know. I see you doing well, invited
In a great chamber in front of the gentry. I
Can see them with their dresses settling in
And bored mouths beneath moustaches sizing
You up as you are, a lout from the canal
With big ears but an angel's tread on the flute.

But you will be all right. Stand in your place
Before them. Remember Johann. Begin with good
Nerve and decision. Do not intrude too much
Into the message you carry and put out.

One last thing, Karl, remember when you enter
The joy of those quick high archipelagoes,
To make to keep your finger-stops as light
As feathers but definite. What can I say more?
Do not be sentimental or in your Art.
I will miss you. Do not expect applause.

10

The Poetry of W.S. Graham

EDWIN MORGAN

Although he has not reprinted all his early poems – there are a fair number omitted from *Cage Without Grievance* and *2ND Poems*, and *The Seven Journeys* is not represented at all – the uncompromising chronological arrangement of his 'Collected' presents Graham's readers with a dense initial verbal blast or barrage redolent of the whole heady iconolatry of the 1940s, and they must persist through these vatic voluntaries until they reach the clearer air of *The White Threshold* (1949), *The Nightfishing* (1955), and the later work of the 1970s. In the early poems, the word is king but meaning is not; and yet, as in the similar poetry of Dylan Thomas, there are frequent lines which stand out and refuse to be forgotten:

Gone to no end but each man's own

or

Through all the suburbs children trundle cries

or

O gentle queen of the afternoon

or

I walk as a lonely energy at large through my host

– the last of these in a poem unfortunately omitted from the *Collected Poems*. In an essay published in this early period, 'Notes on a Poetry of Release' (*Poetry Scotland*, No. 3, July 1946), Graham wrote:

The most difficult thing for me to remember is that a poem is made of words and not of the expanding heart, the overflowing soul, or the sensitive observer. A poem is made of words. It is words in a certain order, good or bad by the significance of its addition to life [...] Let us endure the sudden affection of the language.

He did not escape the obvious dangers lurking in that view, the overtaking of sense by sound, the over-estimation of subconscious and chance elements, the frustrating of argument and persuasion. Yet no-one can say that sound, and the subconscious, and the progress of a poem through something other than logic, are not important features of poetry, and we have to be clear that Graham's continuing faithfulness to the Word is what gives his whole work its integrity, in that he is a great and cunning craftsman, with a very particular skill in rhythm, and in the movement of a poem from line to line, a skill that stood him in real stead from *The White Threshold* onward, when control and clarity began to attract him more than they had done when he set out. A good Graham poem is an exceedingly well made poem (and hearing him read it impresses this fact even more strongly).

The White Threshold and *The Nightfishing* contained examples of the new clarity in fine lyrical pieces like 'Since All My Steps Taken' (where 'hobnail on Ben Narnain' and 'the creak of the rucksack' accompany the speaker's own quest to find himself and his poetic language) and 'Letter VI' (a love poem); in suggestive, memorable, powerful, almost-understood short poems like 'Night's Fall Unlocks the Dirge of the Sea':

> The surge by day by night turns lament
> And by this night falls round the surrounding
> Seaside and countryside and I can't
> Sleep one word away on my own for that
> Grief sea with a purse of pearls and debt
> Wading the land away with salt in his throat.

and in the two longer title-poems, 'The White Threshold' and 'The Nightfishing', both of which combine Graham's obsessional interests in the sea and in trying to define the communicative act and art of poetry itself. The former poem, as the title suggests, envisages the sea as a vast source of beginnings, of voyages and discoveries, physical and mental, of life and livelihood and yet equally of death and fear and awe, a place stained with the blood of hunted whales and rich with the bodies of drowned sailors yet also and perhaps inexplicably 'always the welcome-roaring threshold' – and this sea is also the perilous medium of language the poet sets out on, again and again, filled with the 'drowned' writers and works of the past and with the submerged, struggling, ascending hopes and cries of the poet himself which call up, in their turn, the memories and hopes of his readers:

Always these all sea families felled
In diving burial hammocks or toppled
Felled elm back into the waving woods,
Wear me my words. The nettling brine
Stings through the word. The Morven maiden cries.

Your heartlit fathoms hurl their ascending drowned.

Very end then of land. What vast is here?
The drowning saving while, the threshold sea
Always is here. You may not move away.

'The Nightfishing', generally and rightly regarded as the better poem of the two, gives itself the benefit of a largely narrative structure – leaving the quay at night on a herring boat, casting the nets, waiting, hauling the catch in, returning in the morning through rough seas to a calm harbour – and by this method hopes to keep the reader less anxious, to make of him a companion, a co-voyager, a co-fisherman who will feel that he has seen and brought back his catch. The poem is carefully put together, with a night bell striking from a buoy far out at sea, as the speaker now back home remembers where he has been. Both bells are described as 'gentle' or 'faint', and this seems important. The poem, for all that it is concerned with a rough, cold, sometimes dangerous, often noisy human occupation has as its aim the extraction of an almost mystical stillness. It may be the stillness of a moment when a man bends to blow out an oil lamp, and with the exhaling of his breath is suddenly made aware of the whole chain of time and history, and of himself as no longer even the same person rising from the lamp as the one who bent down:

I bent to the lamp. I cupped
My hand to the glass chimney.
Yet it was a stranger's breath
From out of my mouth that
Shed the light. I turned out
Into the salt dark
And turned my collar up.

Or it may be the stillness at the centre of the poem, at the point when the boat has stopped and the men have cast their nets and are sitting back waiting, not long before daybreak. Describing this pause, this moment (as it appears) out of time, a very Eliotian moment one might call it (and the passage has echoes of Eliot's 'Marina'), the poet is at his most vulnerable, since he has virtually to say why the nightfishing is important to him, and in what way it is something more than a nightfishing. The abstractness of the language, and the repeated use of rather question-begging words like 'grace', show his struggle, his self-consciousness. On the naturalistic level, the pause is a period of inactivity between the skilled work of casting and hauling in the nets; on the level on which the nightfishing is 'going out to catch a poem', the pause represents the moment at which much of the work has been done, and from which the end can be glimpsed but has still to be fought for, a moment of brooding survey, a kind of 'death' within the 'life' of the material, a necessary abstraction. But how to write about it without making the self-absorption seem extreme, even imperceptive?

> And I am illusioned out of this flood as
> Separate and stopped to trace all grace arriving.
> This grace, this movement bled into this place,
> Locks the boat still in the grey of the seized sea.
> The illuminations of innocence embrace.
> What measures gently
>
> Cross in the air to us to fix us so still
> In this still brightness by knowledge of
> The quick proportions of our intricacies?
> What sudden perfection is this the measurement of?
> And speaks us thoroughly to the bone and has
> The iron sea engraved to our faintest breath,
> The spray fretted and fixed at a high temper,
> A script of light.

As Norman MacCaig says in his 'Culag Pier', another poem about herring-fishing, 'And ropes seem tangled, but they are not so'. No doubt the 'intricacies' have 'proportions'. But what is the 'sudden perfection', what are the 'illuminations of innocence'? Is there an innocent pause between the hunt and the kill? At that very moment of stillness on the boat, the sea underneath is beginning to churn and twist with thousands of living creatures, some already caught on the meshes, some realizing in panic that their swimming-area is no longer free, all about to die in half an hour's time. This is not the fishermen's worry, since it is their livelihood, since people eat fish. Yet the poet is not a fisherman, and it might be argued that his use of words like 'innocence' and 'grace' and 'perfection' is likely to be counter-productive, making the reader restless, by their withdrawing of imaginative sympathy, at the very point where the reader's cooperation is most needed. But whether or not that objection is sustainable, I think it is certainly true that Graham has found the greatest difficulty is stitching together the outer and inner demands of the poem at some points, whereas at other points they may swim easily and beautifully into our acceptance. Whatever its faults, 'The Nightfishing' has seriousness and grandeur, and it remains for me at the centre of his achievement, even if excellences of other kinds were attained in his later volumes.

This seems not to be the general critical view, especially on the part of those of a younger generation who came to discover or rediscover Graham during the 1970s, after the appearance of *Malcolm Mooney's Land* and *Implements in their Places*, both of which were Poetry Book Society Choices. Although there were many poems in both volumes which I liked and admired, I found some disappointment in these books – and I believe this disappointment was shared by others of my generation, the generation contemporary with Graham, which had grown up with his poetry – because they contained so much repetition of themes familiar from his earlier work: the problems of communication, the relation between poet and reader, the nature and status of language. I thought that someone who came from Greenock and Glasgow ought not to have lived so long in a telephoneless cottage in the wilds of Cornwall. In this, I feel on reflection that I was partly right and partly wrong. Having sea, wife, cat and kitchen table for sounding-board may be no bad thing; one can concentrate on essentials. Yet concentrating on essentials may become a bad thing. Integrity is a lone star state. The struggle to use isolation (Hopkins; Dickinson) is always admirable and instructive, but sometimes the hostages of involvement and mundanity turn out to be good hobgoblins who actually sweep the house and stoke the fire. But as Keats said, 'A man's life of any worth is a continual allegory – and very few eyes can see the mystery of his life'. Without the distancing of Cornwall, Graham would not have brought to fruition the Scottish and family material which is threaded through all his books but which finds its most moving expression in the volumes of the 1970s.

In an early volume like *The White Threshold* he establishes a sort of map of varied recollections of childhood and youth in Scotland. He climbs Ben Narnain in 'Since All My Steps Taken', recalls high tenement and peevered pavement and 'Clydeside, / Webbed in its foundries and loud blood' in 'The Children of Greenock', muses on the mixed rural and industrial landscapes of Blantyre, Dechmont, and the river Calder in 'The Children of Lanarkshire', writes 'Three Letters' to his brother, his mother, and his father:

> Yes as alike as entirely
> You my father I see

That high Greenock tenement
And whole shipyarded front.

As alike as a memory early
Of 'The Bonny Earl o' Moray'
Fiddled in our high kitchen
Over the sleeping town

These words this one night
Feed us and will not
Leave us without our natures
Inheriting new fires.

Another letter, 'Letter II' in *The Nightfishing*, begins to take the speculation more deeply into then and now, into the gains and losses of Clydeside and exile, into the acceptance of life as a process of sloughed skins – except that the old skins are not lost, and we live with our dead selves as well as with unknown selves to come.

Younger in the towered
Tenement of night he heard
The shipyards with nightshifts
Of lathes turning their shafts.
His voice was a humble ear
Hardly turned to her.
Then in a welding flash
He found his poetry arm
And turned the coat of his trade.
From where I am I hear
Clearly his heart beat over
Clydeside's far hammers
And the nightshipping firth.
What's he to me? Only
Myself I died from into
These present words that move.
In that high tenement
I got a great grave.

Although the speaker, in becoming poet and not engineer, is a 'turncoat', the very metaphor he uses ('in a welding flash') pays its tribute to the early environment, and the ambiguous and striking phrase at the end implies that whether or not he died to Greenock and the Clyde, and whether or not it was a great loss, the grave he got from it and carried away from it was 'great' in the fecund sense of filling him with images and memories he would never cease to draw from, and in the precise sense of imbuing him with an engineer's love of good construction. 'What's he to me?' Answer: everything.

In the volumes of the 1970s, 'The Dark Dialogues', 'Greenock at Night I Find You', and 'To Alexander Graham' stand out. The second section of 'The Dark Dialogues' evokes in a masterly way the disturbing power of memory to interfuse with the present, and with a Wordsworthian simplicity (but not really simple – a very skilled hand is at work!) and with the sharp pathos Graham's poetry sometimes achieves, it links the accidental visitations of memory into the theme of human communication and understanding:

> I sit with the gas turned
> Down and time knocking
> Somewhere through the wall.
> Wheesht, children, and sleep
> As I break the raker up,
> It is only the stranger
> Hissing in the grate.
> Only to speak and say
> Something, little enough,
> Not out of want
> Nor out of love, to say
> Something and to hear
> That someone has heard me.

'Greenock at Night I Find You' opens with a perhaps unfortunate late obeisance to Dylan Thomas ('loud Greenock long ropeworking / Hide and seeking rivetting town of my child / Hood') but immediately settles down to the speaker's imagining, at night, as in a dream, that he is revisiting the town of his early years, hearing the rattle of the yards, smelling the bone-works, watching the blue welding lights, walking along Cartsburn Street:

> See, I am back. My father turned and I saw
> He had the stick he cut in Sheelhill Glen.
> Brigit was there and Hugh and double-breasted
> Sam and Malcolm Mooney and Alastair Graham.
> They all were there in the Cartsburn Vaults shining
> To meet me but I was only remembered.

The sudden but particularly effective last two lines of the poem suggest many readings: 'I went away as a young man, so all they had was memories of me', 'Even if they are dead now, I like to think they remember me', 'They could not meet me – I was only remembering'. The father who makes his brief appearance in that poem takes the centre of the stage in 'To Alexander Graham', the best of the three. Graham's favourite firmly-written three-stress line without rhyme is used here with a wonderful confidence and delicacy. The speaker dreams he is back in Greenock, at the harbour, and meets his father who seems glad to see him and tries to speak to him although the words have no sound. The dream is so vivid that the dreamer can smell the tar and the ropes on the quay. It reminds him of the time when he left Greenock as a young man, and his father wanted to say something to him but did not do so. He wonders what his father would think of him now – whether he would be proud of him. The bond between them is strong, perhaps all the stronger for being broken. It is almost like an endless recession of images, or repeated shots from a film, of two figures meeting and parting, trying to say what they want to but cannot say, the younger haunted by the older until when he himself is old he dreams of the father as a handsome and still young man.

> You stopped and almost turned back
> To say something. My father,
> I try to be the best
> In you you give me always.
>
> Lying asleep turning
> Round in the quay-lit dark
> It was my father standing
> As real as life. I smelt
> The quay's tar and the ropes.
>
> I think he wanted to speak.
> But the dream had no sound.
> I think I must have loved him.

If there is a repetitiveness in Graham, which comes from the relative thinness of the material he uses, this is something he seems to have wished to qualify in the books of the 1970s, which spread out into a much greater variety of subject than was usual before: poems on friends like Peter Lanyon and Roger Hilton, a poem about first arriving in literary London, a poem in 'ten shots' about a refugee from the concentration camps, a poem about operating a fruit machine. Of such poems, the most impressive is the totally unexpected but delightful sequence 'Johann Joachim Quantz's Five Lessons', in which the eighteenth-century flautist (and composer for the flute) is made to give a series of instructions to a young pupil, 'a lout from the canal / With big ears but an angel's tread on the flute', who is something more than promising. The background of the place and time is lightly but deftly sketched in, and the advice reverberates well beyond flute-playing.

> But you will be all right. Stand in your place
> Before them. Remember Johann. Begin with good
> Nerve and decision. Do not intrude too much
> Into the message you carry and put out.
>
> One last thing, Karl, remember when you enter
> The joy of those quick high archipelagoes,
> To make to keep your finger-stops as light
> As feathers but definite. What can I say more?
> Do not be sentimental or in your Art.
> I will miss you. Do not expect applause.

Graham's *Collected Poems* is a fine volume, and ought to establish his reputation on a firm basis. His is one of the most distinctive and distinguished voices in modern Scottish poetry.

Further Reading

W.S. Graham, *Aimed at Nobody: Poems from Notebooks*, ed. Margaret Blackwood and Robin Skelton (London: Faber & Faber, 1993)

W.S. Graham, *New Collected Poems*, ed. M. Francis (London and New York: Faber & Faber, 2004)

W.S. Graham, *The Nightfisherman: Selected Letters*, ed. Michael and Margaret Snow (Manchester: Carcanet, 1999)

W.S. Graham, *Uncollected Poems* (Warwick: Greville Press, 1990)

R. Grogan (ed.), '"Dear Pen Pal in the Distance": A Selection of W.S. Graham's Letters', *PN Review*, 73 (1990)

Aquarius, 25/26, *George Barker, W.S. Graham* (London, 2002)

Calvin Bedient, *Eight Contemporary Poets* (Oxford: Oxford University Press, 1974)

Constructed Space, City of Bradford Arts, Museums and Libraries Division (Bradford, 1994)

Neil Corcoran, *English Poetry since 1940* (Longman Literature in English Series; Harlow: Longman, 1993)

Andrew Crozier, 'Thrills and Frills', in Alan Sinfield (ed.), *Society and Literature 1945–1970*, second edition (Brighton: Harvester, 1983)

Edinburgh Review, 75, *The Life and Work of W.S. Graham* (Edinburgh, 1987)

Matthew Francis, *Where the People Are: Language and Community in the Poetry of W.S. Graham* (Cambridge: Salt Publishing, 2004)

Damian Grant, 'Walls of Glass: The Poetry of W.S. Graham' in Peter Jones and Michael Schmidt (eds), *British Poetry Since 1970: A Critical Survey* (Manchester: Carcanet, 1980)

Tony Lopez, *The Poetry of W.S. Graham* (Edinburgh: Edinburgh University Press, 1989)

Elizabeth Lowry, 'The Strange Disappearance of W.S. Graham', *Thumbscrew*, 5 (Summer 1996), pp. 15–33

Edwin Morgan, 'The Sea, the Desert, the City: Environment and Language in W.S. Graham, Hamish Henderson, and Tom Leonard', *Yearbook of English Studies*, 17 (1987), pp. 31–45

Rosalie Murphy (ed.), *Contemporary Poets of the English Language* (Chicago: St James Press, 1970)

David Punter, 'W.S. Graham: Constructing a White Space', in *The Hidden Script: Writing and the Unconscious* (London: Routledge and Kegan Paul, 1985)

Iain Sinclair (ed.), *Conductors of Chaos* (London and Basingstoke: Picador, 1996)

Michael Schmidt, *An Introduction to 50 British Poets* (Manchester: Carcanet, 1979)

General Index

Index of Graham's Works